PIONEER FORTS
OF THE WEST

FORT OSAGE, MISSOURI

PIONEER FORTS
OF THE WEST

by Herbert M. Hart

Drawings by Paul J. Hartle

Bonanza Books / New York

This edition is published by Bonanza Books,
distributed by Crown Publishers, Inc.
by arrangement with Superior Publishing Company

h   g   f   e   d   c   b   a

1981 EDITION

Library of Congress Cataloging in Publication Data

Hart, Herbert M.
    Pioneer forts of the West.

    Reprint. Originally published: Seattle:
Superior, 1968.
    Bibliography: p. 187
    Includes index.
    1. Military posts—West (U.S.) I. Title.
UA26.W4H33   1981   623'.1978 81-18153
ISBN 0-517-36953-2   AACR2

PRINTED IN THE UNITED STATES OF AMERICA

WESTERN FORTS had little in common with formal forts of civilization, but from rude huts such as these at Fort McRae, New Mexico, war of West was won.

FOREWORD

"The stockaded works erected in the Indian country are important to overawe the Indians, and to restrain their perpetual disposition to war . . . They command the great avenues of communication into the country; they cover the whole frontier; they protect our citizens in the various employments required by their duties, public and private, and they produce a moral effect upon the Indians, which is visible and permanent."
—Report to the 19th Congress, 1826.

WHEN these words were written in 1826, the term "Indian country" did not mean anything like it would come to mean within a few short decades. Although the geography expanded, the mission of the "stockaded works" remained the same. Before the great adventure had ended, the sites of an estimated 2,000 such places dotted the landscape from the Mississippi to the Pacific.

The *Forts of the Old West* series undertook in 1963 to visit as many of these sites as could be found and for which a reasonable excuse for such a stop could be rationalized. The first three volumes of the series told the stories of about 200 of these historic places.

This volume undertakes to recount the tales of 70-some more, ranging from those that belonged to the Spaniards, English, Russians and Mexicans, to the official forts of the United States. They represent almost a hundred years from an indefinite period in the 18th century to that of the American Civil War. A projected Volume V of the series will pick up the thread to the end of the 19th century.

An attempt has been made to group the posts with others of common interest or mission. The selection of what fort belonged where had to be arbitrary; many belong as well in one section as in another. It is hoped that any reader taking issue with the method will consider that the disadvantages are out-weighed by at least one advantage. The method permits stories to be told of forts that had similar roles in the settlement of the West.

For the first time, the series includes a number of non-military forts and fort-type places. This is partly in response to repeated suggestions that these, too, played a role that had a bearing on that of the official Army posts. On occasion, some had Army connections. It is

FORT LEATON, TEXAS

also difficult, in speaking of forts of the pioneer period in the West, to cover the subject without including these places.

Because of the undesirability of repeating forts that were included in previous volumes, many do not appear here that had a major role in the events that are described in this book. Fort Bridger, Wyo., was all-important in the Mormon War but is not here because it was in Volume I. This same volume had several Washington and Oregon posts that could have been included in the chapter on the "Battle of the Blockhouses." Many outposts of "The Forward Line" and the immediate pre-Civil War are being saved for Volume V because their greatest contributions came after that unpleasantness was settled.

Every installation presented here was personally visited and photographed by the author. Since 1962 this has involved approximately 65,000 miles of traveling back and forth across the West during periods of leave from duties as an infantryman in the United States Marine Corps. Almost 600 fort sites have been visited by every conceivable means: a station wagon camper (complete with wife and four children), horseback, jeep, ferryboat, motorboat, rowboat, seaplane, helicopter, foot, and, infrequently and uncomfortably with camera and trousers held aloft, by swimming. Most of the sites in this volume were visited in the summer of 1965 and the fall of 1966.

The difficulties of visiting some sites are described in the paragraph that concludes each story. Regardless of what others may say or maps may indicate, these are the routes that worked for the author. The many dead ends and trails that lead no where are deleted. These are the routes that worked ultimately, and these are the ones the author would take if he were to return to the sites.

It should be remembered that many of the sites are privately owned. Permission to visit them always should be requested. It is assumed that the visitor will not disturb anything, will reclose all gates, and will leave the site as he found it.

Visits to isolated places should not be undertaken without proper preparations. Maps, a rough-duty vehicle (if the family car is inappropriate), the equipment to extricate this vehicle if it bogs down, first aid and snakebite kits, emergency food and fuel, and signaling means should be included. Solitary expeditions into the back country are not recommended.

In the preparation of the tales that accompany the modern photographs, every conceivable source was consulted. No claim is made that the coverage of a fort is its definitive history. This could not be done in several books of this size. Instead, an attempt has been made to tell how the post once looked and what took place at or near it. Old pictures and a simplified ground plan are included when it was possible to find them in the federal, state, or local sources. In a few cases, the author's field notes had to suffice for ground plans.

It is hoped that the *Pioneer Forts of the West* will show by word and picture a page of Western history; a period when the face of the adventurer was turned toward the setting sun and the Army was at his side.

Palma de Majorca, Spain   H.M.H.
Saint Patrick's Day

CONTENTS

(Nichols Collection)

(PIO Ft. Leavenworth)

(PIO Ft. Riley)

(Calif. State Library)

(Porter Collection)

GENERALS IN PIONEER West included (left to right) Henry Atkinson (1782-1842), commander of Western frontier for 23 years and leader of First Yellowstone Expedition; Henry Leavenworth (1783-1834), leader of Missouri River Expedition of 1923 who died while commanding Southwest. California's conquest brought next three generals to fame: Bennett Riley (1787-1853), John Fremont (1813-1890) and Stephen Watts Kearny (1794-1848). Fremont was a leader in initial revolt in California, Kearney was senior U. S. officer who settled war, and Riley was final military governor who called constitutional convention.

WAR IN THE EARLY WEST

> *"Thus it ever is; the red men of the Atlantic slope must be crowded further west, whilst his race on the far-off Pacific shores, are jostled and pushed toward the rising sun. When at last the great tides of immigration meet midway between the two oceans . . . one shudders at the thought of the many bloody conflicts yet to occur between the contending races of human beings."*
> —Surgeon Glisan in his diary, August 17, 1850.

FIRST came the Spanish and then the French, the Russians and the English. Still when a fledgling American Republic turned westward, it found territory that was virtually virgin.

It was into this vast frontier that a pioneer Army led the way. In the beginning its role was that of an explorer. In 1806 Captain Zebulon Pike investigated what was to become the Santa Fe Trail and wound up a prisoner of the Mexicans. About the same time Captains Meriwether Lewis and William Clark traced a route that ended at the mouth of the Columbia River. From 1817 to 1820 Major Stephen Long went by boat and on foot to uncover the secrets of the middle lands—across which the Platte, Arkansas and Canadian rivers provided access.

Major Bennett Riley took four companies of the 4th Infantry down the Santa Fe Trail in 1829. Between 1832 and 1835 Captain Benjamin L. E. Bonneville temporarily put aside his army affiliations so that he could explore the Northwest and, coincidentally, garner possible profits from fur trading. From 1842 to 1844 Lieutenant John Charles Fremont explored much of what was identified with the Oregon Trail. He happened to be in California when the American settlers decided to revolt against the Mexican rule.

In size it was not much of an Army that tried to exert its influence across the plains, deserts and mountains of the Western frontier. Until the birth of the 1st U. S. Dragoons in 1833 the troops had been horseless. The arrival of dragoons brought cavalry to the West and also a tradition of flowing mustaches and unshorn locks. Annually until the Mexican War, these troops fielded expeditions into the wilderness that resulted in much territory covered but little fighting.

On the eve of the Mexican War in 1846 the Army could count only 5,300 personnel on its rolls despite an authorized 9,000. By the time the war had ended, the records could show that 30,954 regulars had participated in addition to 73,776 volunteers and militia and 7,500 sailors and Marines.

PRESENT OR FUTURE generals in West included (left to right) George Pickett (1825-1875), key figure in San Juan controversy who led famous Gettysburg charge; William W. Loring (1818-1886), one-armed leader of several expeditions who became Egyptian general after Confederate generalship; Benjamin L. E. Bonneville (1795-1878), explorer and Southwestern campaigner; David E. Twiggs (1790-1862), only federal line general to go over to Confederacy, surrendering Department of Texas to cloud his 48 years of U. S. service; John E. Wool (1784-1869), instrumental in Cherokee Removal and, before Civil War, Pacific Coast commander.

Not all of this war was fought south of the Rio Grande. On June 6, 1846, Stephen Watts Kearny led his 1st Dragoons across the plains to Santa Fe. He proclaimed the Territory of New Mexico part of the United States and then moved on to link up with Naval forces at San Diego, California. Part of his force was a regiment of Missouri Volunteers led by their elected colonel, St. Louis lawyer Alexander William Doniphan, who not only maintained military command but used his legal talents to draft a code of laws for the annexed territories.

The rear guard for Kearny was the Mormon Battalion led by Philip St. George Cooke. These "Saints"-turned-soldier escorted Kearny's supply wagons and joined him 90 days after he arrived in California.

When the Mexican War ended in 1849, the army was given the task of guarding the 6,000 miles of frontier. By this time the westward flood of trader, settler, miner and farmer had brought with it a way of life that was unreconcilable with that of the nomadic Indian. Frequent clashes were inevitable.

In 1847 the Pueblo Indians of New Mexico erupted in a violence that resulted in massacres of both white and red races. In 1848 the killing of Missionary Marcus Whitman and his wife ignited expeditions against the Cayuse Indians by a regiment of Oregon Volunteers. The so-called "Navajo Troubles" occupied the Army in New Mexico in making and re-making treaties up to mid-Civil War. At the same time troops in Texas clashed with the Comanches, Cheyennes, Lipan Apaches and Kickapoos.

The decade of 1850 saw 22 distinct "wars" fought by the Army. From 1848 to 1861 there were 206 actions on the part of the regular Army with a loss of 11 officers and 175 enlisted men killed and 37 officers and 329 enlisted wounded.

Every western state had its share of fighting, from the Bannock and Snake tribes of the Northwest to the Utes of Utah and the Apaches of New Mexico and Texas—faced once with little success in 1857 by Bonneville, a former explorer and now a colonel.

Another peaceful war pitted the troopers against the Royal Marine Light Infantry in what the official records term the "San Juan Imbroglio," a disagreement in northwest Washington over the boundry between the United States and Canada. It took 13 years to settle this one. The German Kaiser served as the arbiter.

The Sioux tribe occupied the Army in expeditions in 1855-6, 1857 and into the Civil War. Equally troublesome and just as sporadic were the incidents and counter-incidents that involved almost every Indian tribe and tied down 181 of the 198 companies of the Regular Army before the Civil War. On the eve of the Civil the Army numbered 16,000 officers and men; most of them manned the 79 forts scattered across the Western frontier.

A chapter in American history closed when the Republic split itself into a North and a South. The repercussions were heard across the land and with them a new era that could no longer call itself the true "pioneer" West.

THE FORTS

"A prim little village built around a square, in the center of which is a high flagstaff and a big cannon. The buildings are very low and broad and are made of adobe—a kind of clay and mud mixed together—and the walls are very thick."
—An Army's wife description of Fort Lyon, Colorado.

SELDOM were there high stockades, even less seldom were there stone walls at these scatterings of buildings that called themselves "forts" in the early West. Sometimes a blockhouse or two would be at opposite corners of the perimeters. Maybe there would be some trenches or earthworks with perhaps an underground shelter into which the women and children could be rushed during attacks. Other then these slight nods in the direction of Marshal Vauban and his European fortress theories, the Western fort was designed more to fight away from than to fight in.

Even the matter of what was really a "fort" presented confusion in Western history. The 1857 Army Regulations determined, "Camp is the place where troops are established in tents, in huts, or in bivouac. Cantonments are the inhabited places which troops occupy for shelter when not put in barracks." In 1878 the designation "fort" was authorized for "all posts permanently occupied by troops or the occupation of which is likely to be permanent."

In actual practice, although the fort title usually was given to the major permanent-type places, other designations were used with little regard to regulations. Camp, post, barracks, depot, cantonment, station, detachment, picket post, presidio and sub-post all came into use. Sometimes places with temporary-type surnames lasted longer than those with permanent designations.

In the northern territories the forts were of wooden construction; in the deserts of adobe. Rock was used when the material and the masons to use it were at hand. More often than not the order for a new post directed that it would be built by the soldiers themselves. This dictated much what would be built and how finished the result would appear. More than one soldier could compain with understandable bitterness that he spent more time as a carpenter and stone mason than as a fighter.

In reconstructing the views of each fort that follow, ground plans were consulted from the files of the National Archives, state and local agencies, and any other source that seemed reliable. This mass of miscellaneous notes, blueprints, official reports, and other versions has been summarized into simplifed ground plans.

Minor buildings have been left out, as have other things that seemed important to engineer blueprints but were impossible to transcribe effectively in the space available. Because buildings rose and fell with uncommon frequency, there was no way to provide a plan that held true throughout a fort's tenure. The plats should be considered as faithful only for the date indicated.

Although no scale can be provided for each fort because of the vagueness of the sources, some idea of size can be estimated when typical dimensions are given, such as the parade ground or of a major building.

For ease in identification, here are some of the abbreviations used:

HQ, OFF, ADJ—Headquarters or Adjutant's office	OQ—Officers quarters
S or St—Stables	CO or COQ—Commanding officers quarters
B or EM—Barracks	BLK—Blacksmith
BK—Bakery	TR, SUT, or TRAD—Sutler or post trader
SH—Storehouse of Warehouse	M or MAG—Magazine
H—Hospital	K or KIT—Kitchen
C or Chapel—Chapel	CEM—Cemetery
GH—Guardhouse	COM or COMM—Commissary
EM or NCO Married enlisted quarters	CARP—Carpenter
T—Tower or Blockhouse	CAV—Cavalry
MESS or MH—Messhall	INF—Infantry
PO—Post Office	ART—Artillery
SURG—Surgeon	SHOP or WORK—Workshops
GRAN—Granary	LIB—Library
LAUN—Laundry or Laundress quarters	

POSTS OF THE PIONEERS

"The forts, or trading estab'shments, are 18 in all, and have a large number of hands employed about them, in conducting the fur trade and laboring upon the farms and in the workshops and mills. Each of these posts presents a miniature town by itself, whose busy populace pursue most of the avocations incident to the more densely inhabited localities of civilized countries."

—Rufus B. Sage, writing of Oregon in 1855.

THE common denominator of the pioneer post lay in its claim to the surname "fort." It could be an elaborate stockade complete with blockhouses and cannon or it could be a settler's shanty to which he had affixed the title for reasons probably known only to himself.

Hiram Chittenden, the chronicler of the fur trade, estimated that there were at least 150 fur and trading forts in the West up to 1843. Many more came after that date, some of them on abandoned sites but with new names.

No one has attempted to do more than than guess at the number of other places that dotted the West and lay claim to the "fort" title. Stage stops, Pony Express relay stations, commercial houses, wayside taverns and local refuges from Indian attack all bore the name. Many a pioneer family "forted-up" in a building that the casual observer would describe as a cabin or a barn, but that was not how it was termed locally.

On the banks of the Perdenales in the Texas "hill country" the ancestors of President Lyndon Johnson barricaded themselves in a rock building during at least one Indian attack. Known as "Johnson's Post," that structure remains today.

Most of these pioneer posts exist today only in the diaries of the early travelers and settlers. What follows are a few representative ones of which more than mere memories are left.

FORT CLATSOP, OREGON

The first United States fort in the far West, Fort Clatsop, Oregon, varied quite a bit from the many that were to follow. The only shooting that is witnessed was the celebration of holidays or the killing of game. The Indians that surrounded the post presented a threat no greater than the swarm of fleas that accompanied them.

Rather than fighting off Indian visits, Fort Clatsop's garrison welcomed them. The Americans would have perished without the food received in trade. Without the information obtained from lengthy palavers, the purpose of the fort would not have been served. When, after three months of service, the fort was closed, it was presented to the local chief in appreciation of the help given by the Indians.

Technically a military fort because it was so manned, Fort Clatsop really fit better into the mold of the pioneer posts. Its use was that of an exploring and scientific headquarters rather than a fighting fort, and its ultimate achievement was political: the key to the United States' claim to the Pacific Northwest.

Meriweather Lewis and William Clark, two Army captains—even though the latter was really only a lieutenant—were the fort's first and only commandants. Their garrison consisted of 28 men of the "Corps of Discovery;" a half-breed French interpreter; his Shoshone wife, known variously in historical accounts as Sacajawea ("boat launcher") or Sakakawea ("birdwoman"), and her infant son. It had taken them 18 months to travel the 4,100 miles to the Pacific where they waited out the winter of 1805-06 before returning to the East.

The Lewis and Clark Expedition of 1804-06 was the United States' first sightseeing visit to the West. President Thomas Jefferson had engineered the Louisiana Purchase in 1803 and this was his method of investigating an area that doubled the size of the new republic.

The expedition left St. Louis on May 14, 1804, and arrived at the mouth of the Columbia River in modern Washington on November 14, 1805. By December 8 they had selected a camp site on the Oregon shore of the Columbia, 30 feet above the high water mark, amid suitable timber for construction, and near a fresh water spring.

While Clark led five men four miles westward to search for salt along the seashore, Lewis directed the building of a fort. He was "glad to find the timber splits butifully (sic) and of any length" and within two weeks the fort was ready for occupancy.

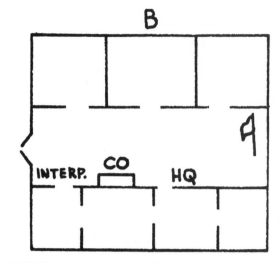

FORT CLATSOP'S rough layout, drawn by Captain William Clark on elkhide cover of his field book, was basis of this sketch. Identifications are uncertain except for three upper barracks rooms. Room in lower right-hand corner probably was storeroom or smokehouse. (Redrawn from National Park Service data.)

PORTS in fort's walls served more for ventilation than as firing slots. Main Indian threat was the flea which was "so numerous as to be almost a calamity to the Indians of the country," Clark wrote. "When they have once obtained mastery of a house it is impossible to expel them. . . Every Indian is constantly accompanied by multitudes of them, and no one comes into the party's camp without leaving behind him swarms of the tormenting insects."

Fifty feet square, the stockade included three rooms along one side, four along the other, and a parade ground in the center. The entire construction period had been one of continual rain so it was a relief to move into relatively dry and sheltered headquarters. With one room set up as a smokehouse, it also appeared that they would be able to preserve the elk meat, which usually rotted quickly in the damp climate.

The local Chinook, Clatsop, Cathlamet and Tillamook Indians were both observers and participants in the work, especially in attempting to profit from this "windfall of wealthy outsiders." Quickly the explorers realized the Indians were shrewd bargainers, usually "asking double or treble the value of the object for sale and decreasing the demand in proportion to the degree of ardor or knowledge of the purchaser."

If an Indian particularly relished something, he would do his utmost to obtain it; one of the frontiersmen narrowly escaped death when he realized that he had been lured into a squaw's hut so that he could be killed for the contents of his pocket. On other occasions Indians were banned from the fort for stealing.

A few days after the fort was dedicated in honor of the Clatsop Tribe, one of the visiting chiefs

(Copyright Clatsop County Historical Society, Inc.)

REPLICA of Fort Clatsop was built in 1955 by Astoria, Oregon, civic organizations with logs donated by Crown-Zellerbach Paper Corporation. Floor plan and design followed descriptions in Clark's records. National Park Service control of site, authorized in 1958, includes museum, interpretive facilities and marked trails to expedition's landmarks.

offered two of his squaws to the captains. When his offer was declined, the ensuing clamor from the Indians made it obvious that their generosity was being insulted.

The holidays of Christmas and New Year's were celebrated by rifle volleys in the air and a repast

of spoiled elk and pounded fish. Clark entered in his journal, "We have no ardent spirits."

Although the party had planned to stay at Clatsop until April, they decided to leave early because of the difficulty in obtaining food. The game seemed to have left, and the stock of trading beads and clothes had dwindled.

The arrival on March 15 of a Chinook chief and his wife probably settled the matter. They were accompanied by "six damsels, who in the Autumn had camped near us on the other side of the bay, and whose favors had been quite troublesome to some of the men," the journal recorded. The captains realized that this might provide an additional drain on their trade goods even though they had stretched them by cutting the ribbons into little pieces.

By March 23 the expedition was back in its canoes. The Indians had complete freedom of the fort, and Lewis and Clark could note unhappily that all of the articles left for bartering on the long trek home "might easily be tied in two handkerchiefs."

TO GET THERE: From downtown Astoria, Oregon, take Highway 101 south across Youngs Bay Bridge. At .7 miles after crossing bridge, turn left at Airport-Fort Clatsop sign. Go 2.4 miles to fort site and reproduction, staffed daily by National Park Service.

GATE WAS CLOSED at sunset when Indians were sent outside. Beginning December 30, guard was established of a sergeant and three privates. Privates took turns standing as sentinel in center of parade and watching for any suspicious actions on part of Indians. After being relieved at sunrise, old guard also had to provide "two loads of wood for the commanding offercers (sic) fire."

ONLY REAL fireplace in fort was in commanding officers' room, though soldiers quickly set up makeshift fires in their barracks. Lewis and Clark had room at left of picture; interpreter and Sacajawea lived in room behind fireplace next to gate. Only female on expedition, Sacajawea was honored by its leaders for her assistance and fortitude. In 1810 Clark became guardian of Sacajawea's son and sponsored his education in Europe.

LANDING SITE below fort includes this reminder of main mode by which Lewis and Clark covered 8,000 miles of Northwest. They had to trade canoes for horses to cross Great Divide, but used water route otherwise. Loss of canoe from Fort Clatsop was considered catastrophe and garrison hunted several days before finding it. Sergeant of guard was required "once at least in 24 hours to visit the canoes and see that they are safely secured."

FORT LEATON, TEXAS

The earliest Anglo-American settler in West Texas, Ben Leaton had a sure-fire formula for getting along with the Indians. Either he killed them or coddled them, depending on which version of the formula can be believed.

Probably a trader with Doniphan's Missouri Volunteers march into Mexico in 1847, Leaton arrived at Presido del Norte in 1848. Four miles downriver on the Texas shore were the adobe remains of a Spanish mission built in 1684, El Apostol Sabriago. It had been re-established in 1773 as "El Fortin de San Jose," abandoned in 1810, and served as the home of Juan Bustillo after 1831.

Leaton bought "El Fortin" from Bustillo on August 19, 1848. Adobe making was started immediately to build new rooms and repair existing ones. Some estimates say that Leaton did not stop his program until approximately 100 rooms comprosed what quickly became "Fort Leaton."

Two months after buying the fort, Leaton played host to a mapping expedition that included Texas pioneers John C. Hays and Samuel Maverick, 50 armed men and ten Delaware Indians. Their camp

LEATON'S BLOODY banquet took place in this patio, if story can be believed. After it ended, supposedly cannon was lifted to roof of fort where it could serve as warning to other Indians.

MASSIVENESS OF Fort Leaton is suggested by this ground plan drawn from remains in 1936 by Mrs. Jack Shipman, editor of Marfa, Texas, newspaper, and revised by Texas fort buff Jack Baughman. Doorways are estimated in many cases, as is identification of "guardhouse" room. Building is 192 feet square in this plan; patio 60 feet by 30; corral 179 feet by 82. Granaries had pillars, 4 feet by 5, to support roof. (Redrawn from Jack Baughman plat.)

was set up a mile east for ten days while Leaton sold them horses and supplies. Maverick's *Journal* included this description of the place:

"Leaton built his fort-type home that contained some 40 rooms, the walls of which enclosed a large court or patio, in true Spanish style. Great hallways, closed by immense doors, allow teams and wagons to enter the court. At the corners of the building were constructed lookout positions with narrow openings for the rifles of the defenders."

From the beginning Fort Leaton gained a reputation for hospitality. Lieutenant William H. Whiting visited the place in 1849. He reported later that he would never forget Leaton's cordial interest in Whiting's expedition and "his reckless profusion and the efforts of both himself and his wife to make my messmates comfortable."

When Whiting left, Leaton insured their safety by insisting that one of his men accompany them.

Leaton seemed to have established rapport with the Indians and they seldom bothered him. As Whiting's official report suggests, this was not the case at the beginning. Noting that Leaton's "eight or ten Americans" worked with weapons at hand, he said, "They have been exposed to the incursions of the Indians on one side, and to a series of outrageous impositions and aggressions on the part of the Mexicans on the other, and forced to mount guard day and night."

Later the Mexican government and the U. S. Army accused Leaton of serving as a middleman for renegades, Indian and otherwise. Supposedly he provided them with food, ammunition and weapons in return for stolen property and rustled stock.

"On inquiry I think there is no doubt that Leaton deals extensively in buying mules and horses, stolen by the Indians from the Mexicans, and trading them off," charged the Army commander in El Paso. As an indication of proof, the officer added that he and Leaton were able to move through 800 Indians "and to his advice to them, not to disturb us, he attributes the fact that they did not molest us."

Another theory was that when he first arrived Leaton taught the Indians a lesson that they would not forget: To establish good relations from the start, Leaton invited all of the Indians to a combination feast and peace talk. After much beef and liquor had been consumed and the Indians swore their undying friendship, Leaton realized that they took with them every one of his horses and mules.

Although he said nothing, the unhappy host decided that a different method would be needed to insure the security of his fort. Several weeks later he invited the Indians back, spread another banquet before them and again was the amiable host. Then he quietly slipped out and the muzzle of a cannon appeared from behind a false wall. Cannister raked the tables. Riflemen on the roof fired into the patio until the tiles of the old Mission El Apostol Sabriago were awash with blood.

If this story can be believed, this was the reason the Indians maintained a respectful distance from Fort Leaton. Doubts have been raised by the fact that tales of similar deadly feasts appear frequently in western lore.

If this massacre was true, it was but the first of several killings in what was to become the tragedy of Fort Leaton.

After the Fort's owner died of yellow fever

during a New Orleans trip in 1851, his wife waited a year and then married Edward Hall, a Scotsman who was the local Mexican customs house officer. Trading and farming continued and apparently the hospitality. A detail of army camels encamped nearby in 1860 and the commanding officer visited "Mr. Leaton and had a magnificent dinner." Leaton's sons were carrying on in the old tradition.

The financial picture was not encouraging under the new master as described in detail by Leavitt Corning, Jr., in his *Private Forts of Presidio County, Texas.* In July, 1861, the fort was mortgaged to John D. Burgess for $1,707.46. The next year a

FORT LEATON ruins are quickly deteriorating, despite restoration attempt in 1930's. Fire hit it in 1936 and farm workers lived in it until late 1940's Treasure hunt holes, such as in left picture, speed destruction. Graves in foreground are of John B. and Paz L. Burgess. Mountains in background are in Mexico, overlooking border city of Ojinaga. It was here that Edward Hall, then owner of Fort Leaton, led Confederate gang in capture of Union sympathizer, hanging him until he was almost dead. Also in Ojinaga William Leaton was killed in gun battle with police in late 1870's. This was same Leaton who killed John Burgess in 1875. Ojinaga was scene of battle between Mexican Federal and rebel troops under Pancho Villa in 1913-14. Villa won.

GUARDHOUSE is suggested by narrow air ports. Legend says Leaton completed cattle-buying deals by luring sellers into this room, then murdering them instead of paying cash.

VANDALISM, in form of bullet holes, has pockmarked state marker in Fort Leaton patio. Place never was military post, but Army was stationed at or near it frequently. Sub-post of Presidio del Norte, official Army name for area, was abandoned in 1883 because no site could be bought, area's importance had decreased, and the climate was too hot.

DESOLATE RUINS are scant reminders of past at Fort Leaton. Note bars in guardhouse window (right). Once rumors came to fort that John Burgess had been killed by Indians. When wife spotted Indian wearing Burgess' coat, Indian and party were arrested. Hangman's noose was not far away when a live Burgess appeared at trial, explained he had given coat to Indian.

new mortgage was floated, this time for $8,000, part of which paid off the first loan.

By this time Hall was embroiled in Confederate politics. He claimed to be the local agent for the Dixie government and supposedly operated a spying and sabotage network out of Fort Leaton. For three years, a leading spy, Captain Henry Skillman, harrassed the settlements as far as El Paso, once holding the plaza there for two hours before he could shoot his way out. A San Elizario patrol finally caught and killed him near Presidio in 1864.

While Hall was being condemned as "a villian" by Federal authorities in the north, he found he had enemies closer to home. Burgess demanded payment of the loan even though there was no due date. Hall refused.

The question was settled when two assassins forced their way into "El Fortin" and shot Hall to death at the dinner table.

Burgess became the new master of Fort Leaton and the Leaton-Hall widow moved her family across the river. Thirteen years later on Christmas Day, 1875, Burgess was shot and killed. The killer: William Leaton, not quite 21, carrying out a vow he made when his step-father was assassinated.

More tragedy for the Burgess family came to Fort Leaton. In 1877, a Burgess son disappeared after being accused of killing a man. Soon the justice of the peace of Presidio was called to the fort by the Burgess family. The son had returned and was hiding inside, using his wife as a hostage.

Justice Richard C. Daly, and his son, Henry, entered the fort. Burgess fired, wounding the elder Daly. Henry returned the fire. Burgess dropped to the floor and was trying to aim his pistol at his wife when he died.

TO GET THERE: Presidio is at the end of U.S. 67 in the Big Bend country of West Texas. From Presidio, go south on Farm Road 170 for 3.7 miles. Ruins are next to road on right (west) side.

RIVER SIDE of fort, 200 feet long, shows erosion where fireplace chimneys and room partitions once were. This agrees with 1849 description that said it was "a collection of adobe, or earth built houses." Description added that Leaton had "a lookout and a wall which encloses also his corral. The rooms are surmounted by a crenelated wall, and the place would make a strong defense against Indians."

FORT ROSS, CALIFORNIA

If $24 was a bargain price for Manhattan Island, the fee paid for the site of Fort Ross, California, could be called a give-away. Three blankets, two axes, three hoes and an assortment of beads convinced the Indians to turn over 1,000 acres of coastal land to the Russian-American Fur Company. Some accounts add that three pairs of trousers were thrown in for good measure.

Despite the fact that they settled there and built a 59-building installation, apparently the Russians were less than convinced that they really held title to the spot.

Regardless of a clouded title, for almost 30 years Fort Ross was a most active representative of the Imperial Czar. It was established for several purposes, not the least of which was to extend the Russian presence beyond her Alaskan borders.

The new fort also could provide food urgently needed by the fur posts in Alaska. It could also be the base of operations for the expeditions hunting sea otter for their furs. This last endeavor had been the main source of profit for the company until the sea otters appeared to have abandoned the Alaskan coast in favor of the waters further south.

It was not long before the otter industry died. The 1819 season gathered less than 1 per cent of the 40,000 pelts taken in 1812 and it appeared

OLDEST RUSSIAN Orthodox church still standing in United States, chapel collapsed in 1906 earthquake, was reassembled in 1917, and completely rebuilt in 1955. Front steeple was bell tower, rear dome is hollow cupola above chapel's altar.

TWO BUILDINGS shown here survive in modern restoration at Fort Ross State Park: the commandant's quarters—now a museum—and the chapel. Stockade enclosed area 275 feet by 312 feet. Highway cuts through fort from northeast to southwest, passing next to well. Total of nine buildings occupied fort's interior, additional 50 were outside. (Redrawn from State Beaches and Parks data courtesy Wayne Colwell.)

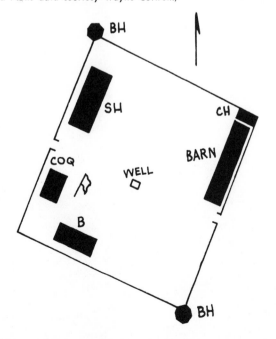

that the otter was headed for extinction. The company had to turn to other sources of profit, and they quickly learned that the Ross coastal location was not favorable to farming.

From Moscow in 1821 the Czar issued a proclamation that barred foreign vessels from the coast north of San Francisco.

The result was unexpected. The United States reacted sharply, issuing the Monroe Doctrine which stated that the American continents were no longer "subjects for future colonization by any European power." Coupled to the Spanish and Mexican opposition to Russian activities in California, the situation of Fort Ross became precarious.

Blockhouses were finished at the northern and southern corners of the stockade and a "fine house" was built for the commandant. Seven other buildings were inside the stockade, including a jail for disciplinary cases who would not bow to the severe punishments; flogging was the most common.

An estimated 400 persons were living in the shadows of the fort but none was more grand than

FORT ROSS in three stages: (left) in 1828 as it was represented in Duhaut-Cilly's **Voyage Autour du Monde**; (below) about 1868 painted later from memory by Henry Raschin, who lived at Ross as 12-year-old; (above) today, commandant's house and northern blockhouse. Seldom seen Raschin painting, used here by special permission of owner David Blumberg, suggests houses were built along southeastern wall.

(Library of Congress)

(David Blumberg Collection)

SEVEN-SIDED BLOCKHOUSE at northern corner of fort was restored in 1956. It did not have musket ports, but it was armed with three cannon. Total of 41 guns in its heydey made Fort Ross impregnable from any Spanish assault. Anchor came from ship wrecked in 1906.

ROUTINE COASTAL fog is beginning to obscure rolling foothills behind eight-sided blockhouse at southern corner of fort. Not far to right is Pacific, 100 feet below fort. Restored redwood stockade is 12 feet high, nine inches thick. It had no catwalk or musket ports.

Princess Helena Gagarin, the wife of the last commandant who was "a very beautiful lady of twenty Aprils who united to her other gifts an irresistible affability." So fascinating was she that the princess was almost kidnapped by one of the Indian chiefs who wanted to add her to his retinue of wives. Her pride was a glass conservatory. It created a sensation among the Indians who had never seen such a collection of glass before.

All of this was impressive to Captain John Sutter when he came in 1841 to bargain for the fort. He especially needed ammunition, arms, equipment and livestock and was persuaded that for a few more dollars he could have everything.

"Thirty thousand dollars, with a down payment of two thousand dollars," was the price Sutter boasted he paid. "The rest I was to pay in produce, chiefly wheat at two dollars per fanega. No time was specified; every year the Russians would send down a vessel from Alaska and receive from me whatever quantity of wheat that I could give them."

This was not quite what the small print of the contract stated. The $2,000 down payment was in addition to the $30,000 in wheat. And the unspecified time for the wheat actually was $5,000 worth for the first and second year and $10,000 for the next two, the final payment being in cash. The wheat had to be delivered to San Francisco at Sutter's expense.

Although beyond Sutter's ability to meet, the deal was consumated. He quickly stripped the fort of everything movable, from all contents of the buildings to some of the buildings. The conservatory was carefully dismantled and taken to Sacramento but was never rebuilt. No one at Sacramento could figure out how to reassemble the complex example of Russian carpentry.

TO GET THERE: Fort Ross' site is almost as isolated today as it was in the nineteenth century. Take California 20 west from Santa Rosa 30 miles to Jenner and intersection with State 1. This highway bisects Fort Ross 13 miles north of Jenner.

PRECISE WORKMANSHIP of chapel hides fact that none of its walls is parallel or equal and there are no right angles in its floor plan. Apparently there were slots in outer walls so that cannon could be fired from inside chapel. Interior, with open dome, is shown below, exterior of 20 by 25 foot chapel, above.

FORT NISQUALLY, WASHINGTON

In 1833 when 21-year-old Doctor William F. Tolmie arrived at the site of Fort Nisqually, he found "a store half finished next to a rude hut of cedar boards" and was welcomed "by a motley group of Canadians, Owyhees & Indians."

Twenty-six years later Doctor Tolmie was to close out the Hudson Bay Company's operation at Fort Nisqually. This would end an era described by U. S. Grant in his *Memoirs* as one "that had brought out the better qualities of the savages. Farming had been undertaken by the company to supply the Indians with bread and vegetables; they raised some food and horses; and they now had taught the Indians to do the labor of the farm and herd."

In contrast to the operation with the Indians of some other trading enterprises, Grant noted that the Hudson Bay Company "always compensated them for their labor, and always gave them goods at uniform quality and at uniform price."

Throughout most of its existence, Fort Nisqually was the principal port for domestic and foreign trade on Puget Sound. It was started 17 miles south of modern Tacoma in 1833, more to make the British presence felt on Puget Sound than for

(Fort Nisqually Restoration Council)

ARTIST'S VERSION of Old Fort Nisqually shows how post probably looked. Modern reproduction has most of these buildings, the main exception being large building in center of post. First building in foreground row was store, followed by granary and blacksmith shop. Factor's house was behind trees; employees lived in houses along far row. Restoration at Tacoma was built from old specifications using uprights, planks, hand-split shakes, hand-forged hardware, nails, and oak pegs salvaged from original site.

big profits in furs. The HBC thought this would counterbalance "the American coasters of later years frequently visiting the Strait of Juan de Fuca."

Although Tolmie was at Nisqually primarily as

NORTHWEST BLOCKHOUSE has construction typical of Hudson Bay Company. Planked logs were fitted into grooves mortized into the upright posts, then oak pegs were driven into holes bored in the horizontal timbers. Result was extremely strong construction.

a doctor, usually he spent more time at the store counter than the medicine chest. Even while the post was being built, trade was brisk and in three weeks 300 beaver skins were shipped to headquarters at Fort Vancouver. With blankets, powder, shot, buckles and other manufactured goods available, the Indians were more than happy to patronize the new post.

Uncertain about the peacefulness of the Indians, Nisqually's builders grouped their few buildings together with high pickets connecting them and a gate in the middle of the front line. When large groups of Indians or strange tribes appeared, a guard was posted so that only a spokesman or two could enter the post.

Occasionally entrance was gained by bribery of the employee tending the gate, something to arouse the anger of other waiting Indians. Once when this happened, a squall blew in suddenly and "laid the line of pickets in front of store prostrate with the ground," Tolmie recorded in his diary.

The clamor that ensued caused Tolmie to institute extra precautions. "Have got three of the men to sleep in my room & shall keep watch all night," he wrote. Whenever the tenor of the Indians seemed to change, the fort's occupants went on the alert. Shortly after his arrival at Nisqually Tolmie noted in his diary, "In my room are five

VIEW FROM blacksmith shop looked out onto parade ground where original post had doubled-story building. Although Fort Nisqually started at site on beach, it was soon moved to higher ground which offered better protection from Indian raids and flood waters.

loaded guns in one corner. Rifle, Gun & Pistols loaded at the head of the bed."

Tolmie in 1833 was in charge of the post whenever the factor was away. His description of the honor was less than enthusiastic: "Commander of a trading post in a remote corner of the New World with only a force of six effective men in the midst of treacherous, bloodthirsty savages, with whom murder is familiar."

One hazard this 21-year-old Briton faced was the desire of the chiefs to marry off their daughters. On the same day six weeks after his arrival, three different chiefs offered him their daughters. He "respectfully declined them all, declaring it improper for a physician to have unlawful dealings with the fair sex."

A week before he had rejected a more vocal offer. He was sitting in the store one evening and noted in the diary, "A paint besmeared beauty outside, is using all her blandishments to obtain admission, but this is truly no temptation, and if never more strongly assailed I shall remain virtuous during my stay in this country without assuming any merit for self-control."

Tolmie stayed at Nisqually for six months. In 1844 he returned as superintendent of the Puget Sound Agricultural Company. This was formed to

EASTERN ROW of Fort Nisqually, as seen from southeastern blockhouse, shows blacksmith shop, granary, and corner of trading store. Cannon in center is reminiscent of time swivel gun was used to beat back Indian attack on fort.

OLDEST WOODEN building in Northwest, granary became especially active when Fort Nisqually's emphasis shifted from fur trading to agriculture. In some years Nisqually shipped upwards of 15,000 bushels of wheat to Russian settlements in Alaska.

AFTER BOUNDARY between United States and Canada was settled in 1846, British at Fort Nisqually were accused of inciting Indians against Americans. Although this was disproved, HBC interest in Nisqually decreased and in 1859 Factor Tolmie moved to Canada. In 1867 U. S. government paid company $650,000 for its holdings on Puget Sound.

handle the farming operations of the HBC. He was at Nisqually when the local Indians under Chief Patkanim tried to take over what by then was an elaborate fort, similar to the modern replica.

Patkanim got into the fort on the excuse that he wanted to look for another chief. When one of the traders accidentally fired a gun, the Indians hidden outside mistook this for the signal to attack. Before the gate could be shut two employees were killed and one wounded, but the attack was beaten back.

U. S. Army troops were rushed to the area—in fact in a British ship—and five months later the Indians responsible for the killings were caught. Two were executed. Patkanim, who claimed he knew nothing of the plot, was exiled temporarily to San Francisco so that he could be impressed with the ways of the white man.

Patkinam returned with the air of one who has been converted. He aided the settlers but apparently it was the old story of "if you can't beat them, join them." Patkanim's biggest chance came when the military offered $20 for the heads of hostile Indians. He led his warriors in a 10-hour battle with other tribes and gathered a few heads. He soon realized their were easier ways to riches. His answer was to chop off the heads of his slaves and turn them in!

TO GET THERE: The original site of Fort Nisqually is near the main entrance of the Dupont Powder Company plant on the beach near Dupont, Washington. In 1934 remaining ruins were moved to Point Defiance Park in Tacoma, Washington, where a full-scale replica of the fort was built. From downtown Tacoma take 6th Avenue West to Pearl Street (in the 6000 series), turn north (right) and continue north until street deadends at park (in 6000 series north). Follow marked road inside park to replica.

FORT VASQUEZ, COLORADO

Love may manifest itself in many ways, but seldom as effectively as it did at Fort Vasquez in 1842.

Here on the eastern bank of the South Platte River, traders, trappers and travelers gathered nightly for protection from the winter winds and "lurking savages." The adobe walls provided shelter from the elements. The solid gate and alert sentinels in the watch towers insured against any surprise threat.

"Rube" Herring, a visiting trapper, soon realized that he had more to fear than Indians and weather. The bold looks and coarse comments received by Mrs. Herring from a trapper named Beer meant but one thing: trouble.

The incident was described by Rufus B. Sage in his 1855 book, *Scenes in the Rocky Mountains*. Referring to Beer, Sage wrote, "Backed by a number of personal friends, and anxious to obtain the lady from her husband, the former had provoked a quarrel and used very insulting language to his antagonist."

When Herring could take it no longer, he challenged Beer. "The preliminaries were arranged in confident expectation of killing Herring, who was considered a poor marksman, especially at an off-hand shot," Sage continued. "The weapons selected by Beer were rifles, the distance fifty yards, the manner offhand, and the time of shooting between 'fire' and 'three'."

Beer shot at the word "fire." His ball hit a tree near Herring.

"At the word 'three' the contents of Herring's rifle found lodgement in the body of Beer, who fell and expired in a few minutes."

That ended that incident, although Sage went on to muse "Upon the frequent deeds of mischief and iniquity that had originated within" the post of the South Platte River, especially "in connection with the infamous liquor traffic. And thought I, were those bricks possessed of tongues, full many a tale of horror and guilt would they unfold."

Vasquez was one of four trading posts that shared the profits and troubles along the river north of Denver. Nearest to Denver was Fort Lupton, 28 miles north, built about 1837 and alternately called Fort Lancaster. Fort Jackson was built about the same time a couple of miles north. Vasquez was built in the fall of 1835 about five miles above Jackson. Another seven miles beyond, Fort St. Vrain was established in 1837. It was also known as Fort Lookout and Fort George.

The competition among the posts is suggested by this 1838 comment of the founder of Fort Jackson, William A. Sarpy: "My object is to do all the harm possible to the opposition and yet without harming ourselves."

Fort Vasquez should not be confused with the log cabin trading post operated by Louis Vasquez five miles north of Denver in 1834. This was known as "Fort Convenience" and, occasionally, Fort Vasquez. It is thought that here Vasquez teamed with Andrew A. Sublette, his partner in the real Fort Vasquez enterprise further north.

This post was built of adobe bricks which were

(State Historical Society of Colorado)

"**MADE OF MUD** or 'dobey' the enclosure is about 100 feet square, tne walls about 12 feet high, upon two corners stand the round guard house running about five feet higher. Around the walls are 'port holes' and so made as to shoot from them in any direction." This is how 1860 visitor described Fort Vasquez ruins. Plat is probably more accurate than WPA reconstruction as shown in 1958 photograph. Exact appearance is unknown because fort was used in 1850's by travelers, in Civil War by Army, and in late 1860's as a stage stop. (Plat redrawn from State Historical Society data.)

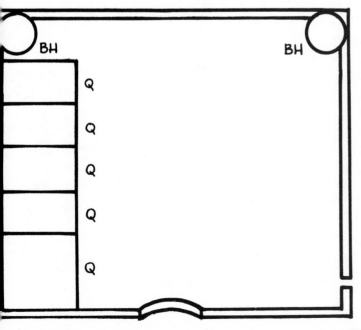

made on the spot by having oxen tramp in the mud and sand to mix the ingredients thoroughly. By the end of fall, 1835, a 100-by-110 foot square had been enclosed and brisk trading was already in progress. One visitor reported, "Vasquez & Sublette had about 50 lodges of Chiens at there (sic) fort on the South fork."

The beaver trade was on the wane by this time so the Indians turned to the buffalo for their liveli-hood. Buffalo skins, robes, blankets, and even tongues were traded at the fort for a variety of items which ranged from finger rings and powder horns to "paper covered looking glasses" and food.

Seven hundred buffalo robes and 400 tongues were shipped from Vasquez by an unusual mode on April 26, 1840. They were loaded aboard a large, flat-bottomed "Mackinaw boat" and floated down river the 2,000 miles to St. Louis. Much

BLOCKHOUSES, or sentry boxes in reconstruction are not quite accurate, most authorities agreeing that sides higher than main wall should be round. Some reports of old-timers claim there was at least one 36-foot tower. Mounds at original site were used in making adobe bricks for replica constructed a few feet away because of nearby highway.

wading and pushing was done by a seven-man crew during the 69-day journey. This was one of the few successful voyages down the South Fork and main stream of the Platte, reputed to be one mile wide and one inch deep in some places.

Business began to drop off and in 1840 Fort Vasquez was sold. Lock and Randolph, the new owners, did not fare well, and it was described as "a recently deserted post" by Rufus B. Sage when he passed Vasquez two years later. The "principals becoming bankrupt through mismanagement and losses of various kinds . . . had caused them to evacuate their post and quit the country."

One boatload of furs had failed to reach St. Louis, the bottom had dropped out of the fur market and an Indian raid had made off with the fort's entire herd of horses and mules, all factors that bankrupt the new owners.

As it turned out no one profited by the 1840 sale of the fort. Not only did the buyers lose, but so did Sublette and Vasquez. They had accepted a note for the post which was worthless.

TO GET THERE: All four posts are near U. S. 85 north of Denver, Colorado. Fort Vasquez reconstruction is between the north and south lanes of U. S. 85 about 1.5 miles south of Platteville. Two miles north of the town of Fort Lupton, some adobe remains are inside a barn, identified by a sign on private property. The unmarked and uncertain site of Fort Jackson is three miles west of Ione. Fort St. Vrain's location is identified by a marker 3 miles west of Gilcrest (.2 miles north of the St. Vrain sub-station of the public service company).

MILITARY DESIGN of Fort Vasquez is challenged by some historians. They say that trading posts did not look this way. WPA architects or Civil War use by Army might account for discrepancies such as extraordinary number of rifle slots in walls. Building along western wall is in most contemporary descriptions, is believed to have been four or five rooms used as quarters. Well was not in actual fort.

FORT ASTORIA, OREGON

Misfortune plagued Fort Astoria, Oregon, even before it was founded. Death was a frequent companion throughout its active years, and dishonor was not unknown. "Ill starred" is probably the best way to describe this trading post that started with great expectations in 1811 and disappeared into obscurity sometime after 1824.

The Fort Astoria chronology really began in New York City when John Jacob Astor prepared a scheme to capitalize on the trading potential of the Pacific coast. In chartering the Pacific Fur Company, his plan was to establish a headquarters near the mouth of the Columbia River in the Pacific Northwest.

A round-robin system of trading would feature a ship leaving annually to resupply this distant fur-gathering outpost. After dropping off her supplies, the ship was to take the furs to the Orient and trade them for goods for the home market.

Two expeditions left for the Pacific Coast, one by the ship *Tonquin* and the other overland along the general trace of Lewis and Clark's expedition.

Tonquin left New York on September 10, 1810 and was almost immediately torn by dissention. By the time she had anchored within the mouth of the Columbia River six and one-half months later, at least eight men had died in accidents and the entire complement was united against the captain.

The captain had ignored the fact that his ship was chartered by the fur company. Technically this made him an employee of the company's directors who were his passengers. Throughout the voyage he tried to impose discipline on them as if they were crew members. The desire to be rid of the captain as quickly as possible probably sped the movement ashore upon anchoring in the Columbia River.

"Not having the captain to contend with," wrote Washington Irving in *Astoria*, "they soon pitched upon a spot which appeared to them favorable for the intended establishment."

As soon as *Tonquin* was unloaded, work started on building a residence, storehouse and magazine and planting a garden. In honor of the founder of the company, the place was designated Astoria.

Progress was slow because immense trees had to be cleared from the site by men who had never done work of that type before. Duncan McDougal, the company's factor ashore, confined his contacts with the captain to frequent exchanges of caustic letters. This ended when *Tonquin* sailed for Vancouver Island on June 1, 1811. That was the last the company saw of the ship and her disliked captain.

Contrary to orders from Astor, the captain permitted Indians to board *Tonquin* after reaching Vancouver Island. It was not long before the tactless captain had infuriated the principal chief by hitting him in the face with a pack of furs and expelling him from the ship.

Several days later when brisk trading was taking place, the warriors edged around until two or three were near each white man. At a signal the Indians turned on the crew. Within minutes all of the officers and men had been slaughtered except for five men hidden in a cabin and the interpreter who jumped overboard.

The Indians left that night but returned the next morning. As soon as the ship was crowded with looting braves one of the surviving crewmen

OLDEST GRAVESTONE in Pacific Northwest is this 1814 burial in tiny Fort Astoria Park. McTavish was chief factor of North West Fur Company and rival of Alexander Henry for love of local barmaid and adventuress Jane Barnes, first white woman in Oregon. Both men were drowned while on social calls. Although neither won the lady, Henry came out second best; his grave is nearby and not even marked!

touched off the powder magazine, blowing up the ship and her occupants.

When word of this disaster filtered through to Astoria, the few men there rushed to finish a strong palisade around their buildings. Work had already started on this because of earlier rumors of an impending Indian attack. Four 4-pound cannons were mounted in the bastions.

To further impress the Indians with the garrison's strength, McDougal tried some psychological warfare. Knowing that smallpox had ravaged the coast in the past, he showed the leading chiefs a small bottle which he said contained smallpox. McDougal announced that at the first sign of hostility he would uncork the bottle and release the disease. The terrified Indians kept the peace.

On January 8, 1812, the first part of the overland expedition arrived. Other groups came in for the next two months but John Day and Ramsay Crooks did not arrive until May 11. They had been captured by Indians and left naked in the wilds. A final party, reduced by desertions and death from disease, completed the journey on January 15, 1813 after a 15-month trip from St. Louis.

Disconcerting to the Americans at Astoria were new rumors that war had been declared with England. This hastened discussions that the project should be abandoned and in October, 1813, McDougal sold the post to the British North West Company for 20 percent of its value. A number of the employees remained loyal to the American company. One was Gabriel Franchere, a clerk

whose diary noted, "McDougal, as a reward for betraying the trust reposed in him by Mr. Astor, was made a partner in the Northwest Fur Company."

A British 26-gun warship appeared a month later and prepared to bombard the fort. The crew had been told that this valuable prize would be theirs as soon as the fort surrendered.

Notification of the British ownership of the fort infuriated the ship's captain. He threatened to bring suit to recover his lost loot. The captain was even more angry when he inspected the primitive place that had kept him at sea for almost five months.

"Is this the fort about which I have heard so much talking?" he exclaimed. "Damn me, but I'd batter it down in two hours with a four pounder!"

Fort Astoria officially joined the British Empire on December 12. Franchere described a formal group that ceremoniously marched to the flagstaff where "the captain took a British Union Jack and caused it to be run up the top of the staff; then taking a bottle of Madiera wine he broke it on the flagstaff, took possession of the country in the name of his Brittanic Majesty; and changed the name, Astoria, to Fort George."

SOLID CONSTRUCTION and friendship with Indians maintained peace at Fort Astoria. When first overland group arrived, after 340-day trip over estimated 3,400 miles, they described "infant settlement of Astoria . . . with its magazines, habitations, and picketed bulwarks, seated on a high point of land, dominating a beautiful little bay, in which was a trim-built shallop riding quietly at anchor." By this time, large company quarters and a small schooner had been added to first construction.

(Paul Rockwood watercolor from National Park Service)

TO GET THERE: Site of Fort Astoria is outlined in paint on the streets and sidewalks centered at 15th and Exchange Streets in Astoria, Oregon. Blackhouse and McTavish graves are in tiny park at that intersection.

FORT GENOA, NEVADA

When Orson Hyde, a 50-year-old "Apostle" from the ruling inner circle of the Mormon Church, was instructed to take charge of Mormon Station in what is now western Nevada, he was promised by Brigham Young that Salt Lake City would provide him with whatever he needed.

He arrived on June 19, 1855, after a month-long trip and reported finding "a most splendid mill and ranch."

Three months later Hyde decided there was a definite lack at his new post. With a cold winter in the offing, Hyde informed Salt Lake City something would have to be corrected or he could not stay. On October 9 he was informed by letter that help was on the way:

"Learning last Friday . . . of your want of a wife," the elders wrote, "we . . . obtained the services of bro. James Townsend, purchased a team &c to go out to Carson County and take your wife to you . . . we have done pretty well as they are going to start tomorrow morning."

Brigham Young had more than kept his bargain. Mary Ann Price, the future Mrs. Hyde, had one child by a previous marriage. She presented Hyde with a ready-made family when she arrived on November 7.

Evidently Hyde was pleased as he not only continued to run affairs for Young but he prospered in his own right at this frontier settlement.

Hyde had not been the first settler. Hubert Howe Bancroft's *History of Nevada, Colorado, & Wyoming* gives this honor to Hampden S. Beatie, a miner who arrived in 1849.

Beatie and several friends built "what is called a double log house," Bancroft relates, "that is, two compartments connected by a covered passage-way, after the style of the Missouri frontier of the past generation. It had neither floor nor roof, but as it did not rain that season it was not uncomfortable.

Beatie had no time to waste on building a more elaborate place. He was too busy trading everything he owned to the parade of pioneers enroute to the California gold fever.

In Salt Lake City, John Reese heard of Beatie's bonanza. Visions of untold riches before him, Reese headed for Mormon Station with 13 wagon loads of eggs, bacon, flour, grain, feed and everything else he thought would command a profit.

Reese built a log cabin, probably the only real house in Nevada at the time, and then spent $2,000 in putting up a stockade. This log barricade enclosed more than an acre of ground and provided protection from marauding Indians and an even greater threat, renegade white men who preyed on isolated settlements and untended herds. In light of the complaints in pioneer diaries of Reese's exorbitant prices, the "fort" probably provided security against irate, over-charged travelers, too.

When Apostle Hyde established his authority at Mormon Station in 1856, he changed the name to Genoa. For some unexplained reason he selected this name to honor the Italian birthplace of Christopher Columbus. The stockade became known as "Fort Genoa" even though there were no soldiers or battles within many miles.

Hyde did not stay long at Genoa but his memory lingered for many years. In 1857 when Brigham Young summoned the faithful back to Utah to resist the invading U. S. Army, Hyde tried to sell his valuable properties for $20,000.

There were no buyers, and Hyde knew that his mill, ranch and other holdings would be taken over as soon as he left. To these squatters Hyde wrote what could be considered a curse: "The people will be visited with thunder and with earthquake, and with floods, with pestilence and with famine until your names are not known among men."

This ominous warning was remembered in 1872 when two different fires in the month of June leveled seven buildings, one of them a brewery. Ten years later the town was almost wiped out when tons of snow thundered down the valley, crushing houses, barns, and people. The destruction was so complete that the exact number of dead could not be determined.

"IMAGINE A CITY with only three houses in it, no streets, tall pine trees and a great high mountain to look strait (sic) up to," is how one Mormon wife described Genoa in 1856. At base of Sierra Nevada Mountains, Genoa was where pioneers rested and re-stocked before tackling this final but torturously steep barrier to gold fields. Five hotels and six saloons gave travelers impression "residents are a social, jolly, bibulous class," 1881 author commented. Mountainside in background, Job's Peak, rises 6,000 feet above town.

TO GET THERE: From Carson City, Nevada, take U. S. 395 south 11 miles to Nevada 57. Turn right (west) four miles where route ends at Genoa.

FORT GENOA was once leading settlement in Nevada, is oldest still in existence. Its legends include tale that $8,000 silver loot from stage robbery was buried by bandits next to a pine tree. Treasure hunters have found the big question to be: "Which pine tree?" World renown came to Genoa when local boy, George Washington Ferris got the idea from a nearby irrigation wagon wheel for his most famous invention, the Ferris Wheel.

ORIGINAL MORMON Station (right) was destroyed by fire in 1910. State and town efforts erected reconstruction in 1947. Genoa was starting point for fabled John A. "Snowshoe" Thompson's mail route from 1856 to 1868. During dead of winter Johnson carried up to 80 pounds of mail on his back in eight-day round trips to Placerville, California. Despite nickname, he used skis. Because mail route was unofficial, he never got a cent for his services.

(Nevada Historical Society)

FORT TYSON, ARIZONA

Reeking "of everything unclean, morally and physically," Fort Tyson so displeased Martha Summerhayes in 1874 that "we slept in our tents that night, for of all places on the earth a poorly kept ranch in Arizona is the most melancholy and uninviting."

In common with hundreds of others, Tyson was a stage station at which riders changed horses, stages changed teams, and passengers changed places. As Mrs. Summerhayes commented, some "were clean and attractive" but the majority were no better than Tyson's.

When Charles Tyson built his fortified stage station in 1856, safety rather than sanitation had priority. Mojave Indians were frequent visitors, and Tyson had no intention of offering them an easy prize. Several adobe buildings provided living, working, eating and sleeping quarters for man

CARAVAN'S END for Hadji Ali, famed "Hi Jolly" of Army's 1850-era camel experiment, is this grave near Fort Tyson. Ali accompanied camels from Africa. was only herder to remain. When project ended with Civil War, he became mule skinner, stage driver, and messenger for General Carleton's California Column.

and beast alike. Walls were thick, roofs and exteriors were as fireproof as adobe plastering could make them, a spring with good water was inside, and everything was connected and enclosed so that each building could protect its neighbors.

Records suggest that Tyson was successful in discouraging attack; either his defenses were too awesome, or his relations with the Indians continuously friendly. It appears that the most violent activities at Tyson's were the reactions of travelers to the accommodations.

Michael Welz bought the "fort" from Tyson and added a post office. The menu improved when his widowed half-sister arrived from New York and took over the cooking chores. This was the best change in the history of Fort Tyson, travelers and stage drivers unanimously agreed.

"RANCHES IN that part of Arizona meant only low adobe dwellings occupied by prospectors or men who kept relays of horses for stage routes," commented early traveler. "Wretched, forbidding-looking places they were! Never a tree or a bush to give shade, never a sign of comfort or home." Fort Tyson easily fit this description.

TO GET THERE: Fort Tyson is on U. S. 60 and 70 at the western edge of Quartzsite, Arizona, 82 miles north of Yuma.

THICK ADOBE walls and ceilings provided maximum protection from desert heat. Sign quotes early desert guide report that accompanied camels from Africa, was only herder to remain. had slight boom in 1896 that caused reopening of post office and re-naming of town as Quartzsite.

ARMY CAMP on the frontier is depicted in this undated pencil sketch of un-named forward post in Texas that seemed to incorporate adobe, jacal, stone, frame, and canvas materials in its construction.

THE FORWARD LOOK

"I start this morning with the dragoons for the Pawnee country, but God only knows where that is."
—Painter George Catlin writing from Jefferson Barracks, 1834.

THE forts that came first had at least one thing in common, the fact that they were the only traces of civilization on a frontier that consisted mainly of forts.

As the nation moved westward, the Army and its camps led the way. Chains of forts were established along the Ohio, then the Mississippi, then the Missouri. A giant steap into the wilderness, and an outpost was established far beyond the forward line, becoming the forward line itself.

Along the Rio Grande, then the Pacific shores and the Columbia, these tiny but powerful instruments of government authority and legality were established. Their missions were manifold: to explore or to survey the unknown; to subjugate or to pacify the Indian; to protect or to discourage the settler.

The success of the forward line — and of the Army mission itself — could be measured by the speed with which civilization and settlements passed by and put the outposts behind them.

What follows are some of the forts that led the way in the early days of westward expansion.

PRESIDIO OF SAN ELIZARIO, TEXAS

"Site of the first military post of the United States," may be the claim of the plaque at San Elizario, Texas, but the facts seem to say otherwise.

Next to the Rio Grande, 20 miles south of El Paso, Texas, San Elizario can lay claim to considerable military action, but not to any world premiere role.

The plaque next to the front door of the church at San Elizario says that it was once the "Presidio de Nuestra Senora del Pilar y Gloriarioso San Jose" established in Mexico in 1683 and transferred to the present site in 1773. Actually it had no connection with this 1683 presidio which was moved in 1773, not to the San Elizario site, but to Carrizal far to the west.

San Elizario dates back to a post that 163 Spanish lancers built in 1752 and named "Nuestra Senora de las Caldas de Guajuquilla." This was moved in 1774 from a location deeper in Mexico to the bank of the Rio Grande about 55 miles southwest of El Paso. The 35-mile move northward to the modern site apparently was made in 1780 to provide better protection for the El Paso-bound wagon trains.

Military use of the Presidio of San Elizario, for that was the name it received when it moved to the Rio Grande, seems to have been sporadic with reports in 1814 and 1835.

The old presidio was occupied by the Americans during part of the War with Mexico. In 1849 two infantry companies and a pair of brass 6-pound howitzers were stationed there. Captain Thomas L. Brent reported that the barracks were "in a most dilapidated state, it being with difficulty that quarters could be obtained for two companies and the hospital."

He had definite ideas about San Elizario's value, finding no "military advantages in the situation of this post which make it desirable as a point for troops . . . excepting only the facilities for grazing."

A year later Colonel George A. McCall, on an

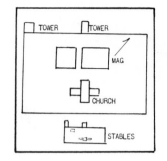

PRESIDIO OF San Elizario looked like this when visited in late 1846 by officers of Doniphan's command. Strong Mexican force evacuated post on Christmas Day, 1846, leaving behind cannon and much ammunition. Square enclosed 1,200 foot area, with inner enclosure including quarters, large chapel, barracks. Outer walls had watch towers. All walls were adobe at least four feet thick and 18 feet high. (Redrawn with permission from copyrighted plat of Roscoe Conkling, courtesy Arthur H. Clark Company, publishers.)

Inspector-General tour, had different thoughts. He said that if he had to choose between El Paso and San Elizario as the location for a post, "this of the two is preferable; for the reason that the old presidio, with little expense, may be made to afford quarters, hospital, and store houses, all well adapted for troops."

His report meant little. It came at the time that the department commander decided to pull the troops out of all the towns so that they could do some soldiering away from the "sinks of iniquity." Other than a short tour there by K Company, Mounted Rifles, to stop some minor thievery among the Indians, troopers were not stationed there until the Civil War.

Two companies of the California 1st Infantry arrived in October, 1862, and stayed a month or so. A year later Companies A, H, F, and C of the 1st California Cavalry apparently took turns at the post. Much of their time was devoted to aiding what their reports termed "Texas Union Refugees," but Rebel activity occupied them too.

In 1864 a 26-man patrol headed down the Rio Grande, surprised "a party of Texas rebels" across the river from Presidio del Norte, killed two, wounded three, and took four prisoner. This did not seem to silence the Southerners. In February, 1865, Company C troopers were approached by Confederate recruiting agents peddling grand rewards in return for desertion. Their headquarters were in Mexico.

Lieutenant Richard H. Orton led five raids across the border to the "recruiters' headquarters," surprised them twice, and put a stop to the business. His personal reward was promotion to captain. Special note was taken of one raid in which he led ten men in an attack on 14, with the casualties — including one dead — all on the opponent's side.

"THE CHURCH and presidio are in a ruined state," observed John Russell Bartlett during Boundary Commission visit in 1850 and reported with this sketch in his **Personal Narrative**. Troops were able to convert old presidio into barracks but government had to rent quarters for two officers at monthly cost of $45. No U. S. Army buildings appear to have been erected.

(Marvin King Collection)

CIRCULAR REAR of Chapel of San Elizario, seen through ruins of adobe residence, is reminiscent of 1780 presido. Round watch-towers were built outside thick adobe walls of fort to guard two entrance gates. On site of original presido chapel, this chapel was built in 1877.

SALT WAR of 1877 ended in front of this building, said to have been headquarters for presidio. Salt War started when rancher, Charles H. Howard, claimed salt beds that had been free to all comers from San Elizario. Mob seized Howard and associates, released them, then was shocked when Howard returned and killed local politician. Texas Rangers took Howard into protective custody, were deceived into finally surrendering him after several days siege. Mob killed Howard and two cohorts in front of this building day before cavalry arrived.

CHAPEL of San Elizario was rebuilt after flood destroyed first building. When Spanish manned presidio, they tried to convince Indians to use firearms instead of bows and arrows. Idea was that Indians would concentrate on firing inaccurate, slow muskets and lose skill in archery. Plan backfired because Indians quickly learned that better firearms were available than Spanish antiques.

TO GET THERE: From El Paso, Texas, take Interstate 10 about 27 miles southeast to Clint exit. Go west three miles to sleepy hamlet of San Elizario, where chapel and adobe headquarters face the square.

RED LIGHT district, only a single block away from Plaza, was headquartered in this stuccoed adobe, local tradition records. For good luck, locks of hair of its future occupants were mixed with mortar when structure was built — and traces can still be seen imbedded between adobe bricks, or so the story goes.

FORT ATKINSON, NEBRASKA

Only one major Indian expedition was fielded from Fort Atkinson. As far as the civilian observers were concerned, it was a disappointing affair.

It was on June 18, 1823, when news reached Fort Atkinson that an Arikara attack on William H. Ashley's trapping company had killed 13 men and wounded ten. Knowing that there was no time to request orders from St. Louis, Colonel Henry Leavenworth alerted six companies of the 6th U. S. Infantry.

Four days later the 220 soldiers and several artillery pieces left Fort Atkinson aboard three keel boats. By August 9 when they reached the Arikara villages 640 miles up the Missouri River, the force had been joined by 80 trappers and enough Sioux Indians to total approximately 1,100 men. The only discordant note so far had occurred on July 3 when a boat capsized and seven soldiers drowned.

An early morning clash between the Sioux and Arikara braves opened the battle on the plain before the villages. When the Arikara saw the soldiers and trappers advancing along the flanks of the Sioux, they stopped fighting and fled into their villages.

A siege of the two villages was carried on by musket and cannon fire for the rest of the day. An estimated 3,000 to 4,000 braves, women and children were believed to be hiding in the dirt villages behind rude palisades.

The Sioux lost interest in fighting when they spotted the Arikara's abandoned cornfields. Leavenworth began to have second thoughts as to how his superiors would react to the expedition, especially if more blood were shed. Peace talks and a treaty

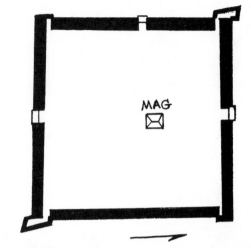

FORT ATKINSON, 1820, was about 500 feet square with stone magazine in center of parade ground. Many buildings were outside of stockade, including store houses, Indian Agency, sutler's store, work shops, and many quarters. From within bastions at northwest and southeast corners cannon were aimed to sweep forward face of fort. Sentry towers were atop each sally port. Underground passage provided exit under center of eastern wall. (Redrawn from National Archives and Fort Atkinson Foundation data.)

followed, despite warnings from the trappers that the Arikara were stalling for time.

At dawn on August 12, Leavenworth was informed that the villages were empty except for the aged mother of one of the chiefs killed the first day. Two days of searching failed to locate the tribe so the expedition boarded its keel boats and returned to Fort Atkinson. Thus, the Army ended its first battle with an Indian tribe west of the Mississippi River somewhat ingloriously.

"The greatest possible contempt for the American character," was how Joshua Pilcher described the Indian reaction to Leavenworth's indecisive campaign. The much-respected head of the Missouri Fur Company and leader of the trappers on the campaign, Pilcher wrote Leavenworth, "You have, by the imbecility of your conduct and operations, created and left impassable barriers."

Officially Leavenworth was praised for his forebearance in not roundly whipping the Arikara. Privately many Army spokesmen agreed with Pilcher that his suggestion of military weakness was responsible for much of the Indian unrest that followed.

The government knew that it could do little to prevent an Indian war. It had only one post west of the Mississippi; founded in 1820 Fort Atkinson was the first fort in the west and was the home of the 6th Infantry Regiment.

From the first, when it was known as Camp on the Missouri, or Cantonment Missouri, things had

NORTHERN SIDE of Fort Atkinson, as viewed from upstream by Omaha artist John J. Svoboda, shows 12 smoking chimneys for the 24 fireplaces in rooms along this side. An estimated 80 rooms were inside stockade.

(Omaha World-Herald courtesy Hollis Limprecht, Max Coffey)

FLAGPOLE STANDS amidst posts erected by Daughters of American Revolution on site of Fort Atkinson. Excavations have located many buildings of fort and large quantity of historical artifacts, some of which are in Fort Calhoun Museum (below). Post was abandoned in 1827 because it was too distant from civilization and not on routes to west.

not gone well. The troops had come from Plattsburgh, New York, 2,628 miles away; the largest trek yet attempted by a U. S. Army unit. The journey finished in a "dispersed state" with troops, families and workmen arriving for a month and a hilf until all were present in the fall of 1819. A total of 1,126 soldiers made up the garrison, the largest in the United States at the time.

The location was near where Lewis and Clark had treated with the Indians in 1804. It was described by William Clark with his own brand of spelling, "Camp Councile Bluff — appears to be verry proper place for a Tradeing establishment & Fortification."

A log palisade 16 feet high formed a square 520 feet on each side. With loopholes for muskets and cannon, the stockade also served as the outside wall for barracks and other buildings within the enclosure. Atop a 20-foot stand and in the center of each wall were mounted three cannons that could cover all sides of the fort.

"When completed, no force will be able to carry the work without the aid of cannon," Colonel Henry Atkinson, the commanding officer, announced.

The fort succumbed to other enemies. Scurvy and illness struck more than 100 men during the winter

of 1819-20 when the mean temperature was eight degrees above zero. More deaths were prevented by sending 100 sick men down the river to civilization. Others were taken to a special rest camp three miles away, Camp Recovery, where the surgeons concentrated on curing them with f r e s h game and wild onions.

When a spring flood inundated the fort, the garrison had no choice but to take refuge on the high ground two miles to the south, Clark's "Camp Councile Bluffs." Here they built a new fort along the same lines as the cantonment. It was named Fort Atkinson in honor of their commander by Secretary of War John Calhoun — after whom the site and nearby town came to be called in later years.

"The good-looking white washed buildings of the fort could be seen at a considerable distance," wrote the Duke of Wuerttemberg on an 1822 visit. "The fort itself was a square structure. Its sides were each 200 American yards long. There eight loghouses, two on each side . . . Each house consisted of ten rooms, and was 25 feet wide and 250 feet long."

The Duke was especially impressed by the fort's farm which supplied most of the fresh food for the post. "The agricultural enterprise near the fort was splendid," he wrote. "Here the finest European vegetables were grown. I saw our common cabbage, beans, onions, and melons of excellent qualbage, beans, onions, a n d melons of excellent quality."

Army Inspector-General Colonel George Croghan had less complimentary views when he visited the post in 1826, a year before it was to be abandoned. After terming Atkinson "certainly the weakest" of the forts along the Mississippi, Croghan said that the farm system "would sink the proud soldier into the menial" and the officer "into the base overseer of a troop of awkward ploughmen."

"Look at Fort Atkinson," he continued, "and you will see barn yards that would not disgrace a Pennsylvania farmer, herds of cattle that would do credit to a Potamic grazier, yet where is the gain in this, either to the soldiers or to the government? Ask the individual who boastingly shews you all this, why such a provision of hay and corn? His answer will be, to *feed* the *cattle*. But why so many *cattle*? Why—to eat the *hay and corn*."

TO GET THERE: From Omaha, Nebraska, take U. S. 73 north 15 miles to town of Fort Calhoun. Museum is in center of town on highway. Fort Atkinson site can be reached by turning east on Madison Street for a half mile to 7th Street. Turn south. Go one-half mile to a side road at the left. Turn left (east) and go a tenth of a mile to the marker. Cantonment site, on the river bottom, has not been exactly determined.

FROM THIS LOCATION Yellowstone Expedition of summer, 1825, was fielded. Atkinson commanded force of 400 infantrymen and two cannon aboard four keel boats, and 50 mounted men along river bank, that made almost 4,000 mile round trip to visit 16 Indian bands, sign 12 treaties. Trip was completed without any casualties, although at one point Atkinson and Benjamin O'Fallon, Indian commissioner, disagreed so violently on policy "they mutually seized, one a knife, the other a fork, and made an attempt to stab each other," observer reported.

FORT WEBSTER, NEW MEXICO

Commissioner John Russell Bartlett did his duty as he saw fit and on June 27, 1851, the decision was clear cut. His camp at the Copper Mines in southwestern New Mexico was being visited by a party of men, and a girl who seemed almost a prisoner. A few casual queries by his soldiers revealed to Bartlett that the visitors had captured the girl in Mexico and were taking her "to some part of New Mexico to sell or make such disposition of her as would realize the most money."

Although his official mission was to establish the boundary between the United States and Mexico, Bartlett "deemed it my duty, as the nearest and highest representative of the United States in this region, to interfere in the matter."

He instructed the commander of his military escort, Lieutenant Colonel Louis S. Craig, to inform the visitors that they were in violation of a treaty between the United States and Mexico and that the girl would have to be turned over to the Army.

After the traders had been sped on their way, Bartlett learned that the girl was 15-year-old Inez Gonzales of Santa Cruz, Mexico. She had been captured by Indians the previous year and purchased several months before by the traders.

Bartlett's group rallied to the girl's assistance. "She was well clad with such materials as the sutler of the escort and the commissary of the commission could furnish," Bartlett recounted, "and besides the more substantial articles of clothing provided for her, she received many presents from the gentlemen of the commission, all of whom manifested a deep interest on her welfare, and seemed desirous to make her comfortable and happy."

Inez stayed with the commission "in a camp of

OLD PRESIDIO was headquarters of Fort Webster Copper Mines location. As drawn in 1851 by Lieutenant Joseph E. Maxwell, this sketch indicates presidio was used as infantry barracks. Dragoon barracks was oblong building with interior patio, right. Commanding officer occupied building at far end of fenced rectangle; sutler store was L-shaped building at near corner. Small building at left of presidio was bakery. All buildings were of adobe.

(Lee Myers Collection)

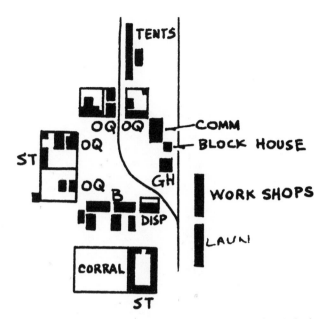

FORT WEBSTER looked like this in 1853, not long after it had moved to banks of Mimbres River. Inspector General said quarters were "quite indifferent and insufficient, the post not having been completed" and noted that one company was living in tents. A tent also served for a hospital, despite fact his plat showed a dispensary (bottom right hand corner of parade). Inspector was pleased to learn that most of the dragoons were in Temperance Society. (Redrawn from Mansfield Report 1853.)

over a hundred men." Bartlett promised to return her to her parents as soon as his work was finished at the Copper Mines.

The commission arrived at the mines on May 2. It was deserted at the time, but once the mines had been the leading source of copper for Mexico. Since 1804 the vast resources had been worked by as many as 600 men, including convict labor supplied by the Mexican government. Coins for the State of Chihuahua were minted there for a period.

Indian raids had stopped all travel with Chihuahua in 1833. The mines had been abandoned, leaving desolate a cluster of adobe huts and an imposing three-sided presidio.

Bartlett described the presido when he found it in 1851 as "of a triangular form, each side presenting a front of about 200 feet with circular towers at the corners. It is built of adobe, with walls three to four feet in thickness, and a single opening on the eastern side."

After a few weeks of labor by Bartlett's escort, the walls were repaired and the roof was restored. The presidio was then able to house all of the men and supplies of the escort. A scattering of 50 or more adobe buildings provided shelter for the commission and their mounts.

Except for a month's trip into Mexico, Bartlett remained at the camp—he named it "Cantonment

COPPER MINES site of Fort Webster is believed to be in this vicinity. Old-timers point out mounds next to pole (in center of picture) as site of "an old fort." Troops sent as reinforcements found "There are 50 men here, all frightened out of their wits. They have old wagons, logs, barrels, rocks, and other articles too numerous to mention, piled around their fort, making it almost impossible to get to it. Their cannon is placed on top of the roof which is flat like all roofs in this country. They expect momentarily to be attacked by Indians."

POSSIBLE WELL at 1853 site has origin unknown to Horace Bounds, owner of ranch. Well is at least 100 feet deep.

Dawson"—until August 27. Early in his visit he had a number of friendly meetings with the Indians but relationships soured as the summer passed. One chief remained his friend and was rewarded with the present of a newly-tailored, blue suit, complete with gilted buttons and a scarlet lining. It is not known whether the chief received the name Mangas Colorado (Red Sleeves) because he like to wear the coat inside out or whether he had been named prior to the gift.

After Bartlett had left the Copper Mines, Chief Mangas Colorado remained in the area. His depredations caused the army to establish an official post at the old presidio. The selection was the result of a search of the area by Major Enoch Steen of the 1st Dragoons who termed it "decidedly the best location I have seen anywhere in the country for a post."

He noted that it in the center of the Indian country and was in such good condition that only a month and little cost would be required to repair it. A company of the 3rd Infantry was assigned at the post to do the rebuilding and housekeeping, and a company of mounted troops from the 2nd's Dragoons came for field service. The official name of Fort Webster was adopted.

The post did not stay long at the Copper Mines. In September 9, 1852, it was moved 12 miles east in order to be closer to the road network.

When Inspector General Joseph K. F. Mansfield visited in 1853, he agreed, "The old post at the copper mines has nothing to recommend it." He did not think much better of the new fort: "The buildings of this post are made of logs and mud and quite indifferent and not sufficient for the command as one company and the sick were in tents."

Fort Webster was abandoned in 1853. Frequently during the next two decades troops were to be stationed at both its first and second sites whenever the Indian troubles exploded. Neither was to be occupied again as a permanent military post.

The story of Fort Webster cannot close without the sequel to its companion tale, that of Inez, the Mexican captive befriended by the Bartlett commission. True to his promise, Bartlett returned the girl to her family. "Words cannot express the joy manifested on this happy occasion," he said. "Their screams were painful to hear."

A year later Bartlett learned the ending of the Inez incident when he stopped at Tubac, Arizona. "To our infinite astonishment and regret" he saw that Inez was living at the dilapidated Tubac presidio as the mistress of its Mexican commander.

TO GET THERE: For vicinity of Copper Mines site take State 316 north from Bayard, New Mexico, 1.7 miles to right at Hanover Junction. At 1.5 miles east, road overlooks supposed site of early Fort Webster. To go to Mimbres River location return to State 316. Head north 2.7 miles to State 90, turn right (east) and follow this former wagon route through "Copper Mine Pass." Bear left at both forks (at 10.5 and 10.7). Road is adjacent to site at mileage 11.3, on privately owned property on the right.

"**THIS IS A** small valley, about one half mile wide," reported Captain William McCleave in 1863. "I marched down the valley about nine miles, when it intersects the 'Rio Mimbres' . . . I expected the cavalry would be at the old fort." By this time Fort Webster was used for occasional outposts, but no permanent details. Dry Mimbres River, on bottomland below post appears below; site of 1853 fort from the north is above.

FORT COFFEE, OKLAHOMA

Just north of Spiro, Oklahoma, the Arkansas River makes a horseshoe bend around a rocky bluff that rises a sheer 100 feet above the water. In the misty past French trappers called it "Roche des Hirondelles" or "Swallows Rock."

After the Army established Fort Coffee atop the bluff in 1834, many a river man was to rue the irony of it all. Here was a place named after "swallows" that was dedicated to the enforcement of strict prohibition throughout the territory. To compound the situation, a brave punster occasionally would add that the Army got rid of the whiskey and put "Coffee" in its place!

Other military posts may have had missions of preserving the peace or defending freedom. Fort Coffee's main objective was to prevent whiskey from being smuggled into the Indian Territory. Its garrison struggled gallantly to do the job against overwhelming odds.

On the edge of "Swallows Rock," Coffee's commander, Captain John Stuart, mounted a brass 6 pound cannon where it could command the river traffic. Sentinels were posted to watch for boats and to put the cannon into action whenever a boat did not stop at the fort's landing. Their orders: fire one blank round of powder. If the boat did not head for the landing, fire a second blank round.

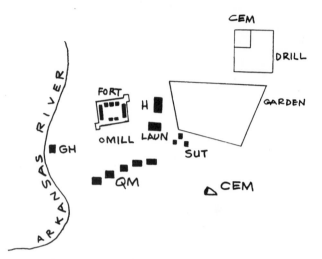

FORT COFFEE, 1837, was built of roughly hewn logs with buildings arranged around three sides of 100-by-100 foot square, identified here as "fort." Barracks and officers quarters were built against inside walls of stockade; latter was actually little more than 10-feet high pickets placed between each building. Magazine was lone building on western side of fort. Key to Coffee's mastery of river was guardhouse overlooking brink of bluff at which cannon was mounted. (Redrawn from plat in Grant Foreman's *Advancing the Frontier.*)

If the boat still did not head in, load up the cannon with six pounds of iron and blast the boat out of the river.

Craft that bowed to the Army's authority—and artillery—were searched unless the captain was known to be of good repute and would certify that his boat was clean of contraband. Boxes were opened, barrels were bored into, and many a gallon of grog was poured into the Arkansas as the owners mournfully watched.

In three months of 1834 Stuart boarded 52 boats. However, this did not seem to have much effect on the liquor consumption upriver. "From the unusual quantity of whiskey which is said to have gone into the Indian country this summer," Stuart reported, "I am inclined to believe that some of the steamboats have in violation of the law and regardless of the certificates of honor . . . in a clandestine manner introduced spirits."

Rum running by another name was not to be countenanced by Captain Stuart, so he announced his determination to head upriver "for the purpose of procuring, if posssible, evidence of the fact, when I will enter a prosecution in every case where the necessary evidence can be had."

If Fort Coffee's success was less than overwhelm-

LITTLE TRACE of Fort Coffee is left at site despite fact it was occupied several times. Choctaw tribe owned buildings until selling them to Methodist Church as a boys school in 1843. Union and Confederate troops used its buildings alternately during Civil War until they were burned by Federals.

TRADITIONAL FORT appearance is presented by this view of Fort Coffee's stockade by Vinson Lackey. Buildings in left foreground were storerooms. Sutler's store was at right foreground. Laundresses lived in largest buildings halfway up hill. Corner of hospital is behind laundresses' cabin. Guardhouse, with flag waving overhead, stands alert on bluff overlooking river, left background.

(Thomas H. Gilcrease Institute)

ing in thwarting smugglers, at least it appeared to be doing a good job on itself. Stuart pointed out that at their previous post "near one half of the men were intoxicated almost every day; a number of the worst men died," but things were now different. "The company has now been three months and a half at this place, and after the first two weeks there has scarcely been a single man intoxicated."

If nothing else his prohibition duties added spice to an otherwise dull routine for the Fort Coffee

(Oklahoma Historical Society)

"FORT KOFFEE on the Arcansas river" is how H. B. Mollhausen identified this sketch when he drew it on July 19, 1853, while on Whipple Expedition. Military post had been abandoned 14 years by this time. Fort Coffee Academy, Methodist school for Indian Boys, had added second story buildings but much construction from Army days still remained. During Civil War Stand Watie, Cherokee Indian who became Confederate brigadier general, operated in area; 150 Southerners were stationed in Coffee buildings in 1862.

trooper. Occasionally a patrol would head inland or upriver to poke around the "blind tigers" for illicit beverages.

Something different occurred in 1835 when a steamboat pulled alongside the Fort Coffee landing and unloaded a wagon full of $36,000 in silver, weighing more than a ton. This was the annual payment to the Choctaw Indians.

An escort from Fort Coffee was assigned to insure that the tempting shipment reached the Choctaws in safety. The destination was only 150 miles away, but the route was mountainous, the flies miserable, the weather torrid, the streams swollen and the low ground boggy. The escort was on its third team of oxen pulling the wagon when destination was reached 20 days out of Fort Coffee.

Four years after its establishment, Coffee was closed. Its whiskey watching role was undertaken by other forts on the river, including Fort Gibson where a red-painted scow poked into likely "blind pigs" along the river bank.

As soon as the Army left Swallows Point, the fort had a new occupant. A quick-thinking Choctaw wasted no time in moving in and laying claim to all he surveyed.

TO GET THERE: From Fort Smith, Arkansas, take U.S. 271 southwest to state line. At mileage 9.4 after entering Oklahoma, turn right (north) on gravel road; historical markers identify intersection. After 5 miles, turn right again. Fort Coffee site is about one mile down this gravel road.

FORT McINTOSH, TEXAS

"It was seldom any one came to their isolated post. No one traveled in that direction for amusement in those days. Nothing but stern necessity and duty took people to such a desolate place, so, when strangers did arrive, they were kindly welcomed and entertained."

Apparently more truth than chamber of commerce went into this description of Fort McIntosh, Texas, in 1854. Written by Mrs. Lydia Lane, it was expanded on when she revisited the post in 1856.

"The heat was dreadful," she wrote. "The houses were mere shells, entirely exposed to the baking sun all day long. Not a green thing was to be seen but a few ragged mesquite-trees. Here and there a blade of grass attempted to grow in the scorching sandy soil, but it was soon burned up by the hot sun."

Inspector-General J. K. F. Mansfield had equally unenthusiastic comments about Fort McIntosh in his report of an 1856 inspection. After noting that one company had just returned from a 700-mile, three week Indian scout and that "most of the men

& 54 horses with sore backs" were grazing away from the fort, he continued:

"At the time of my inspection the thermometer stood at 99° and it was extremely hot & dry & the troops as a body were exposed to the heat in their tents and out of them." He said that the brush shades erected by some companies "were accomplished with difficulty, as the posts had to be purchased out of the company fund which was exhausted with most of them & some companies had no shades at all."

Mansfield blamed the lack of shelter on the fact that there was no lumber "to be had without money as the citizens controlled the limited inferior timber in this quarter" and the department commander refused to spend government money for the purpose. "The suffering of both men and horse was great, yet with quiet submission looking forward to a change for the better."

He did note that some of the officers were living in stone buildings built at their "private expense." As a further illustration of the parsimonious policy of headquarters, he added that many of the troop-

FORT McINTOSH, 1856, included more tents than anything else. Between fortification, at top of plat, and main post were the infantry and artillery camps. Both consisted of tents. The hollow rectangle below main post, labelled MR, was the camp of Mounted Rifle companies. At the time of plat, post had 13 officers and 431 men. (Redrawn from Mansfield Report, 1856.)

FORT McINTOSH, 1875, had improved very little in 20 years. Building ceased when post was abandoned by U.S. troops during Civil War. This is view of main post; fortification does not show but would be northwest of hospital. Only commanding officer had quarters. Other officers lived in hospital or in town; troops in storehouses and tents. (Redrawn from Division of Missouri Report, 1876.)

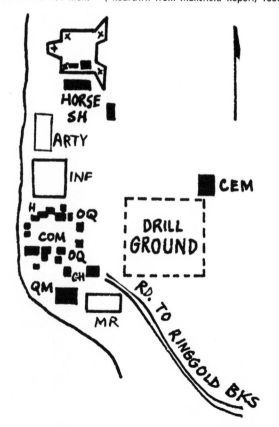

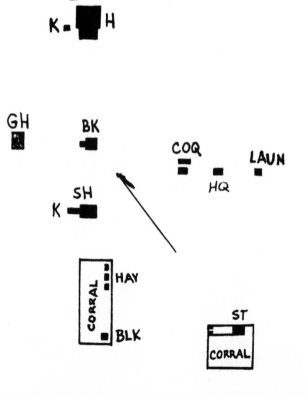

(National Archives)

AFTER 1880 Fort McIntosh took on permanent look. Barracks are at left, officers quarters in center background. Texas Republic had post at Laredo from 1846 to 1848. In March 1849, Camp Crawford was founded at Laredo and renamed Fort McIntosh in January, 1850. Post was given up for a short time in 1858. Confederates took it over from 1861 to 1865. Permanent construction began in 1868, finally finished in 1882. Buildings have been used by Laredo Junior College since 1947.

ers were using their own blankets on their horses because the government had none on hand.

On the eastern bank of the Rio Grande near Laredo, Fort McIntosh had been established as Camp Crawford in 1849. Its purpose was to guard the newly devised border with Mexico. Because the United States had taken over Laredo, founded in 1757, the Mexicans set up Nuevo Laredo (New Laredo) across the river and maintained a small garrison there.

Construction seems to have moved slowly at McIntosh. When Inspector General William G. Freeman visited in 1853, he found the troops living in kitchens because the barracks had not been built. Three years later Mansfield found that the situation had improved only to whatever extent the officers and men could afford to pay for lumber and labor from personal funds.

Another reason for the slow construction may be explained by an Inspector General's report in 1872 regarding McIntosh's weather: "The long continued heat produces an anaemic condition on white men which in one or two seasons destroys the energy."

The bulk of the official time and money was devoted to the fortification at the northen part of the reservation. About this Mansfield had definite

OFFICERS QUARTERS were designed for hot, dry climate. Trees and grass are results of irrigation as predicted in 1872 report, "No crops can be raised except by irrigation, and even with irrigation crops of all kinds are unremunerative on account of the sandy nature of the soil." A story told of fort is that once when barracks caught fire and bugler sounded alarm, troops did not realize there was a fire. Instead they rushed to their defensive positions. While they watched for enemy attack across Rio Grande, barracks behind them burned to ground.

ideas: "I do not consider this small fort of any material strength or importance. The same labor would have put the men in comfortable quarters."

Another reason for the slow construction may have been the actual soldiering requirements that kept McIntosh detachments almost continually in the field.

Mansfield reported that Indian raids from across

GUARDHOUSE, a use suggested by window bars, now is used as warehouse. Even before Fort McIntosh was founded, Army was at Laredo for Mexican War. Legend is that Army once sent supply steamship up Rio Grande during high water period, had it stranded at Laredo for two years until it could be floated downstream.

the border had been the subject of joint action with the Mexicans. Responding to a McIntosh complaint about the raids, the Mexicans captured about 200 Indians, male and female. When 112—including 30 warriors—escaped across the Rio Grande, the U. S. troops pursued and captured most of them.

Fort McIntosh was in its earliest days when Lieutenant Walter W. Hudson went Indian chasing in spring, 1850. They were successful in recovering 30 animals that had been stolen but less successful the next day on the return trip to the fort.

Apparently the horse-stealing Indians had circled around to meet them. The soldiers were drawn into a chaparral thicket where combined rifle and arrow fire killed one private and wounded three men and the lieutenant. Two weeks later Hudson died of four wounds suffered in the fight.

In 1857, Sergeant Charles M. Patrick and a detachment of the 2nd Cavalry came upon an Indian party. After a fight in which six Indians fell and 12 horses were captured, the troopers continued the pursuit for two and a half days. They were 160 miles from the site of the first fight when they had another engagement, finally dispersing the Indians so much that further pursuit was impractical.

The lessons seemed to have little effect on the Indians. In November, 1857, Apaches and Comanches committed depredations right in the town of Laredo. Chased by a McIntosh detachment, they had to abandon their horses, ammunition and loot in order to escape.

The next day the marauders reappeared 16 miles below Laredo. Hearing a report that a boy had been kidnapped, the Army galloped in pursuit, but the raiders had disappeared. This prompted the Corpus Christi newspaper to lament that one 80-man company of cavalry was inadequate to protect the settlements that earlier had been the responsibility of 700 men.

It may have been that the Mexican authorities agreed with the newspaper when they arbitrarily impressed several Americans into the service of one of the revolutionary armies. Goaded by a rally of angry citizens at Laredo, the army acted promptly by dispatching Company I, 2d Cavalry, to the border. When it became obvious that Captain Albert G. Brackett would execute his demands by force if necessary, the Mexicans quickly released their newly drafted "soldiers."

An appreciative citizenry voted a resolution in support of Brackett. It proclaimed that in his actions the townspeople could "find and appreciate the gallant spirit of the soldier and the patriotism which should ever guard our liberties."

ORIGINIAL FORT MCINTOSH was somewhat star-shaped, mounted four 24-pounders and two 8-inch guns in 1856. By 1872, comment was: "This field work is now useless, being located on a sandy bottom which is being rapidly honeycombed by aroyas." General Phil Sheridan visited McIntosh in 1854 during heavy windstorm, noted because parapets of fort were made of sand "the wind was too much for such a shifting substance, and the work was entirely blown away in the storm." He also observed that lumber was so scarce that the wooden bacon boxes were saved "and the boards from these were reserved for coffins."

TO GET THERE: From downtown Laredo, go west on Victoria Street about 15 blocks until it runs into old Fort McIntosh reservation. Recent buildings and parade ground are near entrance. Older buildings are mainly to right (north) of parade ground. Old fortifications can be reached by going north on dirt road that parallels river at far side of post. Mounds are in northwestern corner of reservation.

FROM RIO GRANDE field fort looks like picture above; top of its parapets below. Fort was called upon to defend against Yankee raid in 1864 when it was southernmost defense for Confederacy on Rio Grande. Union advance was secretive, however, and Confederates had to defend from houses in town.

FORT DUNCAN, TEXAS

Indians, bandits, Mexicans, Confederates and Yankees all battled with Fort Duncan at sometime during its existence. The 43-year conflict that occupied Fort Duncan from its earliest days, and at one time seemed to end with no victor, could not be equalled.

When an Army post was established near Eagle Pass, Texas, in March, 1849, the assumption was that a private citizen owned the site. One of the first lessons learned by the Army in Texas was that no matter how desolate or remote the place, title to it was held by someone. Judge John Twohig, San Antonio banker, was that someone in the case of Eagle Pass and the newly established Fort Duncan.

At first, everything was friendly and informal. Twohig told the Army that he had no objection to their use of his land, especially as a fort at Eagle Pass provided protection for the caravans crossing the Rio Grande for points in Mexico and, via Mazatlan, California. He also permitted them to use any timber and coal they could find. For the first four years, there was no formal agreement.

Using sandstone from nearby bluffs the Army erected some buildings, but most of its efforts were limited to rough brush or pole huts.

"The quarters of the men are wretched hovels not fit for occupancy," is how Inspector General William G. Freeman viewed the post in 1853. He added that the commanding officer had been told in 1851 "not to put up any more permanent buildings until a lease was obtained."

Lydia Lane also stopped at Duncan during this period. "It was a wretched place to live in," she

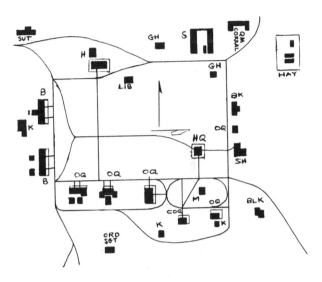

FORT DUNCAN, 1875, was expansive far cry from primitive conditions before Civil War. Although 12 years separate plat from bird's eye view (below) drawn in 1887 by A. Koch, there are only minor differences. Top left corner had sutler's complete with billard room that he had as early as 1856. Barracks were at western end of parade ground. Twenty-bed hospital was on northern edge of parade; officers' quarters along southern. Center officers' quarters was known as "Long House," measured 18 by 80 feet but included only three rooms. Double-storied storehouse kept subsistance and commissary stores on first floor, quartermaster and garrison stores on second. Officers' quarters shown next to bakery actually was occupied by commissary sergeant. Bakery had 300-loaf capacity. Library shown on plat actually was a pair of tents. It had about 200 books and several newspapers and was well patronized, especially after cavalry companies formed competing literary societies in 1875. Differences in location of guardhouse and other buildings in northeast corner of parade indicate some changes between 1875 and 1887. (Plat redrawn from Surgeon General Circular No. 8, 1875.)

(Ben E. Pingenot Collection)

MAGAZINE DATES to first days of Fort Duncan in 1849. Measuring 20 by 20 feet, it has two sets of doors, the lattice work providing ventilation. Adobe officers' quarters can be seen to right rear of magazine. Ordnance at post in 1856 included one 6-pound brass gun, one brass 12-pound howitzer, four iron 24-pounders, and two 8-inch howitzers.

wrote later, "and I am sure some of our companions who were to remain there looked on their future station with sinking hearts when they saw it for the first time."

Twohig offered terms of $1,2000 a year for five years, then a token dollar annually for the next ten. After a total of 15 years, the site and all of its improvements would revert to him. As of Freeman's visit, the Army was studying the deal.

When acting commander of the 2nd Cavalry, Robert E. Lee stopped at Duncan in 1856, the post had taken on a more orderly air and even had a "find band" for parade ground serenades.

Some stone buildings had been erected but at no expense to the government. Officers quarters were built at the expense of the families. The men of Company C, 1st Artillery contributed $80 to build themselves a stone barracks. Ordnance Ser-

geant Thomas Drury built a stone house for his family at a cost of $100.

Lee may not have been aware of this but he did hear how close he came to being ambushed. Only a few minutes before his arrival, the escort for a hay detail had been jumped by Indians within a mile of the post. Before the sergeant in command knew what had hit them, "their mules were cut from the traces under his nose, and jerked into the chaparral," Lee recounted.

About this time, a lease was signed with Twohig: "For 20 years at $130 per month, or $1,560 per annum & $10,000 for back claims," according to the 1856 inspection report.

Life at Fort Duncan was relatively uneventful until it was occupied by Confederates during the Civil War. As a shipping center between Mexico and the Confederacy, it was a target of what the

Confederate garrison of the 1st Texas Cavalry termed "renegades."

In 1864, coincident with an attack on Fort McIntosh at Laredo, a force crossed the Rio Grande and assaulted Fort Duncan. Captain James A. Ware, the commander of the fort, had anticipated the attack and placed his troops in the hospital, comissary, and the town. The home guard was alerted and they barricaded the streets with cotton bales.

Under the cover of darkness, the attackers were able to catch the garrison partly by surprise, even though they were resting on their arms. The hospital force was subdued so quickly that when Ware dropped in to help he was captured. Ware was able to escape before daylight, by which time the defense was split between the commissary building and the arroyo behind the stables. After a short foray against the cotton bale barricades, the attackers re-crossed the Rio Grande.

Another raid was attempted two days later. This did not get past the outskirts of the town because a mounted company arrived to reinforce the fort. In addition, weapons had been provided for the many men who were without them the night of the first attack—their weapons having been rushed to the defense of Fort McIntosh.

When the Federals reoccupied the post in 1868, finding "the buildings were more or less injured or destroyed," the landlord question continued. Until late in the 1870's, the annual $1,560 sufficed. Then the Army decided to buy and Congress appropriated $10,000.

But, said Judge Twohig, the sale price is $10,358. As this exceeded the appropriation, the alternative was to lease the fort at a new rate of $2,400 a year. The sale price jumped to $20,000 . . . then to $30,000. When it hit $36,000 in 1883, the Army's answer was to move the troops to other posts and abandon Fort Duncan.

The criticality of Eagle Pass was such that by 1886 the Army returned. This time it occupied the same site but called it "Camp at Eagle Pass" and paid only $900 annual rent. Finally in 1892 it paid $20,001 and became the owner of what was to become a key troop center during the Villa Revolution and World War I.

Final resolution of ownership came in 1938 when the post was auctioned off to the city of Eagle Pass for $3,760—roughly the annual maintenance cost after it become an inactive post in 1927.

TO GET THERE: From downtown Eagle Pass, Texas, go south on Adams Street to Fort Duncan Park where a dozen of the old fort buildings remain.

ALTERED EXTERIORS have converted headquarters (above) and storehouse (below) to modern uses in Eagle Pass City Park. Recreational nature of area harkens back to 1850's when one Fort Duncan officer was Lieutenant Abner Doubleday, reputedly baseball's inventor.

STABLES PROVIDE cover for modern "horses." In 1865 Fort Duncan was witness to dramatic event when Confederate General Joseph Shelby hauled down "Stars and Bars," wrapped it around plume from his hat, and dropped it into Rio Grande as his Army crossed into Mexico. Another event was 1873 conference at which General Ranald Mackenzie was told by Secretary of War Belknap and General Phil Sheridan to pursue Indians into Mexico, the start of "Mackenzie's Raiders".

FORT LINCOLN, TEXAS

Second Lieutenant Richard I. Dodge and Fort Lincoln were equally brand new to the Army in 1849. A single shot that shattered the midnight stillness and killed a soldier was the baptism of blood for both.

Fort Lincoln was founded on July 7, 1849, on the west bank of the Seco River, a mile or so from D'Hanis, Texas. Previously a Texas Ranger company had been encamped nearby to protect the 29 families of D'Hanis. This became an Army job, no easy matter because the settlers were fresh from European cities and knew little of pioneering. Twenty rough huts, windowless and with dirt floors, made up what Robert E. Lee described as "the smallest and meanest of European peasant hamlets."

The arrival of two companies of the 8th Infantry seemed almost a challenge to the Indians. While the soldiers tried to set up an Army post on a slight promontory overlooking the river, the Apaches and Comanches moved in close.

"For months after the establishment of this little post, there was scarce a night when an attempt was not made on our picket line," Dodge wrote in *33 Years Among Our Wild Indians.* "The sentinels soon learned their lesson, and hiding themselves, watched the ground and fired at every unusual object."

MARKER IS main proof of Fort Lincoln site, although many foundation ruins remain. Until recent years, D'Hanis citizens held Fort Lincoln pioneer celebration annually. Protection was not only reason for town to be grateful for fort; its construction provided jobs at $1.50 a day and saved D'Hanis citizens from bankruptcy.

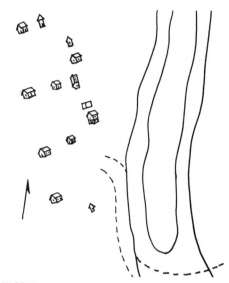

FORT LINCOLN, 1851, looked like this according to old sketch on which this is based. Seco River is at right of sketch with ford and road indicated. General layout of buildings suggests that parade ground and quarters were in area north of road. (Redrawn from data courtesy D'Hanis State Bank, J. P. Ephraim, W. H. Knorr.)

Major James Longstreet, the first commander of Lincoln, and later a Confederate general, frequently turned out the guard to scour the brush for infiltrators. Dodge was not enthusiastic about this idea.

"How often, when engaged in such duty, thrusting my sword into every clump and cover, have I inwardly thanked the Indian for his disposition to put as great a distance as possible between himself and danger," Dodge commented. "Though I hunted faithfully many nights, I never found an Indian."

Fort building kept the days busy. Cyprus logs were cut from along the river bank and stone was gathered from the surrounding area. Nine buildings took shape, including three officers' quarters, two barracks, three storehouses and a hospital. All were enclosed by a stone fence. Protection for the animals was provided by a stable and brush corral.

The latter comes in for comment from Dodge:

"The corral fence at Fort Lincoln, Texas, was made of thorny chaparral brush, tightly pressed between upright posts set by twos. It was impassable for white man or horse, yet scarcely a week passed for the first summer after the establishment of the post, that the Indians did not get over this fence, and cutting horses from the picket line, endeavor to stampede them thoroughly, as to make them break down the fence."

Although the Indians were unsuccessful, and suffered several wounds in the process, they were determined. On one night when Dodge was the officer of the day he heard a shot from the direction

(Peabody Museum, Harvard University)

FORT LINCOLN, 1849, was sketched from across river by Captain Seth Eastman, army officer and artist. In diary of his march for August 2, 1849, Eastman noted that his command moved out at 4 a.m. for Fort Lincoln, 28 miles away. "Warm day and men much fatigued—arrived at the Seco between one and two o'clock." At Lincoln he found a group of 84 new soldiers, 16 of whom were added to his party. "Several of them sick," commented Eastman. Eastman sketched many forts; 17 of his paintings hang permanently in the United States Capitol.

of the corral. "Running at full speed, I entered the corral, to find the sentinel greatly excited. He had not fired; had seen or heard nothing but the shot which came apparently from outside of the corral ... We went outside and almost instantly stumbled over a body, which on examination proved to be that of the blacksmith, a quiet and excellent soldier. He had been shot through the heart and killed instantly."

At daybreak, the sign was obvious. "The Indian had crawled around the corral fence, on to the parade ground, and was probably at work on the gate when the blacksmith suddenly came upon him and was shot, simply to further his own escape."

The Indians were pursued 50 miles until they scattered in the mountains.

Not long after, Comanches raided D'Hanis' sister town, Castroville, 23 miles to the east. Their thievery and terror ended with the murder of an entire family.

Dodge, a guide, and 25 soldiers took up the chase. For a month they followed the Indian tracks over more than 150 miles of killing terrain. Dodge "finally overtook and surprised them in their camp, killing some, dispersing the others and capturing all their horses, saddles and equipments."

"This was so severe a blow that the Comanches almost entirely ceased to frequent that portion of country, and in a very few years after, that post was abandoned, as not longer necessary."

TO GET THERE: D'Hanis is a hamlet on U. S. 90 about 50 miles west of San Antonio. From U.S. 90 in D'Hanis take farm road 1296 north 2.2 miles to where it meets Seco River (left). Dirt road on left goes through gate across river ford and winds up on opposite bank onto site of fort. Private property.

ROCKS FROM fort foundations and old wall are still at site although buildings were torn down and moved to D'Hanis sometime after post was abandoned in 1852. Texas Rangers used post for short period. Cabin (below) is near fort entrance and supposedly was built of fort materials.

CAMP COLORADO, TEXAS

Whether it was serving the Union or Confederate cause, the guardhouse was the busiest activity during the ten years that Camp Colorado, Texas, tried to maintain peace in north central Texas.

Part of that peace was accomplished by locking up the drunk and disorderly types. There was more to it than that. A patrol in 1856 flushed some Indians, killed three and rescued a Mexican captive. He had been with the Comanches so long that he did not consider that he was their prisoner. As First Sergeant Gardner described him, this "naturalized Comanche" had to be locked up so he would not escape from his rescuers and return to his captors. The guardhouse proved to be the best place for him.

Prisoners of a different type exceeded the guardhouse's capacity in 1861, so a compound had to be set up to handle them. By this time Texas Militia were in control of the post. Their prisoners were unhappy Union soldiers whose surrenders at other forts had been accepted with promises of paroles and passage to the east. When Texas officially entered the Civil War as part of the Confederacy, there were second thoughts about giving seven companies of troops still in Texas a chance to fight another day. The paroles were cancelled. Sixty of the troops sat out the first year of the war at Camp Colorado.

Even before Camp Colorado had anything else, it had a guardhouse, and perhaps this was an omen of things to come.

The command that founded the post consisted of two companies recruited from rival regions: Alabama and Kentucky. This rivalry was so pronounced that exchanges of blows were commonplace until

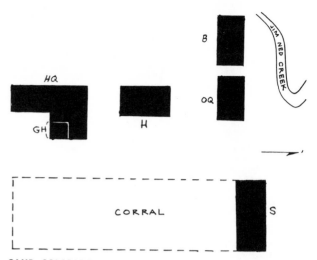

CAMP COLORADO, 1860, had this design according to Henry Rea, Coleman county pioneer. He was past 85 when he pointed out building sites in 1965 to Thomas R. Havins, author of **Camp Colorado.** Headquarters was of limestone, included 12- by 15-foot guardhouse. Other buildings were of adobe with 10-foot wide front porches. Two officers' quarters, 42 by 41 feet, were planned, but only one built. There is no record of any officers' families staying at post. Parade ground was west of buildings. (Redrawn from Mr. Havins' data.)

interrupted by the authority of first sergeants and solitude of damp cells. Nine men were in need of the corrective atmosphere of the latter when they arrived at Camp Colorado's first site on August 3, 1856.

They had made the four-day march from Fort Chadbourne wearing leg irons and riding in wagons. When the column arrived at the banks of the Mukewater in present-day Coleman county, the next step was obvious: build a guardhouse.

Each company erected picket walls four feet high daubed with mud. A fireplace area with a stone chimney of sorts was added to each enclosure and then oval tents 12 by 16 feet put atop the pickets as roofs. For only one day did the prisoners lounge in the impromptu cells. Quickly their routine involved sunup to sunset construction work under close guard. They saw their mud and canvas homes only after dark.

Camp Colorado's progress was hampered by its temporary nature. This was hinted by the fact that it was denied the title of "fort" in the days when the designation was used liberally and with little significance.

The two guardhouses soon were joined by "quarters occupied by the troops, the hospital, and

GUARDHOUSE, most active building at Camp Colorado, is now storeroom in ranchhouse. Englishman bought fort site in 1879, used headquarters building stones in erecting combination residence and store which he attached to old guardhouse. Date 1857 appears over guardhouse door, right; 1879 over side door of residence, left.

PARADE GROUND west of Camp Colorado building saw many officers who later achieved fame. Founder was Earl Van Dorn, future Civil War general, as were E. Kirby Smith, Fitzhugh Lee and John B. Hood. Captain Theodore O'Hara, company commander when fort was founded, was famous as author of "Bivouac of the Dead."

officers" according to an early report. They were similar in appearance, "the pickets being secured from post-oaks, pecan, and hackberry that grew along the creek."

Indian activity also slowed the building program. This turned out to be fortunate for on July 1, 1857, the garrison moved to a new location 23 miles north. Between malaria and mosquitos, the first site had been especially unhealthy and uncomfortable. When the water gave out and a better site was reported on Jim Ned Creek to the north, the decision was made quickly.

Six days of wagon trips moved all of Camp Colorado's possessions. It was on a slight slope in an oxbow of the creek, near to water and to timber. The owners agreed to lease its 6,600 acres for $50 a month for 20 years, or sell it within 40 months for $3 an acre or later at $10 an acre.

Of course, the first matter was to build a guardhouse. Six men were restrained in the same type mud and canvas shelters as before, an alert sentry making certain that the restraint held. Considering that there were only 54 men present at the time, there is little doubt that the prisoners spent little time in their calaboose.

Discipline was taut at the post, too taut as far as many men were concerned. In his *Camp Colo-*

rado, Thomas R. Havins comments that Major Earl Van Dorn's Company A, 2d Cavalry, had only two months in 1857 without men in the guardhouse. Some months there were as many as 14 behind bars. There were also only two months in which Van Dorn did not have any desertions; no less than two occurred each of the other months of that same year. Twenty-four men went to Mexico in the first two months following the move from the Mukewater. In the 24 months after July, 1858, a total of 60 men deserted, more than he had available for duty when he arrived at the second Camp Colorado.

Whiskey dealers had a hand in the disciplinary problems. They arrived at the new site as quickly as did the troopers, and were in business before work was finished on the top-priority guardhouse. As the surgeon had commented at the Mukewater camp, the "lightning whiskey" sold by those who were "squatting amongst us" was "a potent cause of disease as firmly fixed as malaria, and to check its use requires almost superhuman effort."

Aggressive though their patrols might be, the Army was told that was not sufficient. In 1858, the Governor of Texas informed the military commander that some "rangers" would be the state's instrument in Indian-taming. The soldiers were directed to assist the rangers who were, in turn, told that

STONE CORRAL provided security and relative comfort for Colorado's animals. It measured 246 by 13 feet, had walls 15 inches thick and four feet high. Single gate was locked and guarded at night. These rocks are believed to be remains of corral.

(Thomas R. Havins Collection)

CAMP COLORADO headquarters building replica serves as pioneer museum in City Park at Coleman, Texas. This is probably best representation extant, careful searches having failed to find original photographs or sketches of post.

their services would be needed to man the frontier line while the Army went Indian hunting. Army cooperation had not come easily. Only after the rangers discovered the Indian massacre of four members of the Jackson family not too far from Camp Colorado did the Army agree to help the rangers.

Vigorous patroling kept the garrison so busy that on at least one occasion the surgeon, the only officer left behind, was the acting commanding officer. Lieutenant Fitzhugh Lee, nephew of Lieutenant Colonel Robert E. Lee who was acting regimental commander, commanded many Camp Colorado patrols. In 1860 he narrowly escaped death; only his West Point wrestling experience made it possible for him to kill rather than be killed in a hand to hand match with an Indian.

When the Civil War came to Camp Colorado, Captain E. Kirby Smith observed the appropriate amenities. Although he was to resign his commission later and ultimately become a Confederate general, at first he refused Texas Militia offers that he surrender the post to them.

"I could never, under any circumstances, give up my arms and horses, or negotiate upon terms that would dishonor the troops under my command," he insisted. "Were such a demand persisted in, I would mount my command, and endeavor to cut my way through any force opposed to me."

Texas state troops had surrounded the fort, a factor that probably hastened Smith's abandonment once the details of surrender were settled. "The troops marched out with their arms, equipments, horses, ten days' rations, and all of the transportation . . ." reported Smith, adding that the lack of transportation meant that much private property had to be abandoned.

Camp Colorado's history continued under the Confederacy with an occasional interruption when readjustments of policy or boundaries caused it to be abandoned temporarily. Texas Militia manned it most of the time, affording at least a degree of protection against Indian, Yankee and bandit. As civilian-style troopers, lacking training, experience and even uniforms, the garrison's problems were many.

Despite bountiful harvests, the farmers would not sell to the post if they had to accept Confederate money or vouchers. Draft dodgers and deserters became major objectives, including one 500-man, 40 wagon assemblage that was chased unsuccessfully in 1864.

Civilians-turned-colonel tried to impose their brand of discipline. They found the hard way that card playing and horse racing were hard to prohibit. Horse races on the parade ground were stopped, but restrictions against cards had no effect. When courts martial were tried in quantity, headquarters became suspicious and reorganized time and again.

Finally, with confusion on all sides, on May 27, 1865, the commanding officer at Camp Colorado was told to "disband the troops under commands at once. And as they have not drawn any pay for 15 months, it is nothing more than due them that to make an equal distribution among them of all public property you have, allowing each company to retain their company property."

TO GET THERE: Camp Colorado headquarters replica is in Coleman, Texas, City Park. To get to camp site, go north from Coleman on U.S. 283 for two miles, turn right on State 206. After 5.5 miles turn right on farm road 2382. In 2.2 miles route will turn to left but do not follow it; instead continue straight ahead for 4.3 miles more. Site is on immediate left side of road.

FORT CONRAD, NEW MEXICO

The sentry at Fort Conrad thought that perhaps the sun was playing tricks on him. He shaded his eyes for another look. Even shaking his head and blinking did no good. The mirage was still there and, what was more, it was moving slowly in his direction.

A bewildered sentry was the least of the problems for the garrison of this dust-swept, sun-bleached post back in 1852. When the supposed "mirage" drew closer, the apparition took definite form. In front was the battered figure of Fort Conrad's commander, Major Marshall S. Howe. Straggling after him was the bulk of the Conrad command, bereft of shoes, horses, weapons, packs, supplies, in fact of everything but the tattered clothes on their backs.

What started off as a clean sweep of the marauding Apaches, left the expedition swept clean—the blame resting variously on the Apaches, a grass fire, and the Mexican border.

It all began in the fall of 1851, shortly after the cottonwood log fort was established on the western bank of the Rio Grande. A few miles north in the town of San Antonio, a bartender decided to get rid of two boisterous Apache patrons by shotgunning them to death. A third escaped.

Soon after, a band of Apaches appeared in town and demanded that the bartender be arrested. With the alternative obviously being an Apache raid, the sheriff quickly complied. It was not long after, however, that the Apaches learned that the bartender was released as soon as they left town.

A dark period followed for the San Antonio-Fort Conrad area. Amid demands for the militia to be called out and arms to be shipped to the town, citizens found that it was deadly to wander into the countryside. A rancher minding his milk cows was found dead. Even a Conrad patrol was ambushed a mile from the fort, certain death being averted only by the dramatic arrival of reinforcements.

In the face of these conditions, the Army had little choice but to launch an expedition. Howe drew more than 300 men from Conrad and other posts, and stocked up with 30 days rations. He set forth on February 12, 1852, under orders from General Sumner, "Inflict upon these Indians, if possible, a signal chastisement."

The fort's location was such that every movement could be observed by anyone watching from the surrounding hills. As soon as Howe's force moved out, the word was passed Indian style and his expedition was carefully skirted by the hostiles. About 90 miles southwest of the fort the first contact took place, the advance guard receiving fire as it descended into a ravine.

Howe decided that an ambush probably awaited him, so he had the one wounded man picked up and the expedition pulled back to the nearest post, Fort Webster. The Webster garrison, alerted to the advance of an enemy force, was ready to fire. Fortunately at the last moment the uniform was recognized.

The expedition continued its march. The rough terrain took a terrible toll on footwear. Leather had to be fashioned from the hide of slaughtered cattle. The makeshifts of stiffened, brittle leather were less than comfortable.

Near the end of his tortuous march, Howe was drawn by the smoke of what was obviously an Indian rancheria. As an attack was readied, Howe suddenly realized that his wanderings had taken him across the border into Mexico. Thinly disguised comments regarding Howe's courage and ancestry greeted his order to pull back toward the Rio Grande.

Here came the final blow of the wild goose chase as a grass fire trapped the expedition. Everything had to be abandoned and the soldiers raced for the protection of the river's waters. Everything—equipment, weapons, food—was burned, the ammunition exploding as it was devoured by the flames.

There was no other choice. Discouraged, disarmed, and disarrayed, the expedition returned to

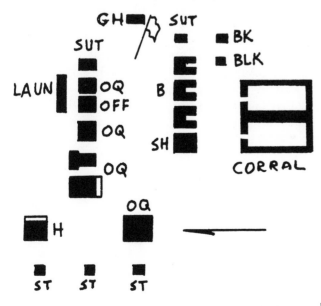

FORT CONRAD, 1853, consisted of cottonwood pole buildings except for 50-foot square adobe quarters of commanding officer. Other officers' quarters were plastered with adobe. Report in 1852 said "surrounding country is anything but interesting . . . little less than a great sterile mountainous desert, not calculated for the residences of man in a state of civilization." (Redrawn from Mansfield Report, 1853).

BLACK MESA, background, overlooks probable site of Fort Conrad. Area is almost as isolated as it was in 1850's when governor complained that it was too far from any town. Placing it distant from vice centers was intentional, but defeated by enterprising individuals who set up "hog ranch" north of post. Surgeon complained that diseases "from the shocking low state of morals here, are very prevalent in both sexes," including "from the same immoral source . . . the adulterated, poisonous liquor . . . that is vended to, and drank by, the soldiers." Hog ranch did not close when fort moved; in 1862 soldier noted in diary "a great number" of women were there and "object in stopping here is well known to all the 'bucks' in this command."

Fort Conrad, a complete blank to show for the efforts at Indian taming.

One explanation offered for the soldiers' poor showing was that they had been doing everything but soldiering for several years. The product of the 1850 decision to move the troops out of the town "sinks of iniquity," Conrad was selected so that the garrison could feed themselves with gardens and watch over the grazing camp. Its location had something to do with protecting routes of travel and preventing Indian depredations, but farm-like pursuits seemed more important.

Several hundred dollars worth of farming implements arrived at Fort Conrad at about the same as did the first troops. While some men were busy putting up buildings, the remainder became cowboys and farmers.

Major Daniel H. Rucker, Howe's predecessor as commander of Conrad, tried to maintain a semblance of military functions along with the agricultural demands. Reports that armed civilians were on an Apache-chasing expedition caused him to locate and disarm the settlers—and immediately feel the wrath of the governor.

"Is it possible that the murderers of our people are to go unpunished . . . and the people are not to be permitted to go in pursuit of these demons . . . without incurring the risk of having pointed at them, by the troops of the United States, the very arms placed in the hands for our defense and protection . . .?" demanded the governor.

Rucker said that he had received no reports of depredations. The governor's reply was to furnish a lengthy list. This goaded Rucker into sending a patrol to one area where a band of Indian rustlers was surprised and dispersed. Then the problem was to determine the ownership of the cattle,

especially when more claimants appeared than there were cattle. Rucker let the governor figure out that one.

When Inspector General Joseph K. F. Mansfield inspected Conrad in 1853, his immediate reaction was to recommend "the breaking up of the post and building an entire new one." He said that the buildings were so rotted and falling down that some of the troops were living in tents. He saved his special comments for the favored project, the farm.

The farm "had been in operation on hired ground," he said, "where 37 1/2 bushels of wheat and 50 bushels of corn were raised the past year, at a cost of 100 dollars for the use of the farm and 102 dollars for repairs of 'acequia' and 45 dollars for hired labor and repairs and other expenses besides the loss of one quartermaster's mule. In short it had proved a failure."

Mansfield's recommendation to abandon the location had been anticipated by departmental headquarters. As a result of an earlier inspection in 1852, the decision had been made to reestablish the post under a new name several miles to the south. Half of the 156-man garrison was already building Fort Craig at the new location.

Five months after Mansfield's visit the men at Conrad received word that their new quarters were ready at Craig. With little delay and no regrets, the garrison willingly abandoned unpleasant Fort Conrad.

TO GET THERE: Nothing is left to indicate Fort Conrad site, but its approximate location can be determined. From San Antonio, N. M., take U.S. 380 for one mile east to U.S. 85. Turn south for 15.5 miles to dirt road, left side, after climbing out of wash. This road heads toward Rio Grande across table land, approximate site of Fort Conrad. On opposite side of Rio Grande is ghost town of Valverde where Confederates defeated Fort Craig troopers in 1862.

FORT ORFORD, OREGON

"There is not a more healthy spot on the globe than Fort Orford," is how Surgeon Rodney Glisan described this far Western outpost in 1855. He added that his only medical business was "the result of some species of intemperance" or "an occasional accident."

Glisan had only been at Fort Orford a week when he entered those words in his diary, published later as *Journal of Army Life*. Had he waited a bit longer, he would have found that the greatest threat to long life and good health was an inhospitable local Indian population.

That word "inhospitable" undoubtedly would have been challenged as too mild by the first arrivals at the spot in July, 1851. Nine men led by J. M. Kirkpatrick, they were supposed to locate a townsite. No soner had the men waded through the surf and piled their baggage on the beach, than the Indians let loose a barrage of arrows. No one was hit, but in view of previous assurances that the Indians were friendly, this sign was more than a blow to morale.

Kirkpatrick congratulated himself on having insisted that the sponsors of his party provide weapons and ammunition. They also had agreed to his last minute demand for the ship's ancient cannon and the three powder rounds that were available. All of this was quickly gathered and the nine men lost no time in taking refuge at what appeared to be the safest point around: a sheer rock that rose starkly from the water about 20 yards from shore.

The next morning more than 100 braves stormed

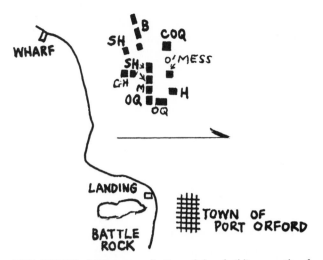

FORT ORFORD, 1854, was collection of log buildings north of battle rock and 35-house town of Port Orford. There was delay in completing fort because materials and part of first garrison were shipwrecked 60 miles north. Everything was brought ashore in a temporary Camp Castaway where they spent four winter months. During height of Indian scares, Fort Orford's buildings were protected by eight-foot high double wall that had dirt packed into six-inch space between, and firing ports every few feet. (Redrawn from Mansfield Report, 1854.)

the rock. "The air was full of arrows," Kirkpatrick said later. "James Carrigan had picked a pine board, and held it in front of us both. Thirty-seven arrows hit the board, and at least half of them penetrated nearly two-inch thickness."

The Indians were almost on top of the cannon when it was fired. "The execution was fearful," Kirkpatrick said. "At least 12 or 13 Indians were killed outright, and such a tumbling of scared Indians I never saw before or since."

After a hand-to-hand melee, the Indians were driven back. Seventeen bodies were counted on the blood washed ridge. Only four of the white men had been wounded, none seriously. Later the men learned that 20 Indians had been killed and 17 wounded.

For 14 days the Indians lay siege to the rock but maintained a respectful distance from the cannon. When their ship failed to return on schedule, the defenders decided that their only hope would be to escape. On the fifteenth day they made especially elaborate improvements to their defenses, but this was strictly for the benefit of the Indian onlookers. After dark the group slipped down from the rock and into the woods to begin a grueling two-week journey to Portland.

The ship arrived at Orford the day after the escape. Seventy men brought ashore several cannon.

GRAVES ATOP battle rock (foreground) are of "Jake" Summers, 1815-1909, veteran of original Indian fight, his wife and son. Defenders' landing site in Oregon is in background.

The blood-soaked and ravaged "battle rock," atop which they found Kirkpatrick's little cannon and a note describing the desperate situation, left little doubt that the first group had been massacred. On the beach they found teeth and charred bones in the ashes of a bonfire. This convinced them, not knowing that the fire was where the Indians had disposed of their dead.

When a 10-man party was ambushed with the loss of five dead and a sixth partly scalped but alive, it became obvious that the Indians had not backed down. An appeal for Army protection was sent to Astoria. The answer was the establishment of Fort Orford by 20 men of the 1st Artillery on September 14, 1851. At longitude 124 degrees, 28 minutes west, during its five-year career the post was the westernmost Army fort in the United States.

The Army built in a clearing in the dense forest north of battle rock. Inspector General Joseph K. F. Mansfield inspected the new fort in 1854 and thought so little of its value that he called it "Port" rather than "Fort" Orford when he recommended it be abandoned as being of "no military merit" and "of doubtful utility." His reaction to the garrison itself touched on sarcasm The buildings, he said, "are all of a character and of logs, but they are comfortable and the place is healthy, and the sick well provided." Just how he meant "character" was not explained.

Mansfield was not a good prophet. Indian depredations were frequent. In as early as its second month of service Fort Orford was the headquarters for a two-month Indian chase conducted by three companies of dragoons. A year after the inspection, a patrol was attacked by Indians who killed two men and wounded Lietutenant August V. Kautz, the post commander, and another man.

Kautz had similar troubles with the new citizens of Port Orford. On at least one occasion he was taken to court for "putting a civilian, who had been creating disturbances among the Indians on the government reserve, in the guardhouse . . . six days," Glisan recorded.

The same source tells of a quarrel Kautz had with the local justice of the peace.

"The lieutenant had been shot through the heart," was Glisan's first warning of the argument, but when he arrived at the scene he found Kautz alive and unharmed. The justice's pistol had been fired at such close range that the gasses gave Kautz the sensation of being hit even though the ball imbedded itself harmlessly into the floor.

The Rogue River Indian War of 1856 found Fort Orford in a critical location. Troops were rushed into the area from other points, Major General John E. Wool set up his departmental headquarters and attempts were made to "put our post in a condition for defense against the enemy should they attack us," noted Glisan.

Most of the garrison, now reinforced many times over, were in the field the first half of 1856. Only a few men were left to guard the fort, so few that the townspeople were thrown into near-panic at every rumor of an impending Indian attack. False alarms were common: a sentry firing at the man coming to relieve him; another firing at a cow; the citizens running for cover at the sound of the fort's cannon, which was merely announcing the arrival of the supply steamer. At the height of the troubles, the tiny garrison was powerless to prevent a town mob from lynching a captured Indian, burying him at the foot of his gallows atop "battle rock."

When the war ended in July, 1856, Fort Orford's last duty was to return to various reservations almost 2,000 captured Indians. All of the troops were gone, but for 40 days more the buildings were used as a hospital until Surgeon Glisan also left and the place was abandoned.

TO GET THERE: Port Orford, Oregon site of old fort, is on U.S. 101 about 83 miles north of California border. Battle rock is on the beach south of town.

BATTLE ROCK is probably little changed from early appearance. After Army left Fort Orford in 1856, town declined and then almost died in fire of 1868. Residents commemorate Battle of Battle Rock annually.

LANDING AT MONTEREY, July 7, 1846, brought United States forces to California and soon ended Mexican control of what became 31st state in four years.

CONQUEST OF CALIFORNIA

"We are about to land on the territory of Mexico, with whom the United States are at war. To strike her flag and to hoist our own in the place of it is our duty. It is not only our duty to take California, but to preserve it afterwards as a part of the United States at all hazards."

—Commodore John D. Sloat to his fleet, July 7, 1846

For almost two centuries a distant and disinterested Spanish government had tried to run the affairs of "Alta California" only to be dispossessed by a Mexican revolution in 1821. Mexico City then provided the seat of government but with no greater success.

The tides of emigration were sweeping at California's borders. Great Britain, Russia and France all contemplated annexing the vast area despite a "Monroe Doctrine" by which the United States reserved the American continents for Americans.

Yankees took the matter into their own hands by over-throwing the Mexican authorities of Northern California in the so-called Bear Flag Revolt in June, 1846. The die cast, the United States moved quickly and landed a fleet at Monterey on July 7, 1846.

The conquest of the new territory went smoothly at first. With the north under the Stars and Stripes, troops were landed at Los Angeles and San Diego. Initial successes were reversed when the Americans suffered defeats that threw them out of Los Angeles and temporarily besieged the troop columns coming overland from New Mexico.

When it was learned that the war included all of Mexico, California became only a side issue. The support from Mexico City ended. Shortly the native authorities made choices between escape or swearing allegiance to a new government.

Rival factions jockeyed for power in the new military government of the era that followed. John Fremont assumed a self-proclaimed role of leadership and had troops that answered only to him. In an attempt to retain power, he went so far as to challenge the designated military governor to a shotgun duel. Not even the Army or Navy could agree on who was supreme. Naval forces had been the first to land and to set up governmental functions, but Army forces were not only senior in rank but, by tradition, supreme on the land.

Finally, diplomacy and tact—plus firm directives from Washington—settled the matter. Gold provided the final answer. The swarms of Yankees answering the lure overwhelmed the old way of life and the conquest of California was complete.

POSTS AT SAN DIEGO, CALIFORNIA

As far as Sergeant Arce was concerned, he and the six members of his squad were in truly an unfortunate predicament. Not only did they have magnificent hangovers, but all seven Spanish soldiers were lashed to the masts of the gringo ship *Lelia Byrd*. And she was making for the open sea with Arce and company as hostages so that the troopers in Fort Guijarros would not blast her out of the water.

It had started a few days before when the United States trade ship stopped at San Diego for water and wood. Sergeant Arce and his men were posted aboard as a guard to make sure nothing illegal took place, especially fur smuggling.

The Yankee captain had been very hospitable and his rum very free flowing. The Spanish soldiers told freely of recent confiscations of furs. Then the previous night, the guard spotted the Yankees carrying arm loads of pelts aboard.

And that was how Sergeant Arce found himself tied to the mast and the *Lelia Byrd* making her best speed for the harbor's entrance. He could see the soldiers in Fort Guijarros standing next to its ten guns, and he could also see the *Lelia Byrd's* seamen standing next to her three 6-pounders.

Ten puffs of smoke from the fort were quickly followed by the whine of shot falling around the ship, and missing. Almost simultaneously, the 6-pounders opened on the thick-walled adobe fortress. Their aim was more accurate and the Spanish gunners took cover.

As the *Lelia Byrd* sped past the fort and into the open sea, the first and only naval action at San Diego concluded. No more rounds were fired from the shore. The shipboard hostages considered themselves fortunate when they were put ashore, until they remembered the wrath that undoubtedly would be their punishment for permitting themselves to be taken.

This was one of the first, but not the last, military events at San Diego. Founded in 1769 as Spain's first colony in California, San Diego began as a presidio that was little more than a parapet of earth and brush protecting two cannon. At first on the beach, the presidio was moved halfway up a hill overlooking the harbor. Governor Gasper de Portola then took most of the garrison north to the site of Monterey, leaving a handful to defend his headquarters.

Father Junipero Serra built a mission nearby. A month after Portola left, the mission was raided by Indians. Several raiders were killed as the six

POST AT Mission San Diego was established on January 20, 1847, by General Philip St. George Cooke and his Mormon Battalion. Mission had been abandoned in 1834 and when Cooke found "the buildings being dilapidated, and in use by dirty Indians, I camped the battalion on the flat below." Chapel later was used as barracks and hospital. Sketch (below) from Bartlett's report of his boundary commission visit in 1852 shows tents next to chapel. Mission was given up by army in late 1850's, returned to Catholic church by President Lincoln in 1865, and restored in 1931. Take I-8 east from I-5 about eight miles; turn north on Murphy road ¾ mile, east on Friars lane, one-half mile.

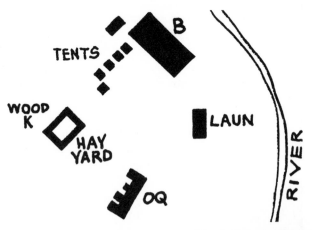

(Marvin King Collection)

PRESIDIO was actual though not official capital of both Upper and Lower California when Governor Echeandia occupied it in 1820's because he liked climate. In 1828 Kentucky trapper Sylvester Pattie and his son, James, were imprisoned in bastion (right). Sylvester died there, James was released when he promised to vaccinate all of California against small pox.

"IRREGULARLY BUILT on very uneven ground, which makes it liable to some inconveniences without the obvious appearance of any object for selecting such a spot," is how English navigator Vancouver described Presidio in 1793. These mounds cover fallen walls north of restored area (shown above). Three cannon were mounted at Presidio when Vancouver visited. Relations with civilians were similar to other army posts: in 1833 when soldier was put in civil jail, his release was secured by a corporal and seven solders who simply marched in and spirited him away.

SAN DIEGO MISSION was at this site for first five years, then moved inland to get away from military influence of presidio. Quarters of officers and soldiers also were in this vicinity. Only this side, where commandant's family lived, was habitable by 1836. "Twelve half clothed and half starved looking fellows composed the garrison," Richard Henry Dana wrote, "and they, it was said, had not a musket apiece." This was time of Indian uprisings that caused most ranches to be abandoned because Army was virtually powerless. Site is in Presidio Park above Old Town, San Diego, and intersection of I-5 and I-8.

EL JUPITER, cannon in center of Fort Stockton site, was cast in Manila in 1783; unsuccessfully tried to prevent **Lelia Byrd** escape in 1803; was spiked by American in 1846. Landscaped earthworks of old fort surround it on hill above Presidio Park.

CAMP RILEY, where Boundary Commission escort camped in 1849 at southern end of San Diego Bay, was at this site in vicinity of Palomar turnoff from I-5 south of Chula Vista. Bartlett's 1852 boundary escort also camped at San Diego—and 20 of its 25 men deserted.

(San Diego Title and Trust Company)

POLITICS ENTERED into selection of New San Diego Barracks site in 1850. Engineer was supposed to locate it near old Fort Guijaros, but selected plain to south in return for share of property. It was supply depot and barracks periodically until 1921, sometimes had only few supply personnel on rolls. Magazine is shown above with convenient saloon just across street. Marked site is Kettner and California streets.

FORT ROSECRANS site was reserved in 1852, taken over in 1870, but not occupied until 1898. Its coast artillery batteries defended San Diego Bay against naval attack until after World War II, but now only abandoned emplacements and watch towers are left. Site includes that of Fort Guijaros (below), now busy Naval base. Post is at end of Chatsworth Boulevard, an extension of Barrett Avenue from I-5.

"ONE OF THE most beautiful posts in the Army" was 1926 description of Fort Rosecrans when it had 27 sets of wooden quarters. Some of these remain today, are used by army reserve and National Guard for training meetings. Post was deactivated after World War II. Army may have done this in self defense: records are full of occasions when officers of San Diego posts "lost their hearts" to local senoritas and resigned in order to marry. One who did not marry still had reason to complain in letter home that parties—called "bailles" kept him up all night "and we did not get home until sunset the next morning . . . but I had quite a pleasant time." His problem: he had to go on duty upon return to post.

FORT STOCKTON originally was Spanish earthwork for defense against rumored Indian plot. Indian leaders were betrayed and ten key conspirators executed. Plaza below fort was witness in 1846 to attempt by Commodore Stockton to organize "Horse Marines." He had soldiers pass their horses to Marines from USS Portsmouth, but, as sailor later wrote: "Long Marines got short horses, and Short Marines, long horses" and gentlest horses went to experts, unbroken to amateurs. Result ended Stockton's resurrection of horse marines, as men went over both ends of horses, "muskets flew in all directions" and equipment was "strewed in promiscuous heaps from one end of town to the other."

soldiers drove them off with the loss of one boy.

When Portola returned, he found a strong presidio surrounded by a stockade of thick tree trunks. By 1782, 28 soldiers under a sergeant comprised its garrison. By 1800, a thick adobe wall had replaced the stockade and an artillery battery had been built at the entrance to the harbor. This was known as Fort Guijarros, Spanish for cobblestones, after the

NEW SAN DIEGO Barracks, 1879 (left) and 1911 (right) show basic similarities, though functions of some buildings had changed. Barracks was double-story, originally built as supply warehouse, condemned by inspector in 1852 as being too small and too weak for quantity of stores it should hold. (Redrawn from Inspector-General Reports, 1879 and 1911).

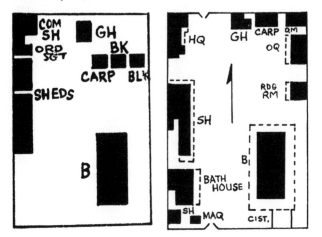

cobblestone ballast that was piled up at its site. Although not elaborate, work on the fort had taken several years because the commandantes would not agree on whether to make it square or round.

By the late 1830's both the presidio and the fort were in ruin. When the 1838 Castro revolt threatened the town, earthworks were thrown up hastily on the nearby hill. At least one cannon was brought up from Guijarros. When the Americans under Fremont arrived in 1846, the San Diegans were apathetic about it all. As soon as Fremont left, however, his rear guard was besieged and forced to take refuge on a ship in the bay. One American swam ashore and spiked the cannon on the hill.

Presidio Hill then became Fort Stockton ten days later when it was retaken by the Americans. The rest of the cannon were dragged from the old fort and two bastions were built of salvaged adobes. Three hundred one-gallon casks were filled with sand and set to form a rectangle 60 by 90 feet.

The Americans were firmly in charge by 1850. The Mission San Diego, six miles inland, was manned by a small garrison. A supply depot was built on the plains south of Fort Stockton. It was in this location that the Army held forth until the circle was complete and Fort Rosecrans was built in 1899 at a site that included Fort Guijarros.

CAMP SAN LUIS REY, CALIFORNIA

Sailors turned soldiers may not have liked the unaccustomed routine of being plodding infantrymen, but at Camp San Luis Rey they found that it had at least one advantage.

The story was told by Ordinary Seaman Joseph T. Downey in *The Cruise of the Portsmouth*. This was a personal account of the tribulations of the 200 shipboard sailors and Marines who joined Kearney's advance in Los Angeles.

More enthusiastic than effective, the seagoing troopers had swung out of San Diego on December 28, 1846, "with a cheer that made the heavens ring." They had not been daunted by Commodore Stockton's inglorious attempts to make "Horse Marines" out of their brethern in the Corps. Nor were they discouraged when their oxen gave out before they had crossed the dry San Diego river beds. Men replaced oxen as the prime movers for the 30 or 40 wagons during the five day hike to San Luis Rey where new oxen were obtained.

"One of those ancient and massive structures found all over Mexico and California," San Luis Rey impressed Downey as "at once wonderful and pleasing to the weary traveller." Although "the gardens and fountains were overgrown and choked with weeds, tall grass and mud," the men found "some splendid vineyards close by the mission, and more grateful than all to us, there was found after inspection a quantity of good wine, which was served out to us, at the rate of a pint to each man in the evening and the same quantity on the next morning."

The landing force was quartered in the square next to the mission. Care was taken to respect the 50 year old adobe buildings. This respect did not prevent the party from memorializing its visit by "leaving as momentoes the names and effigies of our separate ships, done in charcoal upon the whitewashed walls of each separate companies rooms."

It also did not prevent "some lawless fellows, who

MISSION SAN Luis Rey, as it appeared when Bartlett's border survey commission visited it in 1852, impressed Bartlett, "with such a range of buildings and cultivated grounds, a prince or a nabob might luxuriate to his heart's content." In absence of "the officer in command," commission "was hospitably entertained by the sergeant in charge." At that time Army had "placed a file of soldiers here to protect the property and keep off plunderers and squatters."

certainly deserve not the name of men" from breaking into the church. Downey said that "a deep stain" was cast "upon our little army" when these men stole "a lot of the gold and silver utensils used in the celebration of the rites of this sect and feloniously carried them off and sold them at the pueblo."

Punishment of other culprits was the occasion that revealed that the soldiers lot was not all bad. It also established that the landing force, as a ground command, was to be governed by the Rules of the Army rather than the Navy.

The incident started when an officer from *USS Cyane* instructed a petty officer to fashion a set of "cat of nine tails" to punish several men for minor infractions. General Kearny heard about the plan and "cooly walked into the room, and taking up the articles in question, he asked in his easy manner what they were and what they were for," wrote Downey.

" 'Then,' said Lt. H------, 'why General, them are cats and are for the punishment of sailors when they are unruly.'

" 'Well, well,' says the General, deliberately taking out his knife and cutting the cats to pieces, 'if you find it impossible to curb your Jacks, without resort to these things, allow me to tell you, that you shall punish none of *My* Jacks with any such articles, and allow me to inform you at the same time young man, that every Jack in this battalion, is heart and soul mine.' When having finished cutting off the tails, he deliberately threw the handle into the fire, and turning on his heel, left the young officer, with something very like a flea in his ear."

Commodore Stockton supported Kearney's actions. This won for both officers the approval of the Tars of the Pacific Squadron. When the expedition left after an overnight stay at San Luis Rey, the sailors were calling Kearny "Our Old Soldier" and

BARRACKS from days when Spanish soldiers protected mission had this layout, according to adobe remains in front of mission. U.S. Army occupation used tents and mission buildings in 1847-49 and 1850-52, was mainly to provide protection to travelers between San Diego and Los Angeles. (Drawn from site inspection.)

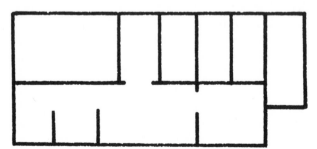

"THIS IMMENSE mission structure, with an imposing church in an angle, built about 60 years previously, was found in good condition," reported General Philip St. George Cooke when he camped Mormon Battalion at San Luis Rey in January, 1846. "The battalion found ample quarters . . . and immediately commenced a thorough instruction of the battalion in tactics." Without books, Cooke found this difficult "teaching and drilling officers half the day, and superintending, in the other half, their efforts to impart what they had imperfectly learned." Battalion left the mission in April. One soldier died, was buried in church garden. Spanish soldiers' barracks (foreground) are described by sign.

Stockton, "Fighting Bob." The sailors "had now found out beyond all question that there were at least two along, and big bugs too, to whom we could appeal in case of need."

"REQUIRE FROM the soldiers personal labor in erecting the necessary buildings, without murmuring at site or work, and with implicit obedience to Padre Lasuen," ordered Governor Borica in 1798 when guard detachment was provided to protect new mission. Average of 16 soldiers lived here even after padres were ousted in 1835, but were unable to prevent looting and gradual stripping of mission buildings. No Indian attacks took place during mission days, possibly because it was most successful of all missions with several hundred converts living around it.

TO GET THERE: From Oceanside, California, take 2d street, which is Mission Road and state 76, east 3.5 miles to restored mission, now a Franciscan seminary.

MISSION SAN LUIS REY de Francia was described in diary of Mormon soldier, Nathaniel V. Jones: "The whole front is about 10,200 feet in length. There was a beautiful piazza which was separated by beautiful turned arches about 10 feet in width and two and a half feet thick . . . The building covered nearly four acres of ground . . . It is the best building I have seen in California." Dimensions were not quite accurate in Jones' report, actual frontage was 600 feet and buildings covered 6.5 acres. Returned to Catholic Church in 1865, it was used in 1892 as refuge from Mexico's religious persecution.

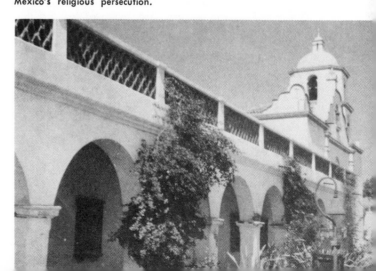

FORT MOORE, CALIFORNIA

Building Fort Moore, California, was a proposition that progressed in direct proportion to the enemy threat. It started in a state of siege, had a short but eventful history, and then quietly disappeared from the Army rolls.

Marine Captain Archibald H. Gillespie was the founder of the first fort. The occasion was somewhat less than premeditated, however.

Gillespie was with Fremont and Stockton when they moved into Los Angeles on August 13, 1846. Their 500-man force met no opposition and the enemy was described by Fremont as "having more the effect of a parade of home guards than of an enemy taking possession of a conquered town."

Four days later word was received that war had been declared between the United States and Mexico. All was quiet in Los Angeles so Stockton and Fremont took most of the troops away early in September leaving Gillespie and 50 men.

Some authorities charge Gillespie with attempting to establish a military dictatorship which precipitated a revolt on September 22, 1846. Gillespie's untactful handling of affairs may have contributed to the unrest, but it is unlikely that in only two weeks he could have been wholly to blame for the revolt. The fact that he had only 50 men to oppose a hidden revolutionary army was undoubtedly the major reason for the uprising.

The first attack on Gillespie was at 3 a.m. against "my small command quartered in the government house," he wrote later. "We were not wholly surprised, and with 21 rifles we beat them back."

The attackers were driven out of the town after dawn, but within 24 hours a force of 600 men surrounded Los Angeles. In addition to a cannon, they were armed with shotguns and lances.

A surrender ultimatum was answered by Gillespie by taking three "old honey-combed iron guns" from the corral of government house, unspiking them, and mounting them on cart axles. Then as quickly as he could do so, he moved to a hill overlooking the town. A temporary barricade of earth-filled sacks was erected, the cannon were emplaced, and the siege started.

Despite his gunnery advantage, Gillespie could see that his situation was less than desirable. He dispatched a messenger, Juan Flaco, for Monterey with word for Commodore Stockton. Nothing was put in writing; instead, Gillespie gave Flaco a package of cigarettes, writing on each cigarette wrapper "Believe the bearer" and stamping them with his official seal.

Flaco's horse was shot from under him while he was trying to cross the Mexican picket line, but he was able to escape on foot and secure another mount. On September 29, 600 miles and five days from Los Angeles, Flaco found Stockton in San Francisco and reported the Gillespie predicament.

Meanwhile Gillespie's situation had worsened. A final ultimatum on September 29 guaranteed the safety of the Gillespie force if it would surrender. Upon the advice of several American civilians, on September 30 Gillespie led his men from "Fort Hill" and marched out of the city, drums beating, colors flying, and two pieces of cannon following.

Supposedly Gillespie was to turn over his cannon to the Californians before he went aboard ship. He did not quite follow the spirit of the agreement, what he left on Fort Hill were spiked, and what he took to the pier, he rolled into the bay.

On October 8 Gillespie joined a Navy-Marine landing force under Navy Captain William Mervine. When the initial advance back to Los Angeles went unopposed, Mervine sent 80 of his men back to the ship. He was to regret this. By mid-afternoon, the detachment was under almost continual rifle fire. During the night this was reinforced by a small cannon that the Californians moved from place to place every time the Americans tried to capture it.

In the face of the illusive cannon and a rumor of 600 opponents Mervine noted that he had 10 sailor and Marine casualties—four of them fatal—and decided to retire from what history called the Battle of Dominquez' Ranch. He did not know that the deadly cannon was out of ammunition.

The war shifted to other parts of Southern California until January 8, 1847, when 600 men under Commodore Stockton and General Kearny defeated the Californians at the Battles of San Gabriel and the Mesa.

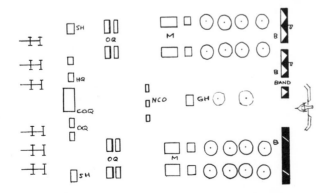

CAMP FITZGERALD plan approved in July, 1861, probably was made more compact and adapted to Camp Latham tent site occupied in September, 1861. From wagons to band tent was 250 paces, cannon on right actually was 100 paces beyond tents. Inspected in 1862, Latham's tents were found to be worn out, soldiers' uniforms shoddy, and almost all 100 horses present unfit for use. (Redrawn from National Archives plat.)

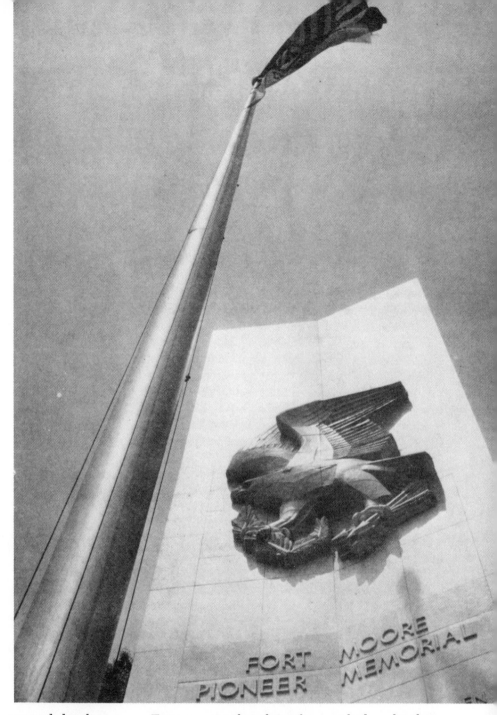

FORT MOORE memorial is elaborate stone marker on Board of Education hill near downtown Los Angeles. Behind this flagpole is 40- by 60-foot stone wall on which scenes depict first 4th of July celebration, when fort was dedicated, and other events important to Los Angeles.

"The streets were full of desperate and drunken fellows, who brandished their arms and saluted us with every item of reproach," was how Lieutenant William H. Emory described the condition of Los Angeles when the troops entered. With rumors that the Californians planned a counterattack, Emory added, "I was ordered to select a site and place a fort capable of containing 100 men." The site was that of Gillespie's Fort Hill.

Seaman Joseph T. Downey wrote that as soon as the combined sailor-Marine-soldier force was assigned to barracks, foraging for food began all over town "and woe betide the house that had no occupants for it was sure to be ransacked from clue to earring . . . for what they called Belly Timber."

Emory wrote that the sailors worked on his fort "which was performed bravely and gave me great hopes of success." Downey's account differed: "Parties were detailed to go on the hill and commence the foundations of a Star Fort . . . This arrangement the Jacks kicked strongly against."

Kearny, Emory, the sailors and most of the original captors of Los Angeles left before the fort was completed. Emory did not take credit for the installation that finally was dedicated on July 4, 1847. "The entire plan of the fort was changed, and I am not the projector of the work finally adopted for the defense of the town," he said.

The Mormon Battalion did the final labor. Nathaniel V. Jones' diary is replete with entries in

FORT MOORE in 1847 overlooked Pueblo of Los Angeles. It was breastwork 400 feet long with bastions and embrasures for cannon. Main purpose was to prevent rebellion so its principal embrasure commanded church and plaza, most probable rallying points. Two hundred men were planned to garrison it. Army incident of 1851 occurred when dragoon company passed through town at same time hoodlum gang was threatening to storm jail and lynch some prisoners. Soldiers were secretly sworn in as posse and settled matter.

spring, 1847: "Hard at work on the fort." When the place was dedicated, a cannon salute was fired, the colors were raised, and the name Fort Moore made official, memorializing Captain Benjamin D. Moore, killed in the Battle of San Gabriel.

Indian chasing and rumors of plots kept the garrison busy, although daily it got smaller as men deserted for the gold fields. A dragoon squadron that had lost many men in this fashion was ordered to San Luis Rey, and immediately the remainder deserted. Another group of soldiers tried a different way to get rich quickly, but were soon arrested for counterfeiting gold pieces.

At Fort Moore the night of December 7, 1847, an overzealous sentry failed to extract the password from a passing cow or horse. He called the garrison to arms and in the rush, a lighted fuze was dropped into an ammunition chest. The explosion partly destroyed the guard house and killed several troopers.

By 1849 the few soldiers left in Los Angeles were garrisoned in the town and Fort Moore was abandoned. Ten years later, Captain Winfield Scott Hancock was the sole military force at Los Angeles. As the department quartermaster, he maintained an adobe house and corral on the edge of town.

With rumors that secessionists were plotting to capture his ammunition and supplies, Hancock "began his preparations for defense, by concealing the boxes of arms and ammunition under innumer-

BY 1883, Fort Moore memory lived only in name "Fort Moore Hill" on which this house stood. Photographer William H. Jackson visited site on February 1, 1867, writing in diary: "Went upon the hill back of the city, the site of some old earthworks and had a fine view of the city and its suburbs." Commercial houses of downtown Los Angeles now cover entire area of this picture.

able bags of grain and, in addition, placing his wagons in such a position as to improvise a quite formidable barricade, behind which he intended to contest every foot, aided by a few loyal friends," his wife wrote later. Their last ditch stand was to be conducted from their house, where Hancock had collected 20 derringers.

The Civil War saw many troops passing through Los Angeles for the East, and militia taking their place. Colonel Albert Sidney Johnston visited Hancock enroute to the Confederacy. With him was Major Lewis A. Armistead who presented Hancock with a new major's uniform which was never to be worn; Hancock jumped the grades to brigadier general. Armistead died at Gettysburg in a charge on Hancock's position.

A training post, Camp Fitzgerald, was established near Hancock's corral in May, 1861, but was moved in August after reporting the site too dusty and too far from water. The new site was still objectionable. The commander reported, "The men are being demoralized here, and I suspect are being tampered with. The vitality they expend on debauch would be spend on .. manly exercises" if the post were moved.

In September, 1861, Camp Latham was established on Ballona Creek near modern Culver City. Colonel James H. Carleton mounted his California Column from here and it served as the troop center for a year. Frequent details had to be sent to arrest secessionists.

By late 1862 the military left Los Angeles in favor of Wilmington to the south. By this time its main enemy had become the whiskey dealers doing business in violation of a prohibition against being within three miles of Camp Latham. One ingenious food dealer was doing a big business in watermelons until the post commander learned the melons were filled with whiskey.

TO GET THERE: Fort Moore monument is on Hill street near Sunset Boulevard in downtown Los Angeles. Three-quarters of a mile to south, near 3d and Main, is probable site of Camp Fitzgerald. Camp Latham site is on Ballona creek. It is across from Willow Grove in Culver City where in 1862 5th California Infantry had Camp Kellogg, named for its first regimental commander.

POST AT MONTEREY, CALIFORNIA

A day out of Lima, Peru, on September 8, 1842, the American ships *Cyane, Dale* and *United States* hove to and two captains' gigs made for the flagship. Captains Armstrong, Stribling and Dornin gathered in the cabin of Commodore Thomas Ap Catesby Jones.

Jones recounted the reports he had heard while in Lima: not only did a state of war exist between the United States and Mexico, but English and French fleets were competing to occupy Northern California. From his nearer location, Jones' fleet had the advantage. Disregarding the rumor that Great Britain had bought California for $7 million, Jones proposed to make full sail for Monterey and take California for the United States.

Jones said it was their "bounden duty" to prevent violation of the Monroe Doctrine by any European power "but more particularly by our great commercial rival England."

Dale returned to Panama to report the plan to Washington. The other ships set full sail for Monterey.

"During the battle and strife," Jones said to his crews, "every man must do his utmost to take and destroy; but when the flag is struck, all hostility must cease, and you must even become the protectors of all, and not the oppressors of any."

At 4 p.m. on October 19, Captain Armstrong was sent ashore under a flag of truce to demand the surrender of Monterey's defenses "to avoid the sacrifice of human life and the horrors of war."

With time to consider until 9 a.m. the next day, Juan Bautista Alvarado asked his military commander about the possibility of defending the place. This same Alvarado had led a revolt against the Monterey redoubt in 1835, taking it easily with

PRESIDIO CHAPEL of San Carlos Borromeo was founded in 1770 by Father Junipero Serra. First chapel was behind palisades next to Presidio, but Father Serra moved to present location to be away from military influence. Six soldiers guarded and helped build church. Serra died here in 1784 and is buried in church. Chapel was presented with barrel organ by English explorer Vancouver in 1793. Address: Church street near Figueroa.

a mixed force of 125 Californians and Americans. His one cannon had been handled by a lawyer who consulted the instruction book for the firing procedures, but its single shot was sufficient to frighten and force out the governor. The attackers had taken an additional precaution: sending a gift of whiskey ahead to the presidio to "pacify" its garrison.

Seven years later after he seized power, Alvarado knew that little had been done to improve the defenses. His captain's opinion was expected: the fortifications "were of no consequence, as everybody knows." He had 29 soldiers, 29 militia, 150 muskets, and 11 rusted cannon with little ammunition.

"The next morning at half-past ten o'clock about 100 sailors and 50 Marines disembarked," a pioneer wrote in his diary. "The sailors marched up from the shore and took possession of the port. The American colors were hoisted. The *United States* fired a salute of 13 guns; it was returned by the fort, which fired 26 guns.

"The Marines in the meantime had marched up

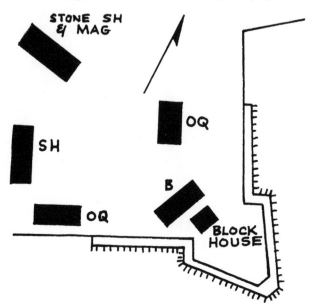

FORT MERVINE was built by Americans in 1846, was first known as Fort Stockton. It included blockhouse, earthen redoubt, a 100-by 17-foot barracks, six-room double-story log officers quarters, and 75- by 25-foot stone magazine. By mid-1850's, inspectors said it was worthless, guns were too small to cover Monterey Bay, and its only commendable attribute was that barracks had been turned over to library society. (Redrawn from Mansfield Report, 1853.)

to the government house. The officers and soldiers of the California government were discharged and their guns and other arms taken possession of and carried to the fort. The stars and stripes now wave over us. Long may they wave here in California!"

Thirty hours later, the Mexican flag was back on the flagpole. Newspapers and other papers located in Monterey convinced Jones that there was no war with Mexico at the time. The garrison was quickly withdrawn to the ships and a salute was fired in honor of the Mexican flag. Relief was mutual that the erroneous invasion had cost neither lives nor anger.

Jones noted that even though "we had 150 seamen and Marines on shore 30 hours, not one private house was entered, or the slightest disrespect shown to any individual; nor was any species of property, public or private, spoiled, if I may except the powder burnt in the salutes, which I have returned twofold."

Later the Mexicans tried to get Jones to reimburse them for the expenses incurred by the Los Angeles garrison that had left to reinforce Monterey. A formal demand for 1,500 infantry uni-

(Marvin King Collection)

MONTEREY is pictured in Bartlett's **Personal Narrative** as it appeared when boundary commission visited in 1852. Bartlett admired "large and well built adobe buildings" and noted that troops were occupying "the old presidio or garrison on an elevation back of the town." He especially admired the "fair daughters" of Monterey, many of whom were marrying American military.

EL CASTILLO, noted on sign, actually was built mile away in 1807 to defend against pirates. In 1818 two privateers attacked town and fort was hurriedly abandoned after firing single round from cannon. Town was ravaged; pirates included Hawaiians who were naked upon landing but soon were clothed in best clothing empty houses could offer. In 1793 Vancouver found guns of El Castillo mounted on "sorry kind of barbet battery, consisting of a few logs of wood . . . cannon, about 11 in number . . . work cost $450 . . . was entirely useless."

WHEN SHERMAN arrived in Monterey, he first lived in Customs House (below) while serving as quartermaster. This double-story end dated from 1814; center single-story was built in 1833; double-story at opposite end was added by American consul at Monterey, Thomas Larkin. From 1847 to 1849, Sherman lived in plastered adobe house (above) also built by Larkin. Custom House is at Alvarado and Scott streets; Sherman house on Main street near Jefferson.

forms, $15,000, and a set of musical instruments was ignored by Jones and not repeated by the Mexicans. Washington relieved Jones of his command of the Pacific Squadron, but a few years later found him back at the same helm.

Monterey learned no lesson by the easy capture of its defenses. Four years later, Commodore John D. Sloat anchored in Monterey Bay and was not bothered in the least by the supposed challenging artillery on the hill. Sloat had learned a lesson, however, and delayed landing until he was told that John C. Fremont and the Bear Flag Revolt had started. Assuming that Fremont was acting as an American agent, Sloat sent a landing party ashore on July 7, 1846, and hoisted the United States flag on the government buildings.

The shift of authority was greeted mildly by the citizens of Monterey. Troops poured in—some of them being dropped at Monterey rather than other

FORT MERVINE is remembered by these original earthworks and cannon 145 feet above Monterey. Third Artillery manned it, called it "Monterey Redoubt" at first, though other names later included Fort Hill, Fort Halleck, Jones' Fort, and Fort Fremont. Initially it had 20 mounted 24-pound guns and four 8-inch guns on platforms. It is now part of U.S. Army Presidio, founded in 1902, overlooking Lighthouse avenue. Army also was at Monterey for short time in 1865, mainly to see if government buildings were still there.

ports in order to keep them from the distant gold fields. Lieutenant William Tecumseh Sherman arrived at this time aboard *USS Lexington*.

Sherman's men expected to do battle as soon as they landed. In his *Memoirs*, he expresses pride that each man had been sufficiently exercised on the 200-day voyage so that upon arrival at Monterey "every man was able to leave the ship and march up the hill to the fort . . . carrying his own knapsack and equipments."

The rumors of an impending attack on Monterey may have spurred on the troops, as it did the officers. Not knowing how far away the fighting was, Sherman said, "Swords were brought out, guns oiled and made ready, and everything was in a bustle."

Records indicate that less than decisive battles were fought at Monterey. In 1847 Sherman incurred the undying enmity of some townspeople by destroying two barrels of contraband whiskey on the pier. A year later he led the chase to recapture a mass desertion of 28 soldiers for the gold

fields; he had to include only officers in his eight-man "posse" because he was afraid that bringing enlisted men would only invite more desertions.

TO GET THERE: Monterey is on State 1 and 68 about 17 miles from Salinas, California. Specific locations are described in picture captions.

TWO EARLY actors in Monterey drama are memorialized here. Commodore Sloat Monument (left) is part of Fort Mervine ruins. Sherman's house (right) shows ravages of time that revealed adobe under plaster. Sherman lived here after officers' mess had to be abolished because cooks deserted for gold fields.

SONOMA BARRACKS, CALIFORNIA

Good friend or not, as the symbol of the established government, General Mariano Vallejo would have to be brought to terms. On that point the 33 rebels outside his house were in agreement. So before dawn on Sunday, June 14, 1846, the general and his family were awakened in their "Casa Grande" on the plaza of Sonoma.

Vallejo did not speak English and the guerilla leader, Ezekiel Merritt, did hardly better in Spanish. Neither the language barrier nor early hour caused Vallejo to forget his manners, though, and he invited Merritt inside to talk. After all, Vallejo reasoned, he knew that the military barracks next door had no soldiers and his rusted cannon no ammunition, so what could he lose by being friendly?

Merritt's rebels lounged outside until the sun became a glowing reminder that several hours had passed. Another man was sent in but he, too, failed to return. Then, with a trap being suspected, William S. Ide volunteered to find out what was wrong and what kind of a rescue party was needed.

Ide returned in a minute. The rebels gathered around him to learn that all negotiations had been stalled by a full-scale counterattack of Vallejo's wine cellar. The affable commander had poured both freely and well, and the rebel spokesmen were too happy to do any talking—if, indeed, they remembered the reason for talking!

On these less than auspicious circumstances the California Bear Flag Revolt began. Possibly in recognition of his breaking the negotiation stalemate, the rebels elected Ide their first president. Not one to let history record a revolt without drama, Ide sent Commodore Stockton a report that provided excitement where it lacked fact:

"We charged upon the Fortress of General Guadaloupe Vallejo, and captured 18 prisoners (among whom were three of the highest officers in the California Government and all of the military officers who reside in Sonoma), eight field-pieces, 200 stand of arms, a great quantity of cannon cannister and grape-shot . . . the soldiers were set at liberty."

Ide's next act was to draft as a flag maker, fellow conspirator William L. Todd, nephew of Mrs. Abraham Lincoln. Todd took a yard-wide strip of unbleached muslin, bi-sected it with a four inch-wide strip of red, and in the top left corner drew a star and a bear. Under the stripe he painted "CALIFORNIA REPUBLC". Before the flag was run up on June 14, the spelling of republic was corrected by squeezing an "I" between its last two letters.

Although Captain John C. Fremont and his exploration party were camped nearby, it does not appear that at first he was actively involved with the revolt. His sympathies obviously lay with the Americans who were reacting to rumors that Mexico was preparing to oust all foreigners from California. When two men were tortured and killed, Fremont assumed that the Mexicans were to blame. He actively joined the revolt—first going through the formality of mailing his resignation to Washington. Joining with Fremont was Marine Captain Archibald Gillespie, unaccountably with Fremont although supposedly on some type of courier mission.

The Bear Flag Revolt lasted 26 days. Its short-lived history was marred by several unnecessary deaths and illegal seizures of private property, but it had one redeeming factor. Off of Monterey lay the flagship of indecisive Commodore Sloat; news that a revolt was in progress finally caused him to land troops and proclaim the annexation of California.

SONOMA BARRACKS was built in 1830's by Mariano Guadalupe Vallejo, "Commandate-General of the Northern Frontier of Alta California," as key to Mexico's strategy to stop Russian spread into California. At right of barracks can be seen edge of Mission San Francisco de Solano, northernmost California mission and only one founded under Mexican rule. A wooden mission structure 24 by 105 feet when built in 1823, it was replaced by adobe building in 1840. Despite secularization order in 1834, Vallejo kept chapel active.

SHERMAN LIVED here when stationed in Sonoma in 1849. Known as Ray House and also Adler Adobe, double-story frame and adobe residence served as officers mess until Army left Sonoma in 1852. It was also site of Masonic Lodge organized by several officers of garrison. Sailors stationed at Sonoma in 1846 were supplied by boats from San Francisco. Mystery still shrouds one boat that completely disappeared during trip with loss of 10-man crew, including two sons of **USS Portsmouth's** captain.

PACIFIC DIVISION headquarters was in this building, Leese-Fritch House, now well-disguised by commercial advertising. General Persifor Smith coordinated affairs of California and Oregon Departments from here 1849-50. California Department was headquartered here for two months in 1850. Sherman's replacement as adjutant general here, Major Joseph Hooker soon resigned to become Sonoma farmer and beachcomber. Legend has it that his associates here and later as Civil War general caused his last name to become slang term for certain class of women of questionable repute.

The removal of the Bear Flag was assigned almost ironically to Navy Lieutenant Joseph W. Revere, grandson of Paul Revere of Revolutionary War fame. Sent from *USS Portsmouth*, Lieutenant Revere raised the Stars and Stripes in Sonoma on July 9, 1846, and "all hands gave up to an excess of joy," Seaman Joseph T. Downey remembered.

"Bells were rung, guns fired, whisky barrel tapped, and hilarity became the order of the day."

Revere returned to Sonoma on August 1 to command the American forces. He stayed during the fall, 1846, as one of Commodore Stockton's land-bound Naval officers.

Sonoma's double storied adobe barracks became the home for various contingents of United States soldiers, sailors, and militiamen. Volunteer Captain John E. Brackett was in command in 1847 when Alcalde John H. Nash refused to surrender his justice-of-the-peace-type position to Lilburn W. Boggs. This was a direct challenge to the authority of the Colonel Richard B. Mason, the military governor. Brackett asked to be excused from forcing the issue; he said that the people who favored Nash might take revenge when Brackett left the service and settled in Sonoma.

Mason's reaction to this excuse was described as "wrath" by Lieutenant William T. Sherman who was sent to Sonoma to correct the situation. Accompanied by six sailors and Navy Lieutenant Louis McLane, Sherman arrived at Sonoma and easily found Nash. Any thought the deposed alcalde had of resisting evaporated when one of the sailors, inexperienced with hand guns, accidentally and harmlessly fired his pistol.

Several days later a bedraggled and seasick Nash arrived at Mason's Monterey headquarters. When Mason kindly explained the facts of life and told him "to go and sin no more," Nash eagerly agreed. His return to Sonoma to assist Boggs in assuming the alcalde duties marked the end of resistance in that area to American authority.

TO GET THERE: Sonoma is about 45 miles north of San Francisco via U.S. 101, and state 37 and 121. Barracks is in plaza at Spain Street East and 1st Street East. Leese-Fritch House is at 493 1st Street West and Ray House at 209 Spain Street East.

SONOMA PLAZA, 1851, was drawn by George Gibbs. Don Salvador Vallejo, brother of General Vallejo, occupied house at far left; general's "Casa Grande," center, was complete with several-story wing from which he could oversee range lands and farms through telescope. Army barracks was to left of flagpole, former mission behind pole, and shops to right. When Bear Flag rebels attacked Sonoma, they expected 80 to 100 soldiers and 200 Indians would be in garrison but "when the charge was made . . . there was no resistance, simply because there was no one to resist," said one report.

(Colonel Fred B. Rogers Collection, Smithsonian Institution)

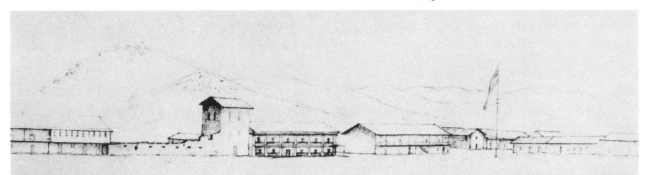

FORT SUTTER, CALIFORNIA

"Riding up to the front gate, I saw two Indian sentinels pacing to and fro before it, and several Americans . . . sitting in the gateway, dressed in buckskin pantaloons and blue sailor shirts, with white stars worked on the collars. I inquired if Captain Sutter was in the fort. A very small man, with a peculiarly sharp red face and most voluble tongue, gave the response. He was probably a corporal. He said, in substance, that perhaps I was not aware of the great changes which had taken place in California—that the fort belonged to the United States, and that Captain Sutter, although he was in the fort, had no control over it."

Thus Edwin Bryant, author of *What I Saw in California*, learned that a new order was on the land. This was in 1846, just a few days after the Bear Flag Revolt had collapsed at Sonoma.

Inside, Sutter was the unhappy host to a detachment of American soldiers and sailors. He was also in the process of becoming a lieutenant of dragoons at $50 a month with the assignment as second in command of his own fort. In command was Edward M. Kern, 23-year old topographer for Captain John Fremont's survey party, assigned this new responsibility when Fremont became the kingpin of the revolt.

Both Kern and Sutter were performing another role at that moment, one for which neither had much enthusiasm. When the Bear Flag revolutionists took Sonoma, they captured General Mariano Guadaloupe Vallejo, his brother Salvador, and Victor Prudon. The General's brother-in-law, an American named Jacob Leese, had accompanied them to Sutter's Fort as interpreter—and somehow became the fourth prisoner by the time the party arrived.

The situation was especially uncomfortable for John Sutter. The Vallejos were his friends, even though in recent years they had become suspicious of the military nature of his fort. To them, and especially to Governor Juan Bautista Alvarado, Vallejo's nephew, Sutter owed much of his success.

It was in 1839 that John Sutter arrived in Cali-

(California Division of Beaches and Parks)

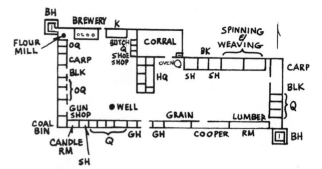

SUTTER'S FORT, 1847, was about 330 feet long, 183 feet wide on west side and 120 feet wide on east. This did not count extensive corrals between front gate and southeast blockhouse that extended almost 300 feet to south. Fourteen-room barracks for Indian soldiers was outside eastern walls; another dwelling was to southwest of fort. Cannon were mounted in each blockhouse and in southeastern corner of interior corral (where rectangle appears). Brewery apparently had four stills in it. (Redrawn from plat by Heinrich Kunzel, 1848.)

fornia, armed with a carpetbag full of letters of introduction and the hint that he was a former captain in the French Army. Actually he was a bankrupt shopkeeper who had outrun his European creditors four years previously. The letters he carried had been obtained through his smooth-talking meetings with government and commercial leaders—all based upon an initial few letters that he was able to parlay into many.

The Sutter self-confidence and his credentials combined to open the official doors when he arrived in California. He presented to Governor Alvarado a plan to establish a colony in the interior of the state, and asked for permission and land. Alvarado saw several advantages to the proposal. The settlement would push the frontier and authority of the government much deeper inland; an additional barrier would be placed to the incursions of Americans from the east, British from the north, and Russians from the northwest. And a presence inland might divert some Indian raids away from the coastline!

As Sutter said later, "I got a general passport for my small colony and permission to select a territory wherever I could find it convenient, and to come in one year's time to Monterey to get my citizenship and title of the land."

Sutter took his party up the Sacramento river

"WHEN THE Star Spangled Banner slowly rose on the flag staff, the cannon began and continued until nearly all the windows were broken," wrote Sutter of first U.S. flag raising at sunrise, July 11, 1846. He added that his prisoners from Sonoma were confused. "I went to them and said: 'Now, gentlemen, we are under the protection of this great flag, and we should henceforth not be afraid to talk to one another...' They all rejoiced that the anarchy was over." This sketch was made in 1846 by Navy Lieutenant Joseph W. Revere, who raised colors at Sonoma and provided flag for Sutter. Somewhat distorted because it does not suggest broad front of fort, view is otherwise accurate, even to showing out-buildings and slight elevation on which fort stood.

MAIN GATE of Sutter's Fort was welcome view for thousands of travelers in 1840's. Much of Sutter's undoing was his generosity that put him impossibly in debt. He personally underwrote most of aid sent from fort to stranded Donner Party in winter, 1846-7, and the 45 survivors of original 87 were his guests until their health was restored. Site of fort was bought by Native Sons of Golden West in 1890, donated to state, and restored to supposed 1848 appearance. It was "re-restored" beginning in 1947 as new details of its construction were uncovered.

and located his fort site after several mosquito-ridden, Indian-surrounded camps. He was able to explain his mission in Spanish to at least one spokesman for each tribe he encountered. His offer of friendship and future hospitality silenced all Indian opposition.

By mid-August, 1839, the Sutter party was ashore with its supplies and equipment. As his ships turned to return to San Francisco, Sutter had his tiny brass cannon fire a nine-gun salute, the first cannon fire heard in the Sacramento Valley and a thing of amazement to both the Indians and animals crowding close to the camp.

With a few Spanish words and the offer of beads, cloth, and other trade goods, Sutter was able to arrange for Indian labor. The Hawaiians in his original party set up two thatched huts for the oncoming winter, but Sutter saw to it that a solid, one-story adobe rancho was built for him. Adobe making continued as Sutter gathered around him everyone who was willing to stay. Within a year he had "about 20 white men working for me in

addition to a large number of Indians," he estimated. The white men were mostly drifters, deserters and vagabonds whom Sutter said he kept in line "because I gave them nothing to drink but water."

The Indians were controlled with ruthless but fair methods although on one occasion he nipped a mutiny at the last moment by attacking the plotters' camp, killing six. He gave the Indians at least token payment for their work, usually beads or credit to buy items in his store. His pride was a mounted guard of 12 to 15 braves under "the command of a very intelligent sergeant." Sutter outfitted them in "blue drill pantaloons, white cotton shirts, and real handkerchiefs tied around their heads."

These personal bodyguards were quartered near Sutter's bedroom, had special privileges, maintained a semblance of military atmosphere at the post, and were turned out to drill every Sunday and whenever there were visitors worthy of impressing.

A year after his arrival, Sutter was granted Mexican citizenship and, with it, title to his lands. A week later he was also appointed the official representative of the government in the Sacramento River region. This made him the interpreter and enforcer of law in a vast area and, as he said, "From that time on I had the power of life and death over both Indians and whites in my district."

With his ownership of the land confirmed, Sutter then "built a large house near the first adobe building," he wrote later. "This I surrounded with walls 18 feet high, enclosing altogether 75,000 square feet. The walls were made of adobe bricks and were two and a half feet thick. At two

corners I built bastions; under these bastions were the prisons . . ."

After Sutter bought Fort Ross in 1841, his headquarters began to assume an especially military appearance, complete with bristling guns and the designation of "fort." The Mexicans began to lose faith in Sutter. By boasting of his Indian "army," his ammunition stock that at times exceeded more "than the whole California government possessed," and his 10 mounted cannon and two field pieces, Sutter aggravated the government.

Sutter's activities were wide-ranging. He started most of his enterprises on credit, winning confidence and support by maintaining friendships with the authorities and actively assisting his newly adopted country. His fictitious captaincy became official when the Mexican government commissioned him to recruit a militia force to oppose the 1844 insurrection. He served in the field with his command, but ended his active military career as a prisoner.

By 1846, his worries had shifted to meeting the

ARMY PRESENCE at Sacramento after Sutter's Fort was at Camp Union, now marked in Sutterville section of Sacramento. Union was founded in 1861, served as training camp for California Volunteers throughout Civil War and as discharge center in 1866. Troops from it served in California Column, also manned forts in San Francisco Bay and, after Civil War, in Nevada and Arizona. Flood of 1862 put Sacramento "entirely under water," according to Army report, and Union troopers went to rescue. As Brigade Headquarters near end of Civil War, it had several political prisoners in custody but was hard-pressed to supply its four-company garrison; reports indicate there were no horses available nor ammunition for carbines.

demands of creditors. He had patched up most of the political rivalries so it was ironic when Vallejo, with whom he had frequently disagreed, became his prisoner.

"I placed my best rooms at their disposal and treated them with every consideration," he wrote later. "The gentlemen took their meals at my table and walked with me in the evening. Never did I place a guard before the door of the room . . ."

When Fremont heard about the liberal treatment of the prisoners, he ordered that Sutter's assistant, John Bidwell, take charge of them. A future governor of California, Bidwell was Sutter's trusted foreman and had served with Fremont. His treatment of the prisoners was just as liberal until they were finally released upon the direct orders of Commodore Stockton in August, 1846.

By this time the American flag was flying over Sutter's post, Kern in nominal command, 30 men from Company C, New York Volunteers, in garrison, and Sutter's power in an eclipse. The deluge of more emigrants and mustered-out soldiers presented him with a squatter problem hard to fight. His cattle began to disappear for the same reason.

Then came the discovery of gold at his saw mill. Overnight, his agricultural and trading enterprises collapsed, especially when the new and more convenient town of Sacramento diverted settlement and business. By 1849, Sutter lost ownership of his fort. Within 10 years, little more than the central

"PARALLELOGRAM, ABOUT 500 feet in length and 150 feet in breadth," is 1846 description of Sutter's Fort. "The main building, or residence, stands near the center of the area, or court, enclosed by the walls. A row of shops, storerooms, and barracks are enclosed within, and line the walls on every side . . . The principal gates on the east and south are . . . defended by heavy artillery, through portholes pierced in the walls. At this time the fort is manned by about 50 well-disciplined Indians, and 10 or 12 white men, all under the pay of the United States." Not quite accurate as to size or financial sponsorship, description is otherwise correct. View (above) from southeast overlooks area once occupied by corrals. Lagoon once behind fort served as source of water and mosquitos; its occasional flooding damaged for. Area apparently was site of Indian village about 1000 B.C.; archaeologists have uncovered artifacts and 23 graves that date from ancient past. Main building (below) was Sutter's residence and office. Here he entertained visitors, including Lieutenant William T. Sherman. Each in his memoirs mentions that other over-imbibed products of Sutter distillery.

building was left of what once had been described as "the largest and best fortified fort in California."

TO GET THERE: Sutter's Fort State Historical Monument is at 2701 L Street, Sacramento. Site of Camp Union is at northwest corner of Sutterville and Del Rio Roads, Sacramento.

CAMP RANCHO DEL JURUPA, CALIFORNIA

With California safe in the folds of the Union, the Army became responsible for the safety of the new citizens. Settlers, gold rush vagabonds, miners, speculators, gamblers, and rough and ready pioneers were more than the primitive California Indian could take.

The reaction to the white man's ways was violent. When reports of "outrages" reached Washington, D.C., California's Congressmen urged that more troops be sent to their state.

Troops came in 1851 and 1852 and established posts along the northern and eastern frontiers of the state. On September 17, 1852, Company H of the 2d Infantry moved into the grist mill owned by Louis Rubidoux near what is now Riverside.

Under Captain Charles S. Lovell, the troops found that the adobe grist mill provided a ready-made headquarters and barracks for what became known as Camp Rancho del Jurupa. The name, after the ranch served by the mill, was a Spanish version of the Indian word for water.

Ranger Horace Bell had frequent contacts with the Jurupa troopers. He described them with more sarcasm than seriousness in his *Reminiscences of a Ranger*.

Bell termed Lovell "a sedate, methodical, sober kind of officer, who seemed perfectly content to sit in his elegant quarters, issue orders to his little army of a dozen or so well-fed, clean-shaved, white-cotton-gloved, nicely dressed, lazy, fat fellows, who were seemingly happy and content on their $8 per month, while even a Digger Indian would naturally expect to earn even more than that sum in a day in the mines. They all, from Captain to Corporal, seemed resigned to a life of well-fed indolence."

Although the exaggerations in Bell's description are obvious, they probably are indicative of the general feeling of the early California settler. The maintenance of discipline was greeted by the unruly pioneer with derision. Bell accused Lovell of exacting "the utmost military punctilio" and ruling "the military roost at Jurupa with all the rigor of a martinet."

Lovell had little opportunity to distinguish himself during the 1852-54 career of Jurupa, but his name reappears frequently in subsequent endeavors in the West before he won a brigadier's brevet for heroism at the Civil War's Antitam battle.

Bell remembered one Jurupa patrol conducted jointly with a Mormon company and a Ranger detachment. The soldiers were "mounted on wagon mules," Bell wrote, but these soon gave out in the pursuit of a bandit band. It was not long before the troopers returned to the post; the volunteers continued fruitlessly for several more days.

Lovell's main concern at Jurupa was not bandits and Indians, according to Bell, but a lieutenant who was "utterly incorrigible . . . so hard a nut that even Lovell couldn't crack him." He supplemented his Army jacket—the only regulation uniform item that he wore—with Mexican leggings, spurs, sash, hat, horse, and other trappings. "Also inordinately fond of Mexican women," said Bell of the officer, "wine and women didn't begin to express the festive character of this gay son of Mars."

Finally Lovell called upon the District Commander for disciplinary help. This plan backfired. Brevet Lieutenant Colonel John Bankhead Magruder, the dashing "Prince John" of later Confederate fame, was sent to investigate. Bell records that Magruder stayed with the unruly lieutenant but that they "made the night melodious with their roysterings." The investigation was dropped.

ADOBES OF Rubidoux Grist Mill, and equally of Camp Rancho del Jurupa, supposedly are in wall to right of marker. Mill Stone is believed to have been used in Army period. Plaque includes fictitious claim that John C. Fremont was at Jurupa in 1846, leading to occasional unjustifiable reference to post as "Fort Fremont."

TO GET THERE: From downtown Riverside, take Palm avenue north to 7th street, turn west across Santa Ana river to community of Rubidoux. Turn at sign for "Rubidoux Grist Mill Site." This is Fort Drive, only visible suggestion of military past, which ends at mill stone monument.

BATTLES
OF THE
BLOCKHOUSES

"They tried to burn us out; threw rocks and firebrands, hot irons, pitch wood—everything onto the roof that would burn. . . Sometimes the roof got on fire, and we cut it out, or with cups of brine drawn from pork barrels, put it out or with sticks shoved off the fire balls . . . There were 40 men, women and children in the house—4 women and 18 men that could fight, and 18 wounded men and children."
—Contemporary description of blockhouse siege, March 1856.

Turmoil, both politically and militarily, marked the mid-nineteenth century Oregon Territory. England's 1846 boundary agreement on the 49th parallel eroded the peace-keeping authority of the "foreign" Hudson's Bay Company, and the United States had little to offer as a suitable substitute.

Army posts were established, usually at existing trading forts, to offer a modicum of comfort to the settlers and to assert the authority of the United States. The vastness of the Pacific Northwest made it impossible for the Army to give real security to the swarms of settlers who came cross-continent to lay claim to free 320-acre tracts that usually belonged to some Indian tribe.

Civil lines were more clearly drawn in 1853 when the area north of the Columbia River became Washington Territory. Isaac I. Stevens, the first governor, found his treaty-making efforts virtually useless and he called upon General Wool to exert military strength against the tribes. Wool, in turn considered the Indian the wronged party despite Federal government policies that encouraged settlers to come to the new territories.

When Stevens mustered a 1,000-man militia to keep the peace, Wool suggested, "Governor Stevens is crazy." The action of Oregon's Governor Curry in organizing a regiment of mounted volunteers was considered by Wool to be designed merely "for exterminating the Indians." Stevens countered by preferring charges against Wool for his "utter and signal incapacity."

While the governors and generals fought verbally, the settlers were not idle. Encouraged by Stevens to "return to their abandoned farms, build blockhouses, and hold and cultivate the soil," the citizens dotted western Washington with 58 blockhouses or fort-type places. The volunteers built 35 and the settlers 23. By the end of most hostilities in mid-1856, even the Army had erected seven forts.

Many of these places remain in modern day, landmarks in town parks or in lonely fields, sometimes guarding cemeteries or just memories. A token few of these blockhouses are visited in the section that follows.

FORT DECATUR, WASHINGTON

Indian unrest at Seattle dates back at least to 1853 when they displayed active resentment of the white man's arrival. Governor Stevens began treaty making with some chiefs until four separate massacres in the summer of 1855 signalled the start of the Yakima War.

With the settlers in panic and the Army's tiny garrisons widely scattered, the Navy was called upon for help.

The *USS Decatur* was ordered from Hawaii into Puget Sound. Her commander, Captain Isaac L. Sterrett, reported on October 15 that he found "a high state of excitement" with most of the farmers "having reported to town for mutual protection. The presence of this ship has quieted their alarm, which seems to have been in a great measure groundless, and most of them have returned to their farms."

Sterrett was not completely convinced that the fears were groundless. He issued to the settlers all of the spare weapons from his armory, and then undertook a coordinated program for the defense of the town.

"Anchored off Seattle Town, moored head and stern, guns shotted, loaded with grape, shell & cannister, and trained," is how *Decatur* Lieutenant Francis J. Dallas' diary described October 15 to November 20, 1855. "Block House at Seattle garrisoned and everything on the *qui vive*, to repel an Indian attack. Frequent exercise with great guns and small arms at target practice."

On October 28 the White River area south of Seattle was terrorized and several families were slaughtered. Indian loyalties were divided. One friendly Indian carried warnings of the war to the settlements; two others rescued three boys and rowed them to the *Decatur* for safety.

Forty men of the Seattle Volunteers rushed to White River, but could do little more than confirm the atrocities and bury the mangled bodies. The Hudson's Bay Company sent 50 rifles and a large supply of ammunition. At his headquarters in San Francisco, General Wool decided that there may be something amiss, so he sailed for the Columbia river. He ordered Captain Erasmus D. Keyes and a company of the 3d Artillery to Fort Steilacoom, near Tacoma, and placed Keyes in command of the Puget Sound District.

"I found a condition of wild alarm," wrote Keyes of his new territory. "Many families had been massacred, and the surviving settlers were all collected in the small towns. There were only two companies of regular infantry and a few companies

(Washington State Historical Society)

FORT DECATUR in 1856, as painted by eye-witness E. I. Denny of pioneer Seattle family, shows families and militia running to protection of blockhouse manned by Marines of **USS Decatur** (background). Blockhouse was built in 1855, measured 25 by 40 feet with heavy-timbered walls 14 feet high. Inside was a balcony from which defenders could fire through rifle loops under cover of shake roof. Two nine pound cannon also were inside. Unlike most blockhouses, Fort Decatur had no extended portions from which defenders could observe exterior of walls.

of volunteers in the district, and they were widely separated."

Assisting Keyes for a month was Lieutenant Dallas of the *Decatur* "appointed as aide de camp and adjutant of the regular forces about the sound and in the country fighting the Indians," according to his diary.

On December 7, the *Decatur* ran aground on Bainbridge Island. Until January 19 she was on the beach next to the Seattle wharf. Every man aboard acquired a detailed knowledge of Seattle. Their activities were described by Dallas as "actively engaged in repairing ship, garrisoning town in constant expectation of an attack from hostile Indians, having on board at night some 40 or 50 women & children."

Under Orderly Sergeant Charles Corbin, the Marine guard of the *Decatur* along with a Naval detachment reinforced the town militia. Corbin had two corporals, a drummer, a fifer and 19 privates divided between a blockhouse at the north end of Seattle and some outbuildings at the southern edge. Probably in deference to its Naval guardians, the blockhouse soon was given the unofficial designation of "Fort Decatur."

The *Decatur* was re-floated on January 19 with Commander Guert Gansevoort her new captain. She lay in close to shore in order to keep her guns within range of likely attack routes and so that reinforcements could be landed with minimum delay. On the afternoon of January 25 Gansevoort landed the "fighting divisions with their small arms on shore" upon hearing that a body of Indians had crossed Lake Washington, three miles east of Seattle. An attack that night seemed certain.

Gansevoort's so-called "3d Division" was placed forward of the wharf. At the southeastern corner of town the "4th division" and some Marines defended a house and a chicken coop. The "1st division" and a howitzer crew were on their left. To the north a store was occupied by the "2d division." Corbin and the remainder of his Marines manned Fort Decatur.

Gansevoort visited his landing party several times during the night and at dawn ordered them to quietly return for breakfast aboard the *Decatur*. This movement was in progress when sounds of an attack could be heard. Dallas was at the wharf with the southern divisions and took immediate action.

"I moved with my command at double quick with arms at a trail, hammocks on their shoulder, keeping them in rear of trees and houses as much as possible," wrote Dallas. "Gained my old position about 8:20, just in time to have the Indians open from the rising ground and forest on the opposite of a swamp about 200 yards wide—a smart fire. By this time I had occupied a hen coop with half of my men, each man having his hammock in front of him with orders not to fire until the Indians show themselves.

"A woodshed in rear of the hen coop with a hayloft above it I occupied with my men who had rifles. By this time a howitzer had come up and the woods for some two miles in extent were literally filled with Indians, I think at the least calculation numbering some 700 or 800, the woods ringing with their yells and firing.

"The fight began to get pretty warm, one man near my post shot through the temple. I charged out several time to draw the fire from the Indians, leaving a portion of my command with rifles to shoot at the Indians . . . one musket ball went through my blanket between my arm and heart, another knocked the nipple off the musket of the man next to me. Our post was nearly riddled with balls. As yet I had no breakfast."

Meanwhile, Corbin was having his troubles at the blockhouse. The hardened Indian fighters of the militia were used to operating in woods rather than from stockades. They insisted on sharing the protection of the blockhouse, especially after the *Decatur's* guns started to fill the air with balls and shot. Corbin finally had to admit them.

OLD AND NEW are contrasted by cannon-ball marker to commemorate Seattle pioneer days and, in background, 42-story Smith Tower, tallest building west of Mississippi when it was built in 1914. Battle of Seattle cost defenders two dead while Indians later admitted to 39 killed and 35 wounded.

The resistance at the southern part of town caused the Indians to shift their attack to the area of the wharf and blockhouse. Crescendos of cannon and musket, greeting every Indian sighting, soon took effect. By 3 p.m. Gansevoort decided that he could call back his men "for the purpose of affording some rest and refreshment." Dallas could finally have his breakfast after a six hour fire fight.

Corbin and his Marines were left as a rear guard. The Navy divisions carried all of the women and children to the *Decatur* and to the *Brontes*, a bark that had been waiting at anchor for a cargo.

Aboard the *Decatur*, Dallas forgot about breakfast and went to the gun deck. The *Decatur's* guns fired with "shell and round shot wherever any Indians appeared," Dallas wrote, "drove them from

(Superior Publishing Company)

the rear of the town and fired at intervals wherever they lighted fires."

Indian sightings and fire grew less and less. At dawn on January 27 a shot was fired at the place where the Indians last had been seen. Nothing stirred; the Battle of Seattle was over.

For the next month, men of the *Decatur* "were actively employed running a line of breastwork the whole extent of the town, building two block-houses, clearing away the stumps for the howitzer to run, felling heavy timber and clearing the woods in rear of the town and doing garrison duty," Dallas wrote in his diary.

The steamer *USS Massachusetts* arrived on February 24, and on March 29 the *USS John Hancock* dropped anchor, finally fulfilling orders issued four months before by Commander David G. Farragut, commander at Mare Island, Calif. On his own initiative upon hearing in November of the Puget Sound troubles, Farragut had begun to prepare the *John Hancock*. Her boilers leaked so badly that it took a week for her to get up enough steam just to move to the coalyard. It was March 18 before the boilers and a blown water bottom were patched, a propeller replaced, and she left for Seattle.

When the Navy finally left Seattle in August, 1856, the town was well equipped for its own defense. Appreciation for the Naval help was increased by the awareness that much of it was at the initiative of a few men acting independently of official policy.

One of these was Farragut. After *John Hancock* left Mare Island, Farragut was informed that his orders were contrary to the desires of department headquarters.

The answer of the Hero of Mobile Bay may well have been the common basis for many of the rescue efforts of the day. He justified what he had done

BATTLE OF SEATTLE can be followed by comparing Cornelius Colgate Hanford sketch (above) with ground plan (below). Navy's four divisions' locations were at numbers 1, 2, 3, 4 respectively. Howitzer (5) was guarded by sailors and Marines located at chicken coop (6) and Fort Decatur (7). After battle, southern block-house (8) was built. Dashed line from Fort Decatur shows trace of post-battle stockade incorrectly shown in sketch as being present during battle. Ships were **Decatur** (10) and **Brontes** (11). Building at 9 was Conklin House, better known as Mother Damnable's, frontier hotel whose proprietress kept her customers happy with good food and lively entertainment. (Ground plan re-drawn from sketch of Lieutenant Phelps, commander of Decatur's 3d division.)

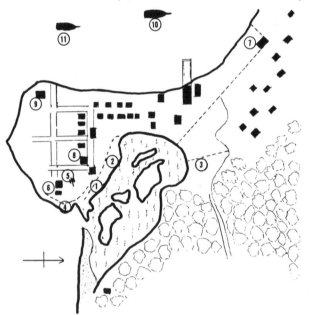

by "the constant calls on me for this vessel by the Commanding Officer in Puget Sound, and the still more pressing calls of the people who were in the deepest distress at the mouth of the Rogue River, together with the outcry against the Army for not doing something for their relief."

TO GET THERE: Fort Decatur, the northern blockhouse, was at what is now the corner of First Avenue and Cherry Street in Seattle. The palisade extended west from this point to the bay. It also went south to modern-day Main Street, the site of the southern blockhouse. Cannonball marker is at Third Avenue and Jefferson Street.

FORT BORST, WASHINGTON

Built in Washington by Oregonians to protect grain instead of settlers, Fort Borst was a fort that was not a fort.

Despite these seeming contradictions, Fort Borst is well-qualified to represent the estimated 58 blockhouse-type forts built in the 1850's by militia, Volunteers, and settlers in Washington Territory. Its design and materials followed the pattern of the other blockhouses, most of which have disappeared at the hands of time or wood scavengers.

Captain Francis Goff and 26 Oregon Volunteers founded Fort Borst in 1856 at the strategic point where the Chehalis River was crossed by the military road between Forts Vancouver and Steilacoom. Officially, the structure was called "Blockhouse on Chehalis River, below Mouth of Skookum Chuck." Unofficially, because it was on the property of Joseph Borst, it quickly became known as "Borst's Fort" or "Fort Borst."

Borst was so enthusiastic about having a blockhouse on his land that he gathered the local settlers so that they could help the state soldiers complete the work. Considering that Borst operated a stopover house next to the Chehalis ferry crossing, there was good reason for him to be pleased by the added protection afforded his area.

Once Goff's men and their helpers finished the double-story, fir log fort, the call to other duties took the troops away. Goff escorted a supply train to Fort Walla Walla, Washington, and then commanded the escort for Governor Isaac I. Stevens.

Fort Borst was not abandoned at this time, however. Nearby was where supplies were unloaded from large canoes for overland shipment, providing Borst with a ready-made mission as a supply depot. This was its function for the remainder of the Yakima War, serving as a forwarding point and a storage house for supplies—mostly grain.

Settlers who felt the need to rush to a blockhouse for safety quickly learned that Fort Henness, 10 miles to the northwest, was the place to go, rather than Fort Borst, the supply depot.

TO GET THERE: Fort Borst Park is immediately southwest of the intersection of Interstate 99 and Harris Avenue in Centralia, Washington. Blockhouse is in park.

FORT BORST was near intersection of Skookumchuck Creek and Chehalis River (below), until threatened by flood waters. Blockhouse was moved northwest to location in park (above). Rude ferry operated across river when blockhouse was built near scene of 1855 tragedy of Governon Isaac I. Stevens family. Cousin George W. Stevens, member of governor's personal staff, drowned trying to ford Skookumchuck Creek on horseback. Body was found several days later in whirlpool a mile downstream, pockets and saddlebags still stuffed with candy and presents intended for governor's children. Blockhouse design included loopholes in upper story, also perforation in floor of second-story overhang so that occupants could fire down on anyone hiding against wall.

(Robert D. Moore, University of Washington Library)

DAVIS' AND EBEY'S BLOCKHOUSES, WASHINGTON

Only one settler died on Whidbey Island in the Indian Wars of the 1850's but that one gruesome slaying was sufficient to put the entire island on alert.

The fact that the Indians' victim was a leading citizen of the island and former Collector of Customs at Olympia, Colonel Isaac N. Ebey, caused the killing to be widely broadcast. Even greater note was taken when it was added that the body had been decapitated and apparently the Indians still had the head.

When the killers were identified as Haida Indians by a farmhand who talked to them just before the murder, a shiver of near-panic raced through the island. There was little doubt that the Haidas would return. Self-defense became all-important and settlers gathered next to the strongest farmhouses or largest families.

Following the example of the mainland, sturdy blockhouses had been thrown up two years before. These were strengthened and more were added, the neighbors taking turns helping each other in the work just as barn-raisings and other major chores were accomplished in times of peace.

The settlers knew there was cause to fear the Haida Indians. The tribe had been frequent terrorists of the island until a detachment of sailors and Marines fought and defeated them after the Battle of Seattle. Twenty-six braves and one chief were believed to have been killed in a two-day engagement, after which the survivors and their canoes were towed to Victoria.

SUNNYSIDE CEMETERY next to Davis Blockhouse includes this grave marker with inscription in Gaelic. Cemetery has many 19th century burials, including Ebey family plot.

Haida tribal law demanded that the deaths be avenged. The settlers could see that Colonel Ebey's murder was revenge for the dead chief. That left 26 more corpses before the "eye for an eye" philosophy would be satisfied.

Colonel Jacob Ebey, father of the dead man, had built one blockhouse near his farmhouse in 1855. It was after dark that the son had been called from the farmhouse to his death. When his groans alerted his family and guests to the danger, their reaction was natural but not particularly heroic. They climbed out a back window and made for the blockhouse. The Indians disappeared in the fog while help was being summoned from neighboring farms.

Ebey built three more blockhouses and put a 12-foot stockade around his home. His neighbor and brother-in-law, James Davis, also put up a blockhouse. Davis felt he needed only one, but he designed it for year-round use with a fireplace.

Two years later Colonel Ebey's head was returned. Captain Charles Dodd of the Hudson's Bay Company recognized it in an Alaskan village and risked his life to bring it back to the family of his late friend. The Ebey grave was reopened so that the head could be buried next to the body.

FIREPLACES WERE not common to blockhouses but James Davis included this one so that his family could be both warm and safe during Indian attacks that never came. Chimney was of mud and sticks, fireplace of stone.

GAELIC GRAVE marker, as seen through Davis Blockhouse window, is interpreted by adjacent sign for benefit of vistors unversed in tongue of Ireland, where stone was made. Cemetery is on slope of hill, has many family plots protected by iron fences or marble walls.

DAVIS BLOCKHOUSE is one of largest of estimated 11 built on Whidbey Island. Sometimes called Cook Blockhouse, it was restored in early 1930's by local Ladies of the Round Table Club, now belongs to Island County.

(Albert P. Salisbury Collection)

TO GET THERE: From Prairie Center at the southern edge of Coupeville, take road to west one block where it deadends at Ebey Road. Go left one block to Cook Road. Turn right one block to deadend at Sherman Road which leads to Sunnyside Cemetery, location of Davis Blockhouse. Continue on road to Pratt farm, 1.5 miles. Request permission to visit Ebey Blockhouse in field.

EBEY BLOCKHOUSE was one of four built by father of slain settler. By 1860's it was used by Winfield Ebey as island's first law office. Other blockhouses, long since disappeared, were used as smokehouse, dairy, store house. Owner Frank J. Pratt, Jr., restored this solitary remainder.

ALEXANDER'S BLOCKHOUSE, WASHINGTON

When the settlers along Penn Cove decided that their safety required a blockhouse, there was nothing halfway about the result. As soon as they had built a double-story fort of tightly-fitted logs, the settlers then surrounded it with a 10-foot high double stockade.

The second floor of the blockhouse was high enough to see over the stockade. The walls were notched every few feet so that riflemen could fire at any attackers. Broken glass and jagged metal fragments were imbedded in the top of the stockade as added deterents to stockade climbing.

Known as Alexander's Blockhouse after John Alexander who directed its construction on a corner of his property, the defensive work provided shelter from Indian attack at the same time that it commanded Penn Cove.

As early as Vancouver's explorations of the 18th century, the cove was known to be significant to the Indians. Vancouver wrote of finding deserted Indian villages and cemeteries in which the coffins stood upright in the ground like sentry boxes. Here, the settlers knew, was a logical point for the Indians to launch an attack.

At the start of the scares of 1855, the settlers first went to the Crockett farm and helped build two blockhouses for local defense. When no Indian attack came, the residents along the cove returned home. The experience in building the Crockett forts helped in designing the Alexander Blockhouse. The Crocketts also supplied their share of the labor to the Alexander work.

Other than an occasional scare, Alexander's Blockhouse weathered the Indian wars without a test. All of the local Indians were friendly. The only threat that they presented was the possibility that they would out-trade John Alexander in the store he maintained next to the blockhouse. Bright cloth and beads at his store counter were the ammunition in his dealings with the Indians.

Mrs. Alexander taught many squaws how to sew. She was so confident of their friendship that she stayed alone without a qualm whenever her husband left the island on month-long buying trips. The solitary crisis was when a doctor had to be summoned in the middle of the night to officiate at the birth of her second son, the first baby born on Whidbey Island. William Alexander, oldest brother of the new arrival, went after help, swinging a torch over his head to keep the wolves away.

ALEXANDER'S BLOCKHOUSE was opened to visitors in 1937 by Abram Alexander, youngest son of John Alexander and first settler baby born on Whidbey Island. After his death, Alexander's interest in blockhouse was continued by American Legion post which helped preserve structure and provide funds for new foundation. Small shelter at right houses part of 24-foot wooden cross erected in field by priest in 1840. Alexander brought it to blockhouse when he found it discarded by new owner.

FORMIDABLE DEFENSE against attack was provided by solid construction of Alexander's Blockhouse. Although site is presently surrounded by thin pole fence, this bears no relationship to original 10-foot stockade torn down long ago. Next to blockhouse an open shed houses examples of Indian canoes that are raced annually.

TO GET THERE: Alexander Blockhouse is on Alexander and Coveland Streets at the edge of Coupeville, Washington.

CROCKETT BLOCKHOUSE, WASHINGTON

A crisis for Washington Territory's first family may have been averted because the Crockett family of Whidbey Island learned their Indian-fighting lessons well.

It was in the East in 1838 that Colonel John Crockett, late of the Virginia Militia, decided that the future lay in the West. Three times elected to the Virginia Legislature and influential in matters both political and financial, Crockett was certain that his family would not suffer by such a move.

In company with other families—including that of Jacob Ebey—the Crocketts learned early that preparation was part of the secret of an Indian defense. Hardly had they started on the Oregon Trail when Indians were attacking them, scattering the cattle. The pioneers were more watchful after that.

Luck had something to do with a good defense, too, they found. When Indians attacked the train near what is now Pocatello, Idaho, the settlers were ready. This did not prevent the attackers from getting off a volley of arrows and bullets. A bullet hit one of the Crocketts and probably would have been fatal had it not glanced off his powder horn.

The Crocketts spent some time on the mainland after arriving in Washington. In 1851 they moved to Whidbey Island not far from the Ebey family. Four years later the Indian scares reminded them of their Oregon Trail lessons. With other families that gathered at their farm, the Crocketts built a blockhouse. John Alexander and his two sons joined them from Penn Cove, providing capable hands that helped fell and notch the logs, making quick work of the blockhouse.

Soon after the first defense was finished, the Crocketts and their neighbors put up a second one on the other side of the farm. The help of the Alexanders was returned by assisting them in building a blockhouse at Penn Cove.

(Yale University Western Collection)

CROCKETT BLOCKHOUSE as pictured in Evans' **History of the Pacific Northwest: Oregon and Washington,** was solid structure occupied as dwelling after Indian scares ended. Second blockhouse was taken from island in 1909 for Seattle Alaska-Yukon Pacific Exposition.

QUILTINGS AND style shows by the Daughters of the Pioneers of Washington attempted to raise money to restore Crockett Blockhouse until WPA took over project in 1938. This is eastern-most blockhouse, moved to site next to road after owner Fred Armstrong donated both building and plot.

After expulsion of the Haidas made Whidbey Island seem safer than the mainland, Governor Isaac I. Stevens sent his family to the Crockett farm. Apparently this was discovered by the Haidas.

Still bent on revenging the death of their chief, the Haidas decided that killing the Stevens family would be just retribution.

Mrs. Stevens and her four children were bathing in the cove near the Crockett farm when a Haida war canoe suddenly appeared. It was filled with braves in full war dress, bending every muscle to speed the canoe between the bathers and the shore.

Grabbing the smallest child, Mrs. Stevens screamed for the others to follow her to shore. The blockhouse was her answer.

The sturdy blockhouse, and the sudden appearance of settlers responding to the screams, settled the matter for the scheming Haidas. They turned their canoe about and raced for the open water.

TO GET THERE: From Coupeville on Whidbey Island, take State 525 and 113 toward Port Townsend ferry. Road passes next to Crockett Blockhouse a half mile from Fort Casey entrance.

SILETZ BLOCKHOUSE, OREGON

Forts without blockhouses were common in the West, but seldom was there an Army blockhouse without a fort. This was the case for several in the 1850-era of Washington and Oregon. Siletz Blockhouse is representative of the rare breed.

Siletz fits easily in the time frame of the blockhouse wars, appearing at the time that the subdued tribes were moved to reservations. Technically it was part of Fort Hoskins, 18 miles to the east by air but double that distance by foot or mule across ten rough mountain passes.

Lieutenant Philip H. Sheridan spent much of his early Army days at Siletz and is credited with building the blockhouse. His *Personal Memoirs* tells of being sent to the Siletz Agency in summer, 1856, to protect the agent from unhappy and hungry Indians, arriving "in time to succor the agent, who for some days had been besieged in a log hut by the Indians and had almost lost hope of rescue."

Sheridan posted four guards to protect the distribution of meat to the starving tribe. Then came trouble. "The Indians soon formed a circle around the sentinels, and impelled by starvation, attempted to take the beef before it could be equally divided."

At the moment before several minor chiefs gave the signal to attack, Sheridan was joined in the center of the circle by principal Chief Tetooney John and two other Indians. John announced to the tribe that he would rather die than permit an attack on the soldiers. His harangue held back the Indians until the remainder of Sheridan's men arrived to supervise the peaceful distribution of the meat.

Fearing "the possibility that the starving Indians might break out," the remainder of Sheridan's company was rushed from Fort Yamhill, 30 miles northeast. Their presence, along with increased rations, stopped the disorder.

Sheridan decided it was "advisable to build a blockhouse for the better protection of the agent." The only level ground he could find was the Indian' cemetery, a small area in which 40 or 50 dead were buried in canoes "which rested in the crotches of forked sticks a few feet above the ground." The chiefs agreed to let the Army have the plot, the canoe coffins were set adrift in the ocean, and a dozen soldiers started on a blockhouse.

A year later the agency headquarters was moved six miles. Sheridan's blockhouse was dismantled, floated down the Siletz River, and reassembled "within two or three hundred yards of the agency and completely commanding and protecting it," a report stated in 1858.

Two threats to the blockhouse came about this time.

The garrison was temporarily increased to 50 men when the agent tried to stop a series of intra-tribal murders by collecting all firearms. Success came only after the ringleader was killed while resisting arrest. He had shot at the arresting sergeant and was immediately felled by rounds from the weapons of both the sergeant and the lieutenant in command.

The second threat was a plan by two tribes to jump the garrison during the meal hour. Supposedly the soldiers left their weapons inside the blockhouse while eating in the cellar. The Indians expected to meet no armed opposition. A friendly Indian exposed the plot and the attackers were welcomed by a row of grinning muskets.

Thirty-man details manned the blockhouse during the Civil War. Corporal Royal A. Bensell, Oregon Volunteers, spent a year at what he called "this prison-like fort." Most of the activities centered on keeping outsiders away from the reservation and in trying to maintain some degree of military decorum.

An unpopular 1864 order required that the garrison hold formal guard mount ceremonies. Bensell's diary notes that he supervised one as corporal of the guard for a guard of two privates, only one of whom was armed. This man also had a semblance of a uniform: "a big hat." Bensell wore "a blouse and my parade cap." He said "such a ridiculous caricature on soldiering I never seen (sic) . . . , as the new guard, consisting of a man with a gun and one without, passed by."

TO GET THERE: From Newport, Oregon, take U.S. 20 east six miles to State 229. Nine miles north on 229 is hamlet of Siletz, site of Agency headquarters and blockhouse. No remains.

SILETZ RIVER passes close to Siletz Blockhouse site, was means by which building's timbers were floated from original site to new location in 1858. Descriptions of blockhouse are vague, Corporal Bensell's diary saying only that it was a gloomy place "40 feet square, lighted by four small windows, 22 inches square." One of his men compared it to "an excellent place to 'fat turkeys.'" An attempt in 1864 to whitewash the building made "the old weather beaten fabric look cheerful," Bensell recorded blockhouse soon disappeared after Army left in June, 1866.

"SOME MUST push and some must pull as we go marching up the hill" sang Mormons as they pushed handcarts from East to the Zion of Salt Lake City in 1850's.

WAR OF THE SAINTS

"An Army was sent to chastise rebels, before it was clearly ascertained whether or not there were any rebels to chastise. It was sent forward in the fall, just when it ought to have reached its destination ... Commissioners were sent in search of the rebel foe, and it was then discovered there was no foe at all."

—New York Times editorial, June 17, 1858

WITH his followers and his wives, Brigham Young went west in 1847 to found Salt Lake City and to establish a Mormon State over which he was governor, military commander and spiritual ruler.

Reports of the prosperous success of Young's followers did not set well with Easterners who thought they had cast the Latter Day Saints into the sterile darkness of the desert. When these reports included exaggerated accounts of Mormon subversion of Federal law, the government decided that firm action would have to be taken.

The White House determined in 1857 that Alfred Cumming was to replace Brigham Young as governor. To make certain that Cumming was successful, a 2,500-man Army accompanied him to Utah. The result was the ill-starred Utah Expedition summarized by one officer: "Wounded none; killed none; fooled everybody."

News that the Army was on the way outraged the Mormons. Young issued a proclamation forbidding the troops to enter Utah. The Mormon militia was mustered. Feeling ran high, one Mormon elder boasting, 'I have wives enough to wipe out the United States!"

The march to Utah went poorly. It took four months for the column to walk the 1,200 miles from Fort Leavenworth, Kansas, to Fort Bridger, Wyoming. Here they found that the Mormons had burned buildings, grass, and even three supply trains and a million dollars worth of supplies. Deep snow and the bitter cold of 25 degrees below zero kept Colonel Albert Sidney Johnston's force in Wyoming for the winter.

The Mormon tactic was to burn everything in front of the invaders, and to harrass them from all sides. Blood was not to be spilled, the only aspect of guerrilla warfare not used.

The army renewed its advance in spring, 1858, after being re-supplied. By this time peaceful overtures with Young convinced him that the Army and a new governor meant no harm. Setting forth conditions that made the Army foreigners on their own soil, Young accepted the outsiders. The bloodless war was over. Opinions vary on the results.

"All in all it was a very expensive and wasteful expedition," wrote General D. S. Stanley, "and its only use was in the instruction the troops received in campaigning on the plains. The White House announced it "had curbed the more open rebellion and had quieted Indian outrages," but Young seemed to have the final word—no one could claim that the Mormons had come off second best.

POSTS OF SAN BERNARDINO, CALIFORNIA

The detailing of Company C of the Mormon Battalion to guard Cajon Pass in April, 1847, had a more lasting effect than just cramping the Indian horse raids. When these men found that Brigham Young would permit them to establish a colony in California, the area below Cajon Pass came to mind.

Early in June, 1851, a 150 wagon caravan of 500 Mormons reached a sycamore grove about 15 miles north of Cajon Pass, the site of the several camps which periodically were established to protect the pass. The Mormons stayed here while negotiating to buy the Rancho San Bernardino, 15 miles to the south. As soon as the $77,000 purchase was agreed upon, they started to build and plant although it was not until February, 1852, that the final papers were registered.

News of an Indian skirmish alerted the newcomers to the dangers of the area. In the center of their new mile-square town of San Bernardino, the leaders set aside eight acres and fenced in a parallelogram, 300 feet wide by 720 feet. Twelve

(Henry R. Huntington Library)

FORT SAN BERNARDINO was sketched in 1852 by William R. Hutton. Ranger Horace Bell described it as "a stockade about a quarter of a mile square with two great gates leading into it. Inside they placed their dwellings, shops and stores. Every night the gates were barred and a sentry kept vigilant watch from the walls against surprise."

foot high walls protected three of the sides. The fourth side was a series of log buildings jammed close together. All exterior walls were loopholed and the gateways were indented to allow for crossfire.

Life for the first year at San Bernardino was centered at this enclosure, known variously as Fort San Bernardino or Mormon Stockade. Weapons and ammunition were loaned to the occupants by the Army garrison at Rancho del Chino. Nightly guards were maintained and an elderly Negro, Uncle Grief, was put in charge of the alarm system: a battered horn which he was to blow in the event of an attack.

"Good industrious neighbors" is how the Los Angeles *Star* hospitably described the newcomers to Southern California. Ranger Horace Bell remembered his San Bernardino visits where "I was benefited by my contact with these serious, rugged people. They set good examples for youth. There were no gamblers tolerated in San Bernardino, no rum sellers, no loud characters offering vice for sale. There were no drones there. Persistent industry, intensive husbandry were the impressive features of life there."

Within a year of their arrival, the Mormons were able to harvest their first crop. It was not long after, however, that they learned that the indefinite land boundaries made their titles somewhat hazy. Some of the properties also were claimed by outsiders. In 1856-57, one of these, Jerome Benson, was not satisfied with debating the matter. West of modern Colton, he mounted an old brass cannon inside of an earthworks, rammed the can-

SAILORS' AND SOLDIERS' Monument in Pioneer Park is dedicated to veterans of America's wars, including those of 1846-48 "who carried the flag of freedom and gave us this beautiful Southwest." Despite its reputation as secession center in Civil War, San Bernardino provided many men to California Volunteer regiments.

FORT SAN BERNARDINO stood at this site, now marked by these tablets in front of Courthouse on Arrowhead Avenue between 3d and 4th Streets. Army frequently passed through San Bernardino on patrols, and in 1855 had post there for short period.

non full of gunpowder and rocks, and challenged all comers to dislodge him.

The loyalties around "Fort Benson" were drawn more along property lines than religious. Mormons and Gentiles alike sided with or against each other, and Benson found he was not alone.

Then in October, 1857, the word came back that took 55 per cent of San Bernardino's Mormons home to Salt Lake City. Brigham Young directed that the saints were to "return to Zion . . . regardless of condition or circumstance" and face the threat of invasion by the United States Army. Many prosperous farms were literally given away, sometimes in exchange for little more than a camping outfit. In at least one case, $40 bought a four-room house complete with furnishings, buggy, cloak and sack of sugar.

With the realization that some of this money and much of the Mormon savings were going to buy arms and ammunition to fight the Army, there was some talk of blockading Cajon Pass, but nothing was done.

Soldiers arrived in San Bernardino on December 27, 1858, when Colonel William Hoffman's "Mojave Expedition" camped near the original Cajon guard post, a site they knew as "Camp at Martin's Ranch." When Hoffman moved to the Mojave river to locate a fort site—and incidentally do

battle with the Indians—his main body remained at San Bernardino.

The camp was moved closer to the town and designated Camp Banning by the time that Hoffman returned on January 19, 1859. Spectacular as the success had been against the Mojaves, "the Indians refuse to allow any white men in their domain," wrote Sergeant Eugene Bandel, "and have more than once made raids quite near us to steal cattle from the neighborhood."

Camp Banning became Camp Prentiss in May, 1859, after Hoffman returned to the Mojave, established Fort Mojave, and decisively whipped the tribe. Until the fall, supplies for the Mojave were forwarded from Camp Prentiss.

Californias took slowly to the populace of San Bernardino and at the start of the Civil War were quick to believe rumors of disloyalty there. Major, later Major General, James H. Carleton made a civilian-clothes spying trip in 1861. He reported that the town consisted of 1,000 Mormons "of a man whose character is such that he could not be tolerated in Utah," and 500 others, mainly "a good many Jew merchants . . . adroit horse thieves and unprincipled desperate men," plus a "few respectable Americans." He recommended that two or more companies of troops be stationed at San Bernardino because "all but the few respectable Amer-

CAMP BANNING and Camp Prentiss, 1859, were in this area at southwest corner of Mill Street and Mount Vernon Avenue. Camp Dolores, 1851 California Ranger post that guarded Cajon Pass, was moved here when 4,301-foot altitude of pass became too cold.

icans would set us at defiance tomorrow if they dared to do so."

Carleton's less-than-objective report was believed. On August 26, 1861, Major W. Scott Ketchum reported that he was at a "Camp near San Bernardino" with the first of four companies of the 4th

EARLY HISTORY comes from this site on Devore cutoff 1.5 miles west of Interstate 15. This was vicinity of Camp Cajon in 1847 and 1857-58 and "Camp at Martin's" from December 27, 1858 to January, 1859. At start of Civil War it was suggested than an officer and 12 men be stationed here to guard Cajon Pass, 15 miles to north.

"NO VACANT buildings to be rented for quarters for either officers or soldiers in this town" was first description of 1861 Post San Bernardino, located in October at this site as Camp Carelton. A tent camp, Carleton was moved to "Emergency Camp" on slight hill north of San Bernardino for short time during flood in February, 1862. This site is northeast of Tippecanoe Avenue bridge over Santa Ana River, next to Norton Air Force Base.

Infantry, his sudden arrival thwarting a plot to ambush him enroute.

Ketchum asked that he be reinforced by two dragoon companies to prevent a rumored plan to attack his camp. The decision for such an attack had been reached at several secret meetings of pro-Southerners, according to the latest rumors.

Ninety dragoons were secretly rushed to Ketchum. To mislead disloyal observers at Los Angeles, the dragoons left their tents in place and moved a howitzer under cover in a wagon.

"The sudden and unexpected appearance of the dragoons had a very beneficial effect," Ketchum reported, especially on election day, September 4, 1861, when the "one or two displays of secession sentiments . . . were promptly checked by the show of a portion of the dragoons."

On October 20, Ketchum's 169 regular soldiers were relieved by three companies of California Cavalry, 272 men strong. Ketchum probably was pleased to leave San Bernardino—where his camp frequently was fired upon by snipers hidden in the surrounding bushes—and go to the battlefields of the East and ultimate rank as a major general of volunteers.

The California cavalrymen were horseless, a situation which gave Major Edward E. Eyre more worry than rebel activities. From the newly-designated "Camp Carleton," Eyre wrote that his men had heard rumors that they were going to be turned into infantrymen.

"For God's sake do not leave me long with this only cause of danger hanging over my head," Eyre appealed. "No exertions would be spared by myself, but should anything like a general mutiny occur, overboard I go, whether my fault or not." Eyre need not have worried; his men spent most of the war as cavalrymen in New Mexico and at San Elizario, Texas.

Troops stayed at San Bernardino until March, 1862. They returned for five months in 1863, partly in respone to reports that a leading secessionist recently released from prison was threatening to kill everyone responsible for his jailing. The previous year he had been arrested for hitting a soldier who protested a toast to "Jeff Davis' health."

Apparently all had cooled by October, 1863, when the troopers were recalled and the newest San Bernardino post, Camp Morris, was closed. In the summer of 1865 an infantry company was sent to San Bernardino to check rumors of a secession plot, but by this time the war was over and the threat seemed anti-climactic.

TO GET THERE: Directions to the many San Bernardino posts are given in the picture captions.

CAMP FLOYD, UTAH

"A hot purgatorial spot where winter was long and rigorous, summer hot and uncomfortable, a place where alkaline water curdled soap, and dust storms proved almost unendurable."

Such was Camp Floyd, the post in Cedar Valley, Utah, that became the final headquarters of the Utah Expedition and the home in 1858 for almost 20 per cent of the entire United States Army.

Camp Floyd was not really in the original plans, although in September, 1857, Colonel Johnston had reminded headquarters of "the necessity of an appropriation by Congress, at the next session, for the building of permanent barracks for the accommodation of the troops . . . should there be a peaceable occupation by them of that Territory . . . There should be an early prosecution of the work next spring, in order that suitable quarters can be provided for the troops by the ensuing winter."

Somehow Salt Lake City seemed to be the objective, but the arrival there on June 26, 1858, was a disappointment. "We marched through the city with colors flying and bands playing," wrote Captain—later Major General—Randolph Marcy, "but, to our astonishment, we only saw here and there a very few persons. The city seemed to have been deserted."

The 3,000-man Army did not go unnoticed, of course. At every corner men were prepared to set fire to the city if the soldiers started to loot. No one broke ranks, Johnson having issued orders that neither troops nor herds were to deviate from the line of march or cross private property.

The march was a painful one for Philip St. George Cooke, leader only ten years before of the Mormon Battalion. His sympathies leaned toward his old comrades in arms and he rode through the

CAMP FLOYD, 1859 (below), included between 300 and 400 buildings, most of them of adobe with clay floors and wooden roofs, covered with canvas and four inches of dirt. One official trace remaining is old cemetery (above). Each command was billeted in its own area with Department Headquarters row at far left, then 10th Infantry, 7th Infantry, 5th Infantry, Phelp's Battery, Reynold's Battery, and 10th Dragoons. Large building centered at top of plat was theater. Distance from theater to flagpole was 1,050 feet, from headquarters stables to near edge of corral was double that. As displeased as Mormons were with Army, they were happy to do business with it; Brigham Young made $50,000 selling lumber to new post. (Redrawn from National Archives plat.)

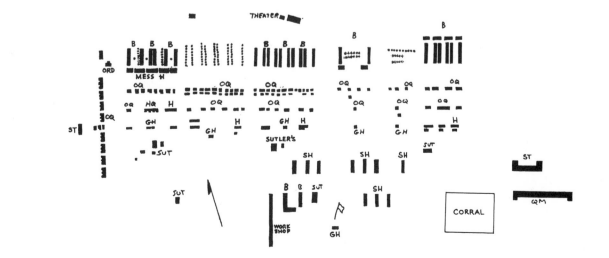

STAGECOACH INN (above) was built on site of Fairfield's first fort, a four-rod square rock fort built by John Carson in 1847. When Army arrived, Carson replaced stockade with this double-story hotel. In accordance with Mormon tenets, he served no liquor and permitted only square rather than round dancing. Colonel Johnston divided his time between Carson's Inn and headquarters office (below). Serving as Johnston's cook was another man to achieve fame in Civil War: William Quantrill, leader of notorious guerrilla gang.

(Utah State Historical Society)

COMMISSARY BUILDING across from Stagecoach Inn, restored at same time as Inn, is only Army building remaining. Army considered returning to site in Civil War but most buildings were gone and owner wanted $15,000 for remainder. Suggestion that Army was afraid to locate in Salt Lake City resulted in final decision that site there would provide better observation of Mormon activities.

city bareheaded as a token of respect for the veterans of his old command.

The march took almost eight hours to pass a single point. It ended at "a church pasture on the other side of Jordan (river), opposite to and about a mile distant from Salt Lake City," Marcy remembered. This is now 21st Street South and Redwood Road. Johnston posted sentries on the bridge to guarantee that no soldiers returned to the city.

Soon after, the command moved 18 miles west of the city to another temporary site. Meanwhile a search was made for a permanent location that met Brigham Young's condition that the Army "must not quarter nearer than 40 miles to any city."

Cedar Valley did not quite meet this requirement. It was 40 miles from Salt Lake City, but less than that to Provo. More so, it was only a few miles from Lake Utah where an estimated 20,000 Mormon refugees were camped. The inevitable occurred: The troop trains and the refugees started on their respective ways on the same day, the troops marched and countermarched trying to find the way to Cedar Valley, and the result was an almost hopeless tangle of saints and soldiers.

About mid-way between Salt Lake City and Provo, the site of Camp Floyd was good strategically. It was an unhappy one otherwise. The five-mile valley neither had enough room for the 3,400 men stationed there in September, 1858, nor sufficient grazing for almost 4,000 horses and mules and many more beef cattle.

The Army had to commandeer forage areas elsewhere, raising a sore point with the Mormons. This mushroomed in March, 1859, into the Spencer-Pike Affair at Rush Valley, west of Camp Floyd. The site of an Army grazing camp, Rush Valley also was where the Spencers ran both their own herd and an illegal saloon. When an intoxicated Howard Spencer challenged the ability of any two soldiers to evict him, and backed up his boast by charging Sergeant Ralph Pike with a pitchfork, Pike bent a rifle over Spencer's head, fracturing the head in the process.

An inflamed Mormon citizenry demanded Pike's arrest, charging that he had mistreated a peaceful civilian who was merely shepherding his private property. Ignoring the saloon and pitchfork details reported in official investigations, a grand jury indicted Pike. The sergeant went to Salt Lake City for trial only to be shot fatally by Spencer during a court recess. Spencer escaped through a crowd that closed in to prevent pursuit.

Despite inflamed passions at Camp Floyd, the Army realized that an attempt to revenge Pike's death or capture Spencer would mean the probable massacre of the small detachment at Salt Lake City. All passes from the post were revoked until the commotion subsided.

Camp Floyd's garrison might well have had a "powder keg complex." The Mormons were as unhappy about the military presence as were the soldiers to be there. The Army's role was so poorly defined that when a troop detachment was sent to Provo to assist the territorial court, it had to be reinforced by ten more companies to counter a suddenly expanded Mormon "police force."

Indian patrolling also occupied much of the garrison's time, but even this was suspect as far as the Mormons were concerned. Every time troops left the camp the Mormons girded for another invasion. Saints posted on the hills south of Salt Lake City watched the approaches from Camp Floyd, ready to light a signal fire at the first signs of an advance.

Johnston never returned to Salt Lake City nor called on Brigham Young, a reason for the absence of rapport between them. Only after Cooke assumed command of Floyd in 1860 were the Mormons inclined to believe their homes were safe from attack.

The final days of Camp Floyd found the garrison reduced to only 700 men and split over the approaching Civil War. "Spirited and almost quarrelsome discussions with Virginians and those who glory with the South in their rebellion" were regular diversions, according to one wife. More official notice was taken on February 6, 1861, when the post was renamed Fort Crittenden, no longer honoring Secretary of War Floyd who had joined the Confederacy.

Five months later the Mormons could breathe more easily. The Army left Cedar Valley, auctioning off its $4 million in improvements for less than $100,000.

TO GET THERE: From Salt Lake City take Alternate U.S. 50 south 26 miles to State 73. Turn west for 21 miles to Fairfield, site of Camp Floyd.

JOHNSTON SLEPT here, according to legend of this room in Stagecoach Inn. Marks on wall are from accidental discharge of shotgun in adjacent room. Such activities might have been in keeping with reputation of Fairfield, nicknamed "Frogtown" in 1859, after it mushroomed to 5,000 population with 17 saloons and other "hog ranch" activities. More uplifting entertainment was provided at camp by Military Dramatic Association, joint venture between soldiers and professional troupe transplanted from Salt Lake City. They built crude theater, painted scenery with shoe blacking and mustard, and had two-year run of such sterling successes as "Sheridan's Rivals," "All That Glitters Is Not Gold," and "My Neighbor's Wife." Salt Lake theater paid $275 for scenery when camp was abandoned.

CEMETERY'S 84 soldier graves were restored in 1959 by Utah Historical Society and American Legion. After fort was abandoned, Fairfield's population disappeared almost overnight. For short time it was Pony Express relay station and, until completion of railroad in 1869, was first western stop out of Salt Lake City on Overland Stage.

JEFFERSON BARRACKS, MISSOURI

Chasing Mormons was just about the least popular idea of 1857 at Jefferson Barracks and 200 troopers expressed disenchantment with it by deserting. Several of their officers were equally unhappy but took the more formal route by penning hasty letters of resignation.

For Jefferson Barracks and its 21-year tradition of supplying troops for almost every major Western expedition, this was an unusual situation. But it was not particularly surprising considering that the men were members of the 5th U.S. Infantry who had just returned from the swamps of Florida. Here they had fought the mud, heat, insects and scurvy of the Big Cyprus Swamp while trying unsuccessfully to round up Billy Bowlegs and other holdouts of the Seminole War. After this, tramping off to Utah was no one's accepted version of a well-deserved rest.

The stay at Jefferson Barracks was only long enough for the remaining members of the regiment to be gathered and rested. Then the 545 men went by boat up river to Fort Leavenworth and, ultimately, by foot to Utah.

More men and supplies passed through Saint Louis as the barracks performed for the Utah War

BOARDED UP former entrance to post recalls decision of General Atkinson to build with lasting materials despite order to use "materials that could be most economically provided by the troops." In 1832 more than 1,300 troops were at barracks for Black Hawk War; defeated chief was brought here by Lieutenant Jefferson Davis and was visited in basement cell by Governor William Clark, Washington Irving and artist George Catlin. Atkinson's problems with militia troops in this war caused him to consider them as much trouble as Indians, despite fact one of volunteer officers was a captain named Abraham Lincoln.

the same role it had played many times previously. When established in 1826 the post was intended to be an "Infantry School of Practice," but this mission was soon overshadowed by the demands of the frontier.

It quickly assumed the functions of its predecessor, Bellefontaine, founded in 1809 as the Army's "most remote post." From its location north of Saint Louis, Bellefontaine had prepared Colonel Henry B. Atkinson and his 6th Infantry for the Missouri Expedition of 1819. Lieutenant William S. Harney headed from Bellefontaine for the Yellowstone in 1824, the same year that Major Stephen Watts Kearney passed through with a battalion of the 1st Infantry. A year later, all three commanders left Bellefontaine for the second Yellowstone Expedition.

By 1826, the post was considered both out-of-the-way and dilapidated. Discipline was no better. Soldiers broke the dull routine with fistfights. At least one lieutenant was killed in a duel with a fellow officer.

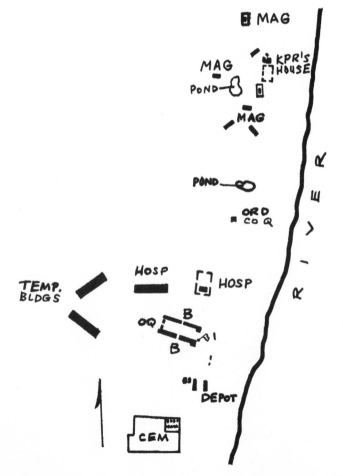

JEFFERSON BARRACKS, 1870, included original site of post in center with Ordnance Depot added in 1850 (at top) and national cemetery began in 1868 (below main post). Temporary buildings and hospital dated from 1862 when barracks had extensive hospital pavilions. Distance from northernmost magazine to cemetery was more than mile and a half. This plat shows only the major buildings. (Redrawn from National Archives plat.)

JEFFERSON BARRACKS looked like this after Civil War, its limestone and brick buildings still in faithful service overlooking Mississippi. River was important to post despite its unpredictability. Philip St. George Cooke's report of 1828 tells how 6th Infantry loaded boat "with their wives and children . . . infants squalled and chickens cackled" and steamer immediately went aground here.

Atkinson charged Kearny and his 1st Infantry troopers with responsibility for building a new post on a 1,702-acre site south of Saint Louis. Kearny started work immediately at what he designated Cantonment Adams, a temporary tent camp.

Two months later Brevet Brigadier General Henry Leavenworth arrived with part of the 3d Infantry and built log huts at Cantonment Miller next to the Kearny camp. Both cantonments lost their names when an Army Order of October 23, 1826, named the post to honor the recently deceased Thomas Jefferson.

Almost every Army officer of the 19th century had at least one tour at Jefferson Barracks. (It appears that all of the officers pictured on pages 10 and 11 served at the barracks, most of them as the commanding officer.)

First Lieutenant Robert E. Lee was at Saint Louis almost continually between 1836 and 1838. He was superintending the construction of dikes to save the city's waterfront. This project did not impress Mary Lee as much as the local mosquitos "as thick as bees every evening."

These swarms undoubtedly contributed to the epidemics that ravaged Jefferson Barracks almost every season. Mrs. Lydia Lane tells in *I Married a Soldier* of how in 1854 Lieutenant Ferdinand Paine faithfully nursed a sick Indian boy to recovery only to die himself. "He had gone on as officer of the day in the morning," she recounts; "at midnight, he was dead."

BUILT IN 1851 and restored in 1959, stables (left) and laborers' house were part of Ordnance Depot. Stables housed four horses and two spring wagons used in unloading ammunition barges at riverside. Ordnance Depot was important tenant of reservation; from 1871 to 1878 entire barracks was turned over to its control.

MAGAZINE now restored, was one of several at Ordance Depot connected by tunnels that also ran to river. Most magazines were built below ground level, natural drainage being provided by crevices in rock formation.

Lee missed by nine years being at the barracks when new Second Lieutenant U. S. Grant reported to his first duty station. Grant's *Memoirs* notes that Colonel Stephen Watts Kearny was in command, "one of the best officers of the day . . . and under him discipline was kept at a high standard, but without vexatious rules or regulations."

His experience with his first commanding officer caused Grant to comment on the other commanders who seemed to "make it a study to think what orders they could publish to annoy their subordinates and render them uncomfortable." He remarked that this same class of officers suddenly discovered they were physically unfit for service at the start of the Mexican War. "They were right," he agreed, "but did not always give the disease the right name."

Grant met the sister of a West Point classmate, Frederick T. Dent, while at Jefferson Barracks, and returned after the Mexican War to make her his bride. Cupid bit others at Saint Louis, too, including Captain John C. Fremont, who met Jessie Benton there. His marriage to the daughter of Senator Thomas Hart Benton played a vital part in his future.

Lieutenant Philip Kearny, the nephew of Stephen Watts Kearny, was aide to Atkinson in 1838 when he met Atkinson's sister-in-law. Diana Bullitt was merely visiting the post at the time, but four years later became the first wife of the stormy officer who later lost an arm in the Mexican War and his life at the Battle of Chantilly.

As the frontier advanced, Jefferson Barracks' role decreased in importance. It fought the Civil War as a hospital and recuperation center for 15,000 soldiers. The original training camp mission was resumed in subsequent wars until after Word War II when Jefferson Barracks was given up by a retrenching Defense Department.

The wife of Winfield Scott Hancock writes in his biography that few persons who were admitted to the hospital "ever left it alive." The then-Captain Hancock "kept on hand a 'cholera specific' in large quantities, which if applied in time, was esteemed infallible. It was given to soldiers who pleaded with my husband not to send them to the hospital. Of those who came to us in season the majority recovered." Casualties were so high, she remembered, that the dead were "carried silently to their graves at nightfull in one wagon, in order to prevent a panic, which needed but the slightest pretext to burst forth."

Robert E. Lee returned in 1855 to Saint Loius as the lieutenant colonel of the newly authorized 2d Cavalry. This tour was for only a short time while the regiment was outfitted with horses and, as an experiment, several different types of carbines.

TO GET THERE: Take Broadway south from downtown Saint Louis, Missouri, to Kingston Road (State 231). Northern entrance is from this road. Southern boundary of barracks is on U.S. 50 (by-pass); Mississippi River is crossed at this point by Jefferson Barracks Free Bridge.

BRICK BUILDINGS at original barracks site are reminders that post was made for 22 companies but remodeled after Civil War to house permanent garrison of 150 men. Barracks (top) is at southeast end of parade ground in front of storehouse (below left). Faded sign still identifies abandoned railroad station (below right) at eastern end of parade near river. After post was given up, some areas were used as historical park by City of Saint Louis. Saint Louis County Housing Authority took over much of parade ground area, renting buildings for apartments, offices and a Catholic school. Famous officers once at barracks included Zachary Taylor, post commander who became U.S. president. Colonel Henry Dodge organized dragoons here in 1833. Dueling was problem in 1830 when Major Thomas Biddle, post paymaster, was challenged by Congressional candidate Pettis Spencer. Biddle was near-sighted, so he selected pistols at five paces. Both principals died. In same year a lieutenant also was killed in duel. Result was official threat of harsh reprisals if practice continued. Lighter activities were described by Surgeon Rodney Glison, remembering "the young ladies there are most accomplished coquettes, and turn the heads and break the hearts of almost every second lieutenant who chances to come this way." He added that young officers frequently borrowed several months in advance on their pay in order to maintain social life, then had "to live as economically as possible in order to replenish their exchequer."

CAMP CONNOR, IDAHO

The solution to the Mormon question, according to Brigadier General P. Edward Connor, commander of the District of Utah during most of the Civil War, was to invite "into the territory large numbers of Gentiles to live among and dwell with the people . . . to disabuse the minds of the latter of the false, frivolous, yet dangerous and constant, teachings of the leaders, that the government is their enemy and persecutor."

Connor also assumed the role of the protector of non-believing Mormons, especially the survivors of an 1861 affair in which Joseph Morris and six other dissident Mormons were slain in a three-day fight with a Mormon posse.

Connor gave protection to 53 Morrisite families, who, he said, "are persecuted by the Mormons to such an extent that they are actually suffering for the necessaries of life." In May, 1863, Connor took them 150 miles north of Salt Lake City to "form the nucleus of an anti-Mormon settlement, and a refuge for all who desire to leave the Mormon Church, and have not the means to emigrate farther."

The site of the experiment was Soda Springs,

CONNOR'S REMOVAL of 160 Morrisites is commemorated by this marker in front of Soda Springs courthouse. At Little Spring Creek, a mile from here, in 1861 emigrant family of seven was massacred in sleep. Wagon box served as single coffin for corpses of parents and five children. It was first burial in cemetery two blocks northwest of this marker.

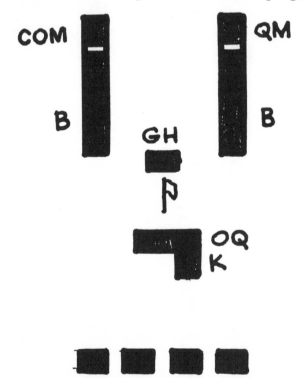

CAMP CONNOR, 1864, probably looked like this, according to Colonel Fred B. Rogers, author of "Soldiers of the Overland." Pine barracks measured 80 feet by 15, were partitioned into messes of eight or 10 men each. "Each mess has a chimney, fireplace, window and door, with bunks; tables and benches, and every convenience that a soldier can devise in habitations of so rude a nature, and so roughly constructed," a soldier correspondent wrote. He added that 25- by 12-foot guardhouse had 3- by 12-foot cell, but "the dwellers in this dread domicile are but few." (Redrawn from Colonel Rogers' plat.)

Idaho, a well-known mineral springs on the Oregon Trail "in the vicinity of the summer resort of hostile Indians," Connor reported. "It is an important point and should be occupied immediately by troops for the protection of overland emigration."

At first Connor planned to establish a fort at Soda Springs with a Morrisite company. They were to be enlisted for 12 months "with the understanding that they are to garrison that post, and meanwhile they could make use of their time when off duty in cultivating the soil and laying the foundaton of their future homes." This part of the plan collapsed when Connor was told that the enlistments would have to be for a minimum of three years.

California volunteers provided the military force for what became Camp Connor on the southwestern edge of the new town of Soda Springs. While the Morrisites laid out their new town nearby, the soldiers built huts of pine logs around a U-shaped parade ground.

Female influences at Camp Connor were provided by "its full quota of laundresses," a soldier observed, and the residents of a building 100 yards from the post "in which is the sole medium through which the followers of Uncle Sam located in the wilds of Idaho, pass from the monotonous routine of camp life, to the Sunday divertisements, amusements, etc., natural to their disposition and inclinations. Within the walls of this building the gay lasses of . . . Soda City swing their crinoline with grace and recherche that would befittingly become a bon ton of Fifth Avenue."

The Army's presence had the desired effect on the Indians. In October, 1863, Connor returned to sign a treaty with the Shoshone Indians. "For the first time in the history of the country it may now be truly announced that the great emigrant roads of the territory may be safely traversed by single persons without danger to life or property or fear of molestation by Indians," Connor boasted.

The status of Camp Connor was uncertain throughout its two-year life. It was in Idaho and technically outside of Connor's district. He settled this by being the first on the scene and then obtaining the concurrences of the appropriate district and department commanders.

On February 24, 1865, Connor ordered the abandonment of the camp "as soon as the roads are passable and the present supplies are exhausted." He explained that Soda Springs' citizens were now "sufficiently numerous to protect themselves" and that he needed the troops to protect the Overland Mail line.

Connor did not add that he had just been informed that his Utah District was transferred to the Department of Missouri. Unless he withdrew his troops in Idaho, they would be lost to him when it became obvious that the camp did not belong to Utah. Headquarters of the Pacific Department disapproved of Connor's action "but as he is no longer under my orders, I forbear saying anything about it," reported Major General Irvin McDowell. "He wanted the troops back, and took this way to secure them."

The Pacific department ordered the non-existent Camp Connor troops to report to the District of Oregon at the same time that the Missouri depart-

(Caxton Printers, Col. Fred B. Rogers, and Bancroft Library)

NINETY-FOOT flagpole "of the most symmetrical proportions" overlooks this sketch of how Camp Connor may have looked in 1863. Correspondent said pole "would be an ornament to a much more beautiful parade ground than the one on which it so majestically stands." He also described barbershop where the celebrated philological, phrenological and spontaneous barber holds forth. He has erected a large and commodious saloon. His chairs are constructed on a manner to insure comfort, ease and luxury to his customers—being a pine bench minus the back." Sketch is from Abraham C. Anderson's **Trails of Early Idaho**, published by Caxton.

ment carried an unlocated "Camp Connor" in its next organizational report.

In his new assignment Connor's attentions were devoted to Indians rather than Mormons. His Camp Connor garrison re-joined him. When next heard from they were in Wyoming on his Powder River Expedition of 1865, building a "Fort Connor" on the Bozeman Trail.

TO GET THERE: Soda Springs is 68 miles southeast of Pocatello, Idaho, on U.S. 30-north. Site of Camp Connor is south of highway immediately west of town.

SITE OF Camp Connor overlooks Soda Springs reservoir and Bear River (background). Probably due to penmanship of period, post frequently appears as "Camp Conness" in official reports. June 30, 1864, official departmental listing included both "Camp Connor, Idaho Territory" and "Camp Conness, Utah Territory." California Volunteer records have frequent entries of troops at latter non-existent post, error probably accepted in belief it was in honor of California Senator John Conness.

H.M.S. GANGES 34 GUNS
Respectfully dedicated to Rear Admiral Baynes, C.B. Cap.t John Fulford and the Officers of H.M.S Ganges by J.Dixon R.N.

(British National Maritime Museum & Gillian Knudsen)

THE FRIENDLY WAR

"Remarks for Immediate Consideration: First, there is in dispute the boundary and dividing line from the parallel of 49° to the Straits of Fuca. The English claim one channel, whereas the Americans claim another as the boundary, the bone of contention being several large islands . . ." —Inspector General Joseph K. F. Mansfield, 1854.

THE Oregon Treaty of 1846 settled the boundary question of "54 40 or fight" with one exception. That exception resulted in 26 years of diplomatic exchanges, caused 13 years of military occupation, and almost precipitated a shooting war between Great Britain and the United States.

Although the treaty said that the Puget Sound boundary would be down the center of the channel between Vancouver Island and the mainland, it did not specify which channel of several. The British assumed the channel was Rosario Strait to the east, charted in 1798 by Captain Vancouver; the Americans were equally positive the boundary was Haro Strait, to the west, the most traveled route. (See map, page 81.)

At stake were most of the 176 habitable islands of the San Juan chain. On the largest of these, San Juan Island, the ever-present Hudson's Bay Company had established a post in 1845. Later, American settlers arrived and Washington Territory tried to tax the company. Collector of Customs Isaac N. Ebey—who later was beheaded on Whidbey Island—had no success in 1853, but the county sheriff was able to drag off 34 sheep in payment of $80 in back taxes a year later.

Diplomatic circles and ineffective boundary commissioners continued the debate until the killing of a hog exploded the issue. In April, 1859, Lyman Cutler, an American squatting near the trading post, announced that he had shot a boar hog that was rooting through his potato patch.

False rumors that Cutler was to be dragged to a Canadian prison caused Brevet Brigadier William S. Harney to rush a total of 461 soldiers to the island. British Columbia Governor James Douglas called on the fleet to land Royal Marines. Five ships were nearby for a total of 167 guns and 2,140 men, but the request was vetoed by Rear Admiral Robert Lambert Baynes.

"Tut, tut, no, no! The damned fools," Baynes reportedly replied. He was not able to start a war over a pig and told his senior captain: "It is now my positive order that you do not on any account whatever take the initiative in commencing hostilities."

Army Commander Winfield Scott was rushed from the East and ordered Harney to stop the construction of a fort and to withdraw most of the troops. Scott talked the British into each providing 100-man garrisons to jointly occupy the island until the ownership was determined. This was followed by 13 years of socializing between the opposing forces of the "Friendly War" until the 1872 decision that the island belonged to the United States.

ENGLISH CAMP, WASHINGTON

"The settlers here are very hospitable and good natured, asking us to their houses and treating us with the greatest civility, so different to the Hong Kong people who think of nothing but dollars," wrote Midshipman William Henry Childers, Royal Navy, in 1859.

Aboard *HMS Tribune*, Childers was writing to his mother, but his words could have been taken as a prophecy of the 13 years to come for the Royal Navy at San Juan. The friendship that seemed to be the key theme was proven by the number of men who returned to the area as settlers.

Despite pressure to assert the Crown's presence by landing Royal Marines, the Royal Navy kept her troops aboard ship during the explosive days of 1859. After the agreement for joint occupation by 100-man garrisons, Rear Admiral Robert Lambert Baynes announced on March 20, 1860, ". . . A detachment of Royal Marines, with their appropriate arms, equivalent in number to the troops of the United States . . . will be disembarked on the north point of the island of San Juan for the purpose of establishing a joint military occupation. . . ."

Marine Captain George Bazalgette—who was destined to remain at San Juan for seven years—was told that he was landing "for the protection of British interests and to form a joint military occupation with the troops of the United States. As the sovereignty of the island is still in dispute . . . you will on no account whatever interfere with the citizens of the United States . . . . American citizens have equal rights with British subjects on the island."

"You will place yourself in frank and free com-

BLOCKHOUSE IS most prominent building at both military sites on San Juan Island. Settlement of boundary dispute in 1872 was rare example of two sovereign nations agreeing to abide by decision of third nation, and marked first time United States had no boundary dispute with Great Britain.

munication with the commanding officer of the U.S. troops," Bazalgette's orders concluded, "bearing in mind how essential it is for the public service that the most perfect and cordial understanding should exist. . ."

Bazelgette was told that he was to use his best judgment in dealing with "offenses committed by any of Her Majesty's subjects" with the authority to banish them from the island if necessary. This order was tested when the American garrison brought in a man peddling a boat load of whiskey to the Indians. The man had been put in the American guardhouse and his cargo destroyed until he claimed to be a British subject.

Bazalgette wasted no time with the professed Englishman. He was shipped quickly to Victoria, stood trial after several months in prison, and was sentenced to the chain gang. Few claims of British nationality were heard thereafter from captured wrongdoers.

Although England usually was unable to maintain the prescribed 100, the garrison had the advantage of continuity. Only two commanding offi-

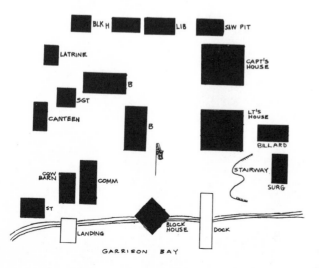

ENGLISH CAMP was remembered this way by James Crook, interviewed at age of 90 by National Park Service. Crook's parents homesteaded site after garrison left and he spent entire life among buildings of which only one barracks, commissary and blockhouses are left. Positions are approximate and not to scale. (Redrawn from National Park Service data courtesy John A. Hussey.)

SUPPLY SHIP apparently was at English Camp—only name by which post was known—when sketched by Frederick Whymper about 1870. Officers' quarters are obscured by ship, but blockhouse is evident. Not quite in conformance with ground plan, buildings at left probably were barracks and commissary. Contemporary newspaper description of post said, "The site of the English Camp is certainly one of great picturesqueness and beauty. The fresh green sward around which the Cantonments of the Marines are erected gives a rural character to the scene that strangely contacts (sic) with military garb of the Marines."

TO GET THERE: From Friday Harbor on San Juan Island—reached by ferry from Anacortes, Washington—take English Camp Road from Second and Spring Streets. Go 8.8 miles to marker; turn left on gravel road .7 mile to parking area. Go straight .2 mile to dirt road. Cemetery is .2 mile near top of hill. All areas are marked.

BLACKSMITH LABORED here at one time although indications are that Royal Marine Light Infantry had few mounts to keep his busy. Captain Delacombe submitted request in March, 1868, for replacement for his personal horse and for "the one allowed for hauling wood and other work in this camp," suggesting only two were at garrison.

ENGLISH CEMETERY, still maintained by British government, is on hill above post. Sign provided by Royal Canadian Navy is at entrance to tiny plot containing graves of seven Royal Marines. Civilian who lived near garrison during occupation also is buried here. Five Marines died from drowning, one "dropped dead" and one was "accidentally shot by his brother." Insignia of world's oldest Marine Corps appears atop each gravestone, most of which were erected by "surviving comrades" or, in one case, "sorrowing brother."

FRAME CONSTRUCTION of barracks (left) and commissary (right) withstood ravages of time because of frequent repairs by Crook family. Barracks was frequent scene of island-wide celebrations, decorated with "evergreen, holly, the Union Jack and other national insignia," as newspaper reported in 1871, when "the attendance of rustic belles was unusually large and the visitors and their gallant entertainers 'tripped the light fantastic toe' until day broke, when breakfast was served and after cheering their hosts lustily the company departed at seven o'clock on Tuesday morning, escorted for a long distance by a band of music and the soldiers."

cers were there in 13 years, Captain William A. Delacombe relieving Bazalgette in 1867. Two lieutenants, an assistant surgeon, and 80 men of the "Royal Marine Light Infantry" provided the garrison without change, except for those caused by sickness or desertion.

Invitations to the English Camp were the accepted way to spend the holidays. American occasions were included, the Englishmen doing their best to out-celebrate the U.S. garrison on the Fourth of July, an ironic joint festival. The Queen's Birthday became such an event that in 1867 the *British Colonist* at Victoria advised prospective celebrators of "the propriety of practicing for the various games which will be open to their competition" because of an audience of "many fair ladies."

"British cheer" was shared at the Christmas holidays of 1871, "the last Christmas the garrison expect to spend on the island." Eleven months later the *Colonist* recorded the departure of the Marines after the buildings were turned over to the United States.

"The flagstaff from which the British ensign had floated for 13 years was cut down, a portion divided among the men, and a long piece brought around to the dockyard as a souvenir," the *Colonist* recorded on November 26, 1872. "The evacuation was conducted in a most orderly manner."

PACE AT English Camp is hinted by this peaceful view in late 1860's outside of messhall. Camp commander, Captain Delacombe, is at left, his son at right. Two surgeons are next to captain, with A. Hoffmeister, post sutler, in center behind mascot. When Delacombe left for England, settlers said he "administered justice to one and all without harshness or severity" and was always "urbane and courteous."

(British Columbia Provincial Archives)

CAMP PICKETT, WASHINGTON

A hint of what was to come was included in General Harney's orders when Captain George Pickett arrived at San Juan Island on July 27, 1859.

"Take into consideration that future contingencies may require an establishment of from four to six companies retaining the command of San Juan Harbor," Harney directed, suggesting he had more in mind than just protecting the settlers from Indians. "Resist all attempts at interference by the British authorities . . . by intimidation or force."

Outnumber 20 to one, the future hero of Gettysburg did not have the air of the underdog as he ordered his 50 men to dig earthworks on the southern tip of the island. He informed the British authorities that he was sent with the "strictest orders to protect the property of settlers on the island, British or otherwise." His proclamation to the island asserted that it was United States Territory and "no laws, other than those of the United States, nor courts, except such as are held by virtue of said joint laws, will be recognized on this Island."

When the English suggested that the Queen might find it necessary to post a garrison to uphold British rights, Pickett calmly replied that there was room enough for both. Privately he added that if the British forced matters, his small force would be merely "a mouthful" for them.

Harney did not delay in trying to even up the odds. Under the cover of fog on August 10 the USS Massachusetts landed the troops and howitzers of Lieutenant Colonel Silas Casey. Then the Massachusetts steamed boldly into the bay behind the

"THE LARGE military force with its eight heavy guns and numerous field pieces which wear the appearance of a menace while crowning the heights of San Juan," according to Governor Douglas' description in 1859, occupied earthworks at crest of hill. This is view from east.

camp and put her cargo and ammunition ashore, disregarding HMS Tribune and her 30 guns.

Casey tried to see Rear Admiral Baynes on August 20 by going to the Royal Navy harbor of Esquimalt on Victoria Island. Baynes refused to go ashore but said Casey would be welcome aboard the flagship, HMS Ganges. "I had gone 25 miles and he would not come 100 yards," Casey complained.

Meanwhile Pickett was pushing the work on a fortification, employing all of his 461 men, representing five infantry companies, four artillery, and a detachment of engineers. Along with some Naval guns from the Massachusetts, the earth-

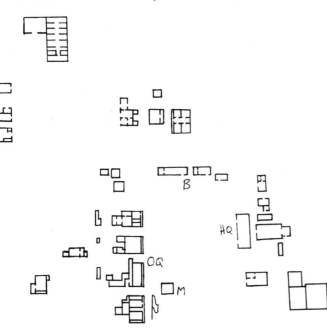

CAMP SAN JUAN ISLAND became official name for Camp Pickett after going through several changes. It became simple Camp San Juan in 1863, but Pickett name usually was used, then Camp Steele after Civil War. Island name was adopted to prevent confusion with Wyoming's Fort Fred Steele, but simple "American Camp" often was used. This 1867 plat shows buildings' room arrangement. Most were of frame, with some log construction, but quarters were considered "quite insufficient for even the present garrison (68)," report of 1871 stated. "They are very low, badly ventilated, and constantly require repairs." This drawing is based on unlabeled plat in National Archives and does not show small blockhouse near flagpole—possibly converted to magazine in final years.

(University of Washington Libraries, Robert D. Monroe)

"CAMP SAN JUAN ISLAND" is title of this watercolor probably made about 1866 by Sergeant A. D. Roland. Combination of military and social activity was regular feature at post, especially in joint entertainments with British garrison. In 1863 both posts turned out for picnic with Vancouverites on plain in front of earthworks, "a shady spot ... where the excursionists were regaled with the good things of this life ..." newspaper reported. "The officers of the American and English garrison partook of luncheon with the pic-nic (sic) party, and made themselves highly agreeable. After the cloth was cleared, dancing was commenced on the grass, but the sun's rays proving too powerful for terpsichorian indulgence, an invitation was given by the medical officer in charge to adjourn to his quarters ..." Fourth of July in same year was celebrated in mess hall; British participated in reading of Declaration of Independence and singing of "Star Spangled Banner," then proceeded to outrun Americans in 100-yard footrace on parade ground.

works boasted eight 32-pound cannon and six smaller guns.

The arrival of General Winfield Scott on October 25 had immediate effects. Most of the troops were ordered back to the mainland and Captain Lewis C. Hunt was put in command of the newly-named "Camp Pickett." The son-in-law of Colonel Casey, Hunt was considered more amenable to the British than the fiery Pickett. The camp was moved from the exposed, windward side of the fortifications to a level area behind them.

Pickett suddenly returned to the island on April 30 and informed Hunt that Harney had restored the original commander. Pickett told the British of the change and also of Harney's decision that the islands belonged to Whatcom County, Washington Territory.

The arbitrary actions passed quickly through diplomatic channels to Washington, D.C. Almost

as quickly Harney was relieved of the District of Oregon command and called to the capitol. His impetuous actions never were satisfactorily explained. Some historians have suggested that Harney and Pickett, both southerners who opposed secession, tried to promote a war with England in the hope that uniting against a common enemy would prevent the Civil War.

Pickett remained at San Juan amid praise from his Royal Marine counterpart and the Royal Navy authorities. "The very cordial and friendly feeling which had existed between the troops of the two Governments . . . the utmost courtesy and friendliness on the part of Captain Pickett," commented a British captain in 1861.

Special Order No. 9 on June 11, 1861, ordered the closing of many Northwestern posts, including that at San Juan. Amidst protests from Pickett, the settlers, and the governor, Colonel George Wright reversed the decision.

"I believe that a strong garrison on San Juan Island, with the aid of a small steamer, would afford ample protection for the whole sound, and that all other posts might be dispensed with," Wright explained. Headquarters agreed, taking

ROBERT'S RULES OF ORDER are indirectly commemorated near earthworks by this plaque dedicated to Lieutenant Henry Martyn Robert, U. S. Engineers, 1859, by Daughters of American Revolution. Author of standard parliamentary rulebook, Robert was second lieutenant in 2d Engineers when at San Juan, retired in 1901 as brigadier general and Chief of Engineers. He died in 1923, last surviving member of West Point class of 1857.

special notice of the "national importance" of the site. It was the only Western post manned wholly by regulars during the Civil War.

Pickett resigned on July 2, 1861, and the post's Company B, 9th Infantry, was replaced by Company H, 9th Infantry, commanded by no other than Captain Thomas C. English. The confusion over the coincidental name ended in December when English's half-strength unit was relieved by Battery D, 3d Artillery. Soon after, Captain Lyman Bissell and Company C, 9th Infantry, arrived at what was to be their station throughout the Civil War.

Whiskey dealers and tax collections occupied most of Bissell's time and resulted in a prolonged series of charges against him. Investigation showed that the commander had taken positive action to prevent illicit whiskey peddling to the troops and his Indians. This was considered an infringement on their rights by the saloon keepers—almost a unanimous occupation on the island at the time.

A defender of Bissell, Edward D. Warbass, reported that the charges against the Army had been drafted in an unlicensed barroom that occasionally passed for a courtroom. One of the drafters was the postmaster who operated his office in the corner of another unlicensed barroom. Warbass was not completely impartial; he was the former sutler of Fort Bellingham.

An attempt to suppress the illicit whiskey dealing was defeated at a trial before the local justice of the peace. The courtroom was an illegal saloon in which the jury sat at the bar and quenched their thirst as they found the owner not guilty of operating an illegal saloon!

Headquarters quieted the civil protest by pointing out that all authority on the island was through the two military commanders, each for citizens of their respective countries. Extreme cases, it was noted, could be ejected from the island if the commander desired, but it was not to be made "a nest for gamblers and drinking shops."

The Civil War policy at San Juan was described by Brigadier General Benjamin Alvord, "to administer opiates and stave off puzzling questions growing out of the joint occupation."

Patriotism stilled some of the problems, but with peace these came into the open. Until the Army left in 1874, frequent conflicts occurred between the civil and military. More than once the Army commander received a summons to appear in court for complying with his military orders.

TO GET THERE: From Friday Harbor, go south on marked route from intersection of Spring and Argyle Streets 6.6 miles to National Park Service site.

EMPEROR WILHELM I of Germany decided that United States was proper owner of San Juan Islands in 1872, event commemorated by this marker at southeastern corner of earthworks. View is along southern crest of work, looking to west; commemorative rock to Lt. Robert is at left background.

EARTHWORKS ARE most prominent remants of American occupation, were described in Bancroft's History, as being 350 feet on west, 100 on southeast and east, and 150 on northeast, "the northside being left open with the garrison ground in its rear. The embankment had a base of 25 feet, with a width at top of eight feet. Inside the redoubt were five gun-platforms of earth, reaching to within two feet of the level of the parapet, each 12 by 18 feet, two of them at corners of the redoubt. The parapet was seven feet above the interior, and the slope of the interior 12 to 15 feet, the exterior slope being 25 to 40 feet, with a ditch at the bottom from three to five feet deep." View (above) is from north and (below) from southwest.

FORT BELLINGHAM, WASHINGTON

Fortunately for the troopers from Fort Bellingham, their presence at San Juan was more political than military. If the need had arisen for the Bellingham soldiers to exchange shots with the English, the Queen's forces probably would have had little to fear.

Seven months earlier, the men of Captain George Pickett's Company D, 9th Infantry, had been tested at rifle marksmanship by Inspector General Joseph K. F. Mansfield. The results were less than encouraging—except to a potential enemy.

"This company . . . fired at the target 6'x22" at 200 yards distant," Mansfield recorded, "one round per 40 men, & put only one shot in the target. This only showed the want of instruction & practice . . . It was armed with the Harpers Ferry rifle & sword bayonet, but the arms were old & much out of order."

Mansfield had an explanation for the poor showing. "Like all posts in this new country the soldiers work more than they drill & they need instruction here as well as other posts in target firing, rifle drills & bayonet exercises."

He drilled the company as skirmishers, too, but could only rate their showing as "tolerable."

Company D was the garrison for Fort Bellingham throughout the post's four-year history. Virtually deserted when Pickett took the company to San Juan for four months in 1859, Bellingham's nearness to the Indian routes required that a detachment be sent back early when hostilities threatened.

The forerunner of the official post was a settler blockhouse on Bellingham Bay during the Indian

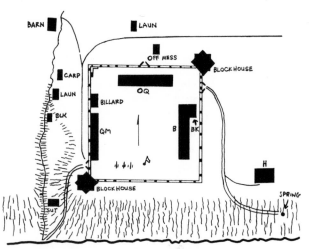

FORT BELLINGHAM's "barracks, storehouses, & officers quarters are within an enclosed square of about 80 yards the side; made of pallisades (sic) set in the ground and loopholed for musketry, and flanked by two Blockhouses two stories high, pierced for mountain howitzers & loopholed," Inspector General Mansfield recorded in 1858. "The officers quarters are a frame building & ample. The barracks a single frame building with mess-hall & kitchen & bakery attached, and ample ... The troops are well quartered & there seems to be nothing wanted of consequence." (Redrawn from Mansfield Report, 1858.)

War of 1855. The Army was rushed to the area and Fort Bellingham founded on August 26, 1856, in response to repeated appeals of the settlers.

Locating a suitable site was difficult on the hilly and wooded shores of Bellingham Bay, and finally Pickett selected the claim of William Roberts. Although offered $800 for the site and its improvements, Robert refused. He and his family finally had to be forcibly evicted so that the Army could build its stockade.

Almost $12,000 was spent in the first few years to provide what Mansfield termed "a cheap and good post, creditable to the parties that performed the duty."

Pickett was absent on leave when Mansfield inspected. Second Lieutenant James W. Forsyth was the acting commander, "a highly meritorious officer . . . who manifested much ability and zeal," the inspector reported. Forsyth continued in the Army, serving as Sheridan's Chief of Staff late in the Civil War, commanding the troops at Wounded Knee in 1890, and retiring as a major general in 1897.

Despite a total of 50 desertions in three years, the Bellingham company was considered "in a good state of discipline." Mansfield noted that 20 of the desertions were in San Francisco, before going to Bellingham, while many of the others could be blamed on the gold fever that decimated most Western garrisons.

Bellingham was evacuated on April 28, 1860.

BLOCKHOUSE REMAINED at fort site long after most other buildings had been taken apart or moved. Each blockhouse was 22 feet square on first floor, slightly larger on second. Cannon available to be fired from large embrasures included one 6-pounder and two 12-pound mountain howitzers. Blockhouse nearest shore was used as quarters for guard, other was prison.

(Washington State Historical Society)

PICKETT LIVED here during his tour as Fort Bellingham commander. He married beautiful Haida Indian maiden and they shared these quarters until she died giving birth to son, James Tilton Pickett. Four-year-old son was placed in custody of friend when Pickett resigned to join Confederacy in 1861. Pickett supported boy and had plans to bring him East, but post-war finances as Richmond, Virginia, insurance agent would not permit before Pickett died in 1875. Son became noted newspaper illustrator and painter in Pacific Northwest.

WASHINGTON'S OLDEST brick building, this single story landmark was built next to fort in 1858 as combination store, bank and commission house for gold rush. It became territorial courthouse and jail in 1863 and was county courthouse until 1891. Bricks were manufactured in Philadelphia and brought around Cape Horn as ballast in sailing ships.

It was never reoccupied despite an appeal in 1861 from the Legislative Assembly that complained of the "unmistakable evidence of hostilities to the whites" by the Indians who had not received their treaty annuities. The Assembly said it was "of utmost importance that Fort Bellingham be reoccupied by at least one company of United States troops for the protection of Bellingham Bay," but the appeal fell on deaf ears.

TO GET THERE: From the center of Bellingham, Washington, take West Hally north to E Street. Turn right, go two blocks east up hill; turn left at Bancroft Street. Pickett house is at 910 Bancroft Street, right hand side in middle of block.

FORT TOWNSEND, WASHINGTON

The fluctuations of military strength on San Juan had a direct bearing on the history of Fort Townsend, causing it to be vacated and then reoccupied during the critical days of 1859. Then when the troopers left the island in 1874, Fort Townsend was re-garrisoned again.

Founded on October 26, 1856, the post was in its third year when the garrison was rushed to San Juan. In company with the other Puget Sound forts of Bellingham and Steilacoom, the troopers responded to General Harney's announcement: "The British Authorities threaten to force Captain Pickett's position and they greatly outnumber him at present."

In command of the combined garrisons was Lieutenant Colonel Silas Casey from Fort Steilacoom. He passed to the other commanders his orders from Harney to "take with you all the ammunition you have on hand as well as your field guns." By July 28, 1858, Fort Townsend was deserted.

Without firing a shot in anger the garrison returned to Fort Townsend on November 16, 1859, in time to spend the winter in barracks that were more substantial than those at the island.

"The buildings all of them seem to be judiciously planned and executed," commented Inspector General Mansfield on his visit only a year previously, "and the soldiers are particularly well accomodated . . . The men were well quartered and slept in double bunks two tiers high, and the kitchen and messroom neat and comfortable. I have never seen soldiers better accomodated."

Company I, 4th Infantry, manned the post before the Civil War under the command of Captain and Brevet Major Granville O. Haller. At the time of Mansfield's 1858 visit the garrison included another officer and an assistant surgeon, three sergeants and three corporals, two musicians and 63 privates.

Mansfield made no comment on the fact five of the privates were sick and 13 in the guardhouse, almost a quarter of the complement. He noted that since payday in mid-November there had been 18 desertions "and some considerable intoxication." The desertion record for three years was 74 partly because of the attractions of the gold fields.

Haller was destined to return to Fort Townsend again as commanding officer in 1879. This time he was a full colonel, a rank to which he was appointed 16 years after an unusual dismissal from the Army.

In 1863, Haller was accused by a Naval officer of making disloyal statements during the Fredericksburg campaign. Without hearing or courtmartial, Haller was dismissed from the Army. Finally after years of letter writing and personal visits, he was able to appeal his case. A Joint Resolution of Congress in 1879 restored him to the Army at the higher rank. He retired three years later.

In its early days Fort Townsend was considered "well-selected for a military post as a protection to all citizens located in this vicinity," commented Mansfield, "and to overawe the Indians, and to afford aid to the customs house officer at Port Townsend in case of necessity, and to the Indian Agent of this vicinity who resides in that place." He noted the closeness to the boundary which "gives to this post at present great importance in a military point of view, as a depot for efficient troops,

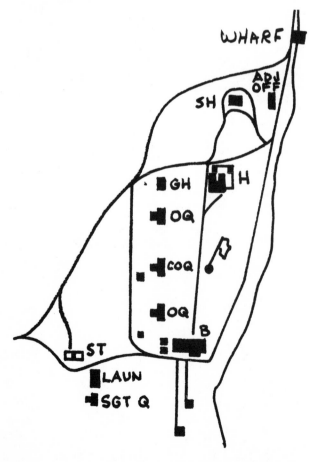

RESTORED TO this appearance in 1877, Fort Townsend closely matched description 20 years earlier when Inspector General Mansfield wrote, "The officers' quarters are three buildings in a line. The center for the commanding officer with the Adjutants Office. That on the right the subalterns quarters and that on the left the Assistant Surgeons. They are roomy and ample and frame buildings, lathed and plastered. Further on the same line on the left is a block or loghouse guardhouse with prisoners rooms and two cells. Further on the right is a block or loghouse bakery, and soldiers library and reading room. Perpendicular to this line on the right stands a two story Barrack, roomy and ample for one company . . . On the left . . . stands the hospital almost finished, roomy and ample." By 1877, adjutant had moved office to bluff overlooking bay. (Redrawn from Division of Pacific Report, 1879.)

(National Archives)

REMNANTS OF wharf are only reminders left of Fort Townsend although state park has marked building sites. Pilings (left) once supported wharf in old picture. Identifiable buildings include waterworks (at head of wharf), adjutant's office (center foreground on bluff), hospital (behind office), and officers' row. Doublestoried barracks is almost hidden by trees at far left.

FLAGPOLE STANDS near barracks site at Fort Townsend. First protection for area was blockhouse at Port Townsend in 1855, manned by Port Townsend Home Guards during Indian troubles. This led to official post in 1856. Military last was there with Fort Worden, coast artillery post north of city from 1898 to 1953; buildings became state hospital after Army left. Across from Fort Townsend on Marrowstone Island was Fort Flagler, another coast defense fort from 1899 to 1953.

ready to be transported to any point, in conjunction and connection with the other military posts in this sound . . ."

Mansfield's prophetic words came true a year later, but are in sharp contrast to that of the department commander in 1894.

"Fort Townsend still remains and is garrisoned by a single company of infantry," it was commented. "The only advantage to be derived from its retention consists in the fact that it furnishes shelter for troops. It might almost as well not exist."

This was not the case in 1858 when Townsend was equidistant from three tribes of 360 Indians and a reservation designed for 700 or more. Many more tribesmen were "scattered over the country in the neighborhood of the reserves," Mansfield commented, providing "about 5,000 souls to be watched over from this position under different demoninate tribes."

"They are not dangerous, and are peaceable," said Mansfield, "but they are exposed to depredations on them by northern Indians, from the British & Russian possessions; and to be captured and

made slaves of, and our own citizens murdered as was Colonel Ebey on Whidbey's Island."

The Ebey murder was brought to Mansfield's attention, along with its solution. He was told that north of the fort's peninsula lived the tribe that "took off the head of Col. Ebey who lived in sight of the post, and it highly important to be able to punish such depredations severly."

When the Civil War closed the post temporarily, its building were used as a Marine Hospital for seamen. Out of the Army's williness to permit this use grew a scandal of comic opera overtones.

Victor Smith was the Collector of Customs at Port Townsend with whom the Army had agreed to use of the fort as a hospital. When Smith was away, the acting Collector of Customs, First Lieutenant J. H. Merryman accused Smith of charging the Marine doctor $218 in rent for the buildings, and then keeping the proceeds. The sum of $4,354.98, was estimated by Merryman to be Smith's embezzlement total.

Merryman refused to turn over the customs records when Smith returned, until the latter threatened to level the customs house—and the town of Port Townsend—with the guns of the revenue cutter. A series of charges and threats followed until both sides agreed to take their difficulties to Tacoma for arbitration.

The Army returned to Fort Townsend in 1874 when San Juan was abandoned. Rebuilding was a major task after more than ten years of caretaker status, but soon the department commander could announce: "The buildings have been repaired and the grounds cleared of the brushwood that covered part of them at my last visit. I think Captain George H. Burton who is in charge has reason to be gratified at the order and beauty of his post."

Except for detachments to fight the Bannacks in 1877, Fort Townsend was quiet. Beginning in 1882 the Secretary of War annually recommended that it be abandoned. This was finally done in 1895, but not through routine Army decision. Fire destroyed the barracks, and there was no place to house the garrison.

TO GET THERE: From Port Townsend, Washington, take State 113 south 5 miles to Fort Townsend State Park, on left side, recreational area where building sites have been marked amidst picnic tables.

TREES TOWER over corral of Fort Crook in this 1859 photograph, showing how foliage served both Army and Indian during 1850-era wars—regardless of whether these are true redwoods.

WAR IN THE REDWOODS

"The Indians would confide in us as friends, and we had to witness this unjust treatment of them without the power to help them. Then when they were pushed beyond endurance and would go on the war path we had to fight them, when our sympathies were with the Indians." —George Crook while at Fort Jones, 1853.

INDIAN fighter that he was, George Crook was able to strike directly at the center of the Indian problem. This was the case whether he was a brevet major general in Arizona or a brevet second lieutenant in Northern California.

Most settlers in northern California felt that the Indian was the aggressor, especially when the red man resisted attempts to undermine his right to traditional or truce-given territories. "Good faith forms no part of the Indian's nature," was a theme expressed by a volunteer colonel as indicative of the local opinion.

The majestic redwoods once extended all of the way to Oregon from 30 miles south of San Francisco. The area was well-defined in terms of trees, but somewhat vague as far as influence was concerned. For the period of pre-Civil War California, the area of disorder was that which centered on the redwoods, and then extended for many miles beyond.

The campaigns of 1855-59 resulted in 100 Indians being killed by soldiers and 200 more by the citizens. Between 1850 and 1860, California spent more than three million dollars on the problem.

During the Civil War, the posts of the redwood region were manned by California Volunteers. When these companies were called to the deserts, special companies of short-time militia—termed "Mountaineers"—were recruited to maintain the posts of their home regions.

The fights of the 1850's and Civil War did not end trouble in the redwoods. In 1867 there was another war that finally culminated in the worst one of all, the bloody Modoc War of 1873.

A reason that the pacification of the redwood tribes took so long lay in the natural obstacles of the terrain. High mountains, deep streams, thick undergrowth all explained why "It should be so difficult a matter to bring to justice a few score of savages," noted the district commander in 1864, "rendering·the rapid and certain movements of troops a matter of difficulty and affording innumerable hiding places to the enemy."

FORT READING, CALIFORNIA

Second Lieutenant Phil Sheridan was stationed at Fort Reading in 1855, but not quite long enough to learn about the disadvantages of the place. His tour there lasted only 24 hours, just long enough for him to be told that he was supposed to be somewhere else.

The Williamson Railroad Survey expedition had left a few days before his arrival, Sheridan learned, with West Point classmate John B. Hood handling the cavalry escort and another West Point associate, George Crook, in charge of supplies. Sheridan was supposed to have Hood's assignment in command of the cavalry.

"The commanding officer at Fort Reading seemed reluctant to let me go on to relieve Lieutenant Hood, as the country to be passed over was infested by the Pit River Indians, known to be hostile to white people and especially to small parties," wrote Sheridan in his *Personal Memoirs*. "I was very anxious to proceed, however, and willing to take the chances; so, consent being finally obtained, I started with a corporal and two mounted men, through a wild and uninhabited region."

On the first night the Sheridan party camped in a cabin. Here they found a sick soldier left behind by the main party "with instructions to make his way back to Fort Reading as best he could when he recovered."

The soldier insisted that he was better. Sheridan agreed to take him along on the condition that "if he became unable to keep up with me, and I should be obliged to abandon him, the responsibility would be his not mine. This increased my number to five, and was quite a reinforcement should we run across any hostile Indians."

By noon of the next day, Sheridan's force was down to three men. The soldier was sick again and had to be left behind. "One of my men volunteered to remain with him until he died," said Sheridan, who could not bring himself to carry out the threat to abandon the soldier.

Four hours later Sheridan heard voices and thought he had overtaken the Williamson party. Fortunately he refused to let his men fire their muskets in celebration. The noise was from 30 Indians who were shadowing the Williamson party.

Sheridan stayed a respectful distance behind the unwanted group and spent the night "somewhat nervous, so I allowed no fires to be built." Supper and breakfast consisted of hard bread without coffee.

The confrontation came the next day. Happily

FORT READING was still unfinished when inspected in 1854, but report stated, "Quarters are good, and there is an excellent stable and the store houses, etc, ample." Unhealthy area and isolated location caused inspector to lament, "It is to be regretted so much labour and expense has been put on a post situated as this is." Rainy season floods came from Cow Creek, causing soldiers to build bridge to connect barracks with kitchens (bridge is large unmarked rectangular behind barracks). (Redrawn from Mansfield Report, 1854.)

MARKER AT Fort Reading site was temporarily at this location next to Cow Creek (background) during 1965 construction of new bridge. Local interests promised that it would be returned to proper location when possible.

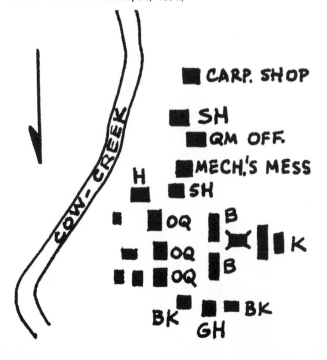

TWO-COMPANY POST of Fort Reading at this site had 91 men present in 1854, representing Companies D from both 3d Artillery and 4th Infantry. Each company also had two laundresses. Post was considered pleasant with "great harmony" among the officers despite 1854 inspection note that artillery commander was under arrest.

for Sheridan, his unexpected appearance behind the Indians disconcerted them. He moved boldly amidst them, his confidence being bolstered when he spotted the Williamson camp a short distance away.

The expedition continued to Fort Vancouver with little incidence. Sheridan's 50-man cavalry escort dissuaded most hostile observers; the discretion of the soldiers prevented an incident that could have been fatal. This took place when the troops camped next to a hastily abandoned Indian village, posted guards to insure that the tepees would not be disturbed, and, fortunately, convinced a lone Indian visitor that no harm was intended.

The soldiers soon realized that the result might have been bloody had they disturbed the village. Almost 400 braves rose up out of the grass "like a swarm of locusts and soon overran our camp in search of food." Sheridan was glad that the intentions were friendly—and the Army force was large.

The Williamson Expedition was one of the major events for Fort Reading. The post was founded in 1852 to control the Indians for 200 miles in every direction but soon appeared to be too isolated to do the job. The hostilities were elsewhere and the other posts which Reading was to supply were too distant.

Reading's location presented two more disadvantages. The site was so unhealthy that sickness was common. The 1852 Inspector General visit found a quarter of the men—including the surgeon —ill with "intermittent fever." The 1854 inspector said that the troops were so frequently ill that they "are powerless in the field with broken constitu-

tions." Only Brevet Lieutenant Colonel George Wright, the post commander, seemed to be spared, added the inspector, "but he tells me that he always takes quinine pills when he feels the attack coming on."

The other complaint about the post was a frequent one for many California camps. Although the creek next to the post was fine for summertime bathing, it often hit flood stage during the rainy season. Not only did the parade ground resemble a lake on these occasions, but the soldiers had to resort to bridges to move between buildings.

In 1856 the Army agreed that there were better sites than that at Fort Reading. The garrison was withdrawn and the buildings used only occasionally until they were sold in 1867.

In 1865 a petition for protection was received from the settlers around Tehama, 30 miles south of the abandoned post. District headquarters suggested that Fort Reading, "at which place we have quarters and a fine stable," would be better than locating at Tehama. The recommendation was not entirely unexpected, considering that by this time the district commander was Brigadier General George Wright, for three years the quinine-taking commander at Fort Reading.

TO GET THERE: From Redding, California—a city that spells its name differently because it is named after a railroad man rather than the fort—take Interstate 5 south seven miles to the North Street exist in Anderson. Go north (left) on North Street across Sacramento River to Dersch Road, about two miles. Site is 5.4 miles directly east of this turn.

FORT JONES, CALIFORNIA

Second Lieutenant George Crook's first food bill at Fort Jones told him that something drastic would have to be done or starvation would be his lot. Stretching his $64 monthly pay was one thing, he knew, but when that sum was even less than the food cost, the answer was more than just stretching.

The answer was a merger of the funds and talents of Crook, a versatile hunter; Second Lieutenant John B. Hood, an experienced farmer; Assistant Surgeon Francis Sorrel, a businessman; and First Lieutenant John C. Bonnycastle.

Their "plan to get along in this country of gold and extravagance" was described by Hood in his autobiographical *Advance and Retreat*. The future Confederate general described how the four organized their own mess and "as we were fond of hunting and game was plentiful [we were able] to supply our own table with every variety thereof and to send the surplus to market for sale. This financial plan worked admirably."

Crook's *Autobiography* goes into greater detail, noting, "I did most of hunting. At the end of the month the mess was able to declare dividends. For over a year we never had any meat on our table except game."

Sorrel arranged for the sale of game in Yreka, 16 miles from Fort Jones, and the revenue helped the partnership to meet their other bills. This was particularly helpful when they found that they could buy ammunition cheaper on the civilian market in San Francisco than through the quartermaster, who had to assess a transportation cost to the basic price.

Hood did some of the hunting, Crook noted, but was a greater asset when "we engaged in ranching together."

CHRONOLOGY ON Fort Jones marker does not mention short period in early 1864 when Company F, 1st California Mountaineers, was organized from local area to fight hostile Indians south of Scott Valley.

"Crook and I were led to secure land and sow a large crop of wheat," Hood wrote. As far as he was concerned, the project was successful even though he was transferred before harvest time. "If my memory betray me not," Hood added, "I received a draft for about one thousand dollars in gold, as my share of the profit in the wheat crop."

Crook had a different opinion of the farm experiment. Although Hood "sold out on leaving in the spring, and made money," Crook commented, "I held on and lost money."

Farming and hunting were not the main reasons that the two young officers were at Ft. Jones, but these supplied their means of livelihood there. Described by Crook as "a few log huts built on the two pieces of a passage plan," Fort Jones was established in October, 1852, a year before Crook's arrival.

Jones was Crook's first frontier fort. Having been filled with tales of Indian fighting and wild animals, the new officer "was prepared to believe many of these stories of bear coming into camp, chewing people, pulling off their blankets when they were

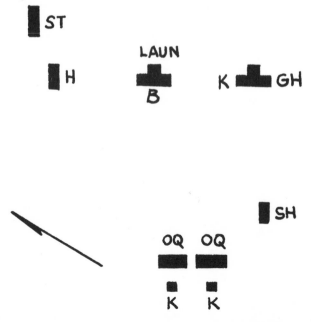

FORT JONES looked like this when visited by Inspector General Mansfield in 1854. He reported that all buildings "were of logs, and erected by the men. Of course quite indifferent, but such as other people enjoy and sufficient for the present." Company E, 4th Infantry, garrisoned post under Lieutenant Bonneycastle; Captain U.S. Grant would have been commander but he resigned before joining company. Mansfield commented that troops "gave a handsome drill at infantry, but the drill as skirmishers was indifferent." (Redrawn from Mansfield Report, 1854.)

asleep ... the treachery and cruelty of the Indians ... I was constantly on the 'que vive' to meet some of these many adventures."

Crook wrote that his first quarters was "one of the pens that was not yet finished. There were neither latches nor fastening of any kind on my door." He quickly corrected this after being awakened one night by a "visiting bear"—that turned out to be the post's mascot Newfoundland dog—and another night by a "stalking Indian."

"The sensation of my scalp leaving my head" was revealed by candlelight to be an equally disconcerted owl that "in its fright lit on my head," Crook found. "His needle-like claws produced the pain in my scalp, as my hair was cut close, and there was no protection."

These imaginary threats to Crook's well being soon were replaced by the actual problem of Indian fighting. He found that this was complicated by his senior officer's love of strong drink, both in garrison and while on patrol.

A two-company post when Crook arrived, Fort Jones soon was reduced to a single company of 30 men, Captain Henry M. Judah's Company E, 4th Infantry, "better known as 'The Forty Thieves'," according to Crook. This officer was a West Point classmate of U. S. Grant and served as a brigadier general in the Civil War, but Judah's combat abilities left Crook unimpressed.

When the command took to the field in January, 1854, leaving a detachment under a non-commissioned officer in command of Fort Jones, Crook led the advance guard. Judah remained with a rear guard, composed mainly of volunteers from Yreka. Crook soon discovered that the volunteers were well fortified with "courage."

"It seemed that the rear guard had gotten some whiskey, and were all drunk, and scattered for at least 10 miles back," he wrote. "Judah was so drunk that he had to be lifted from his horse" when the rear guard straggled into camp. The next day he "was sick all day with the delirium tremens."

Indians were found holed up in a barricaded cave near where they had killed a party of white men. Judah's plan to charge the cave, with Crook and Bonnycastle in the lead, was countermanded by the arrival of a company from Fort Lane, Oregon. Captain—later Major General—Andrew J. Smith took charge, learned in a parley with the Indians that they had killed in self defense, and permitted them to escape.

Crook said, "Our part of the grand farce returned to our place of abode" where there was talk of preferring charges against Judah. The matter was dropped when Judah promised to arrange a transfer.

"ON THE EDGE of a beautiful mountain valley called Scott's Valley, with a beautiful river of the same name running through it," Fort Jones favorably impressed George Crook when he arrived in 1853. Two companies of 2d Infantry were present then, each led by unusual officers. In command was Brevet Major George F. Patten, known familiarly as "He! He! be God! Patten" because of speech mannerism, who lost most of left hand in Mexican War. Captain Bradford R. Alden, company commander, had been Crook's Commandant of Cadets at West Point. When he left East, Alden gave letter of resignation to wife which she submitted to War Department as soon as she heard he had been wounded at Fort Jones. He was shocked but unable to reverse decision upon receiving notification that he had "been resigned." Flagpole (above) marks site on which collapsed building (below) was landmark for years after fort's abandonment.

TO GET THERE: Town of Fort Jones is in Scott Valley, California, 16 miles west of Yreka (described by Crook as "a large ant's nest" in 1854 where "miner, merchant, gambler, and all ... carried their lives in their own hands ... scarcely a week passed by without one or more persons being killed"). From center of town of Fort Jones go south on State 3 to East Side Road; site of fort is a half-mile south of town, left side of East Side Road.

(Colonel Fred B. Rogers Collection)

FORT CROOK, CALIFORNIA

"We invariably charged right in their midst, and confused them, and had them miss me more than once at no greater distance than 10 feet, whereas they could hit a man every time at 60 yards when not under excitement."

As expressed in his *Autobiography*, this could be called the George Crook Philosophy of Indian Fighting. Although there was nothing new about the tactic of aggressive attack, Crook felt that it was ignored by many of his garrison-lazy contemporaries. When left to his own devices along the Pit River in 1857, Crook put action to the words.

The system was not 100 per cent foolproof, Crook found, but perhaps his personal case was the exception to prove the rule. He was one of the first casualties on the Pit River Expedition, taking a poisoned arrow in the right hip. He was laid up for more than two weeks until the poison had dissipated. The arrowhead never was removed.

While he was recuperating at a field camp along the Fall River, Crook was joined by Captain John W. T. Gardiner, 1st Dragoons. Gardiner had orders to take his Company A to the vicinity of the Pit and Fall Rivers and establish a post. As usual, the orders added, "Temporary quarters and stables only will be erected at the post."

Gardiner's first inclination was to name his new post Camp Hollenbush, after his company's surgeon. On July 1, 1857 he settled on honoring his surgeon's most redoubtable patient, George Crook. By this time the fort's namesake was busily demonstrating the worth of his Indian fighting theories.

Problems for both officers came from a new direction, that of Fort Jones and the officer least admired by Crook: Captain Henry B. Judah. It was only through the sufference of Judah that Crook and a detachment of 25 infantrymen were in the Pit River Valley. Judah decided that he wanted Crook and company back at Fort Jones, and on July 11 he made his stand in no uncertain terms. Gardiner was accused of gross disrespect and Crook was threatened with a courtmartial if he did not return at once.

Something caused Judah's temper to cool. Crook was permitted to remain, perhaps because Judah remembered that he never got along with Crook, anyway.

The absence of affection between the two officers had to do with Crook being alone in Pit River country at a time when it was subject to Indian terror. The force originally included both Companies D and E, 4th Infantry, for a total of 65 men under Captain Judah and First Lieutenant Crook. The expedition was to visit the scene of a wintertime massacre and, if possible, run down the culprits.

As Crook's *Autobiography* notes, the affair started badly. "It was as good as a circus to see us when we left Fort Jones," he wrote. "Both companies were mounted on mules, with improvised rigging, some with ropes, and other with equally,

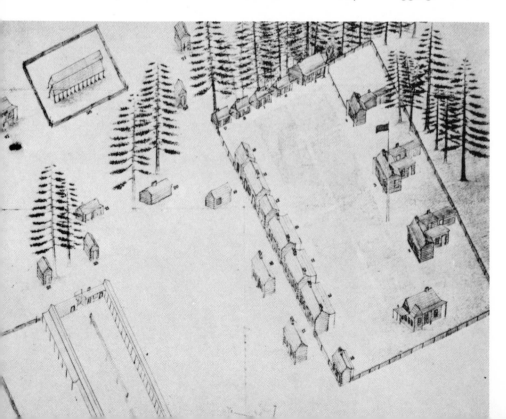

CIVIL WAR appearance of Fort Crook was sketched by Private F. Selby, Company C 2d California Cavalry. It matches earlier plan (opposite page) with few exceptions. Officers' quarters has been added at open eastern end of parade ground; sutler has moved to building at far left of sketch; several small buildings have been added as store houses or shops.

(National Archives)

ARMY ALONG Fall River was at Fort Crook from 1857 to 1869 in this field next to river (background). Army's aggressive patrolling and policy of burning camps of renegades forced Pit River Indians to arrange with distant Piute tribe for sanctuary. Their payment for protection promise was 10 squaws and a cattle herd.

if not worse, makeshifts to fasten the saddles on the mules, and all did not have cruppers . . . Many of our men were drunk, including our commander. Many of the mules were wild, and had not been accustomed to being ridden, while the soldiers generally were poor riders. The air was full of soldiers after the command was given to mount, and for the next two days stragglers were still overtaking the command."

Comedy did not stop when the hangovers passed, according to Crook. Several days later, Judah led the troops in a wild charge against an Indian village that Crook insisted was abandoned.

"It was as good as a circus to look back over the field he crossed to see the men 'hors-de-combat,' riderless mules running in all directions, men coming, limping, some with their guns, but others carrying their saddles," said Crook in the *Autobiography*.

As far as Judah was concerned, that was the close of the expedition. "Capt. Judah had just been married the second time," Crook explained, "and was anxious to get back to his bride. Soon after getting back to our old camp, he returned to Fort Jones, leaving me with only 16 men of my company to accomplish what he failed to do with his two companies. He reported upon his return to Fort

FORT CROOK was drawn in 1859 by Inspector General Mansfield. "A little more improvement in the buildings and stables will make them quite suitable and comfortable," he reported. "These buildings are all of logs and shingled with adobe chimneys and hearths." Mansfield added that guardhouse was empty except for Indian prisoners, barracks did not have bunks, and troops were poorly drilled. (Redrawn from Mansfield Report 1858.)

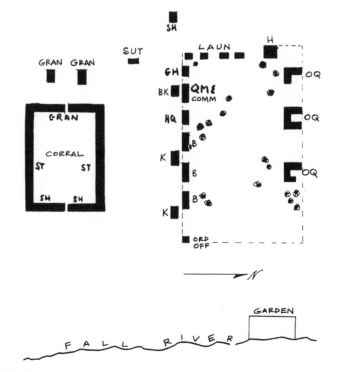

FALL RIVER not far from Fort Crook garden site recalls George Crook's capture of Indian squaw and her baby and unsuccessful attempt to persuade her to guide him to Indian camp. She led troops along river until she was able to dive into the water and escape. Troops left papoose in tree branch, confident its bawlings would attract tribe. In winter, river seldom froze although deep snows cut off outside communication. When mail courier disappeared in 1862, he was branded a deserter until body was found two years later in deserted blacksmith shop on route.

Jones that there were no Indians in the country, etc. etc."

Left alone with his 16 men—or the 25 noted in the official orders—, Crook "knew that there were plenty of Indians, and that my only show was to find where the Indians were, without their knowledge, and to attack them by surprise."

Assuming that Judah's departure with most of the troops was noted by the Indians and that "they would be off their guard," Crook took two men and scouted the area. After finding a rancheria, he tried to take his larger force on a night scout to it, but "by some mistake we became separated." An attempt to do the same the next night was successful except that the Indians had disappeared.

Crook and Dick Pugh, a civilian guide who served Fort Crook for most of its 12 years, patrolled continually. On one occasion, Crook chased several Indians and killed one, then had to turn tail with the Indians in hot pursuit. "A big Indian, seemed to me about 10 feet high, was running his best to catch up . . . his arrows flew around me with such a velocity that they did not appear over a couple of inches long."

Later the same day Crook's command was attacked while in a box canyon. This was the occasion of his wounding and its announcement at Fort Jones resulted in the whole command being ordered out. "As usual they got drunk, Judah included, who fell by the wayside," Crook commented, but a doctor "with all the available men came out."

After returning to duty, Crook continued his aggressive pursuit of the Indians. On July 2 and again on July 27 his command clashed with the Indians. The former was a hand-to-hand fight "so close we could see the whites of each other's eyes."

After peace came, "it became irksome and monotonous to be lying around camp," so Crook spent his time on hunting trips to supply fresh meat. Gardiner's troops concentrated to such an extent on building the fort that two years later Inspector General Joseph Mansfield could blame their military deficiencies on the fact "they have been laborers and mechanics, building log houses, etc., for the past two years."

When Mansfield visited the post, he found it manned by Companies A and F, 1st Dragoons,

GEORGE CROOK was there but he was not founder of Fort Crook. His diary says: "About this time Capt. J.W.T. Gardiner, 1st Dragoons, arrived on Fall River to establish a post, which he did, and named it after the undersigned." Plaque (left) apparently was modelled after old fort building (right), shown as it was 1900.

(Col. Fred B. Rogers Collection)

OFFICERS' QUARTERS at Fort Crook were photographed in late 1850's by Lieutenant Lorenzo Lorain. At start of Civil War, half of garrison was sent to protect San Francisco Presidio. Reinforcements came after reports included typical patrols such as in 1861 when 30-man detachment covered 302 miles in eight days. Commander frequently complained that settlers sent 100 miles for his aid, even though they had more men and better arms and could have started immediate pursuit.

(Oregon Historical Society)

for a total present of three officers, one assistant surgeon—G. C. Hollenbush atfer whom the post was named for a few days—, and 103 enlisted men.

Mansfield was especially critical of First Lieutenant Milton T. Carr, the acting commander of Company A and the quartermaster and commissary officer at the post. The combination of three duties was not happy. Mansfield found that none of Carr's accounts was handled properly, from the $1,542.62 on the company's books that had not been balanced and were "handed to me the evening before I left," to Carr's writing a check for the commissary department "in expectation that a deposit would be made in time to meet it."

Apparently Mansfield was impressed with the fact that Carr could spread himself between three jobs. Still he reported officially, and probably kindly, 'I do not think Lt. Carr had a taste for accounts, and in addition, he has too much duty to perform."

Mansfield was impressed with Fort Crook. "This post is well located to overawe the Indians and protect the emigrants transportation travel between the eastern states and California, and should be maintained and garrisoned with not less than two companies," he reported.

His report recited a "number of murders which have come to light" including five in 1851, five in 1856, six in 1857, two in 1859, and plus considerable looting and animal theft. The stage line also was attacked with the driver escaping after he cut loose his horses "with many arrows shot into him."

The situation improved somewhat during the Civil War although frequently the post was reduced to 25 men. Officially it had two companies of the 2d Cavalry California Volunteers, but the need to place outposts placed a strain on its manpower. The frequent expeditions—usually to settle friction between white man and Indian—kept the post at minimum strength.

William H. Brewer stopped at Fort Crook in 1863 when most of the garrison was Indian chasing. "Lieutenant Davis, in charge of the post, was very kind and gave us hay for our horses," Brewer wrote in his diary. "Except for 10 or a dozen men the troops are all away now, fighting Indians. It must be a lazy life, indeed, in such a place."

Captain, later Major, Henry B. Mellen, commander of Fort Crook through most of the Civil War, effectively carried on its peace keeping mission. "My constant policy has been to treat the Indians justly, and to impress them with the idea that while I will severely punish them when guilty, I will protect them if they keep good faith and are peaceable," he announced.

After several instances of Mellen vigorously defending the rights of the Indians, the local tribes were convinced. Aware that Mellen was fair to both sides, one tribe refused to harbor an Indian renegade who was being hunted for robbery and several three-year old murders. "Fearing that by his acts he would get them into trouble," the tribe surrendered the fugitive. Mellen had him shot. "The tribe express themselves as satisfied with the justice of the sentence."

Fort Crook lasted throughout the Civil War. At the end of the war, it was listed as one of the few camps that should remain for at least "the present winter." When winter ended in 1866, so did the history of Fort Crook as the troops were moved to newly constructed Fort Bidwell in the far northeastern corner of California.

TO GET THERE: From Redding, California (where Fort Reading was the post replaced by Fort Crook), take State 299 about 70 miles northeast to Fall River Mills. Turn left (north) on Farm Road 1220 to Glenburn, 6 miles. At Glenburn post office, turn left (north) on road A19, follow it around 3.2 miles to marker next to fort site.

FORT TERWAW, CALIFORNIA

If the Indians around Fort Terwaw thought they were dealing with amateurs, their misconception was set straight before the new camp was a week old. George Crook and his Company D, 4th Infantry, were quick to demonstrate that they were old hands at keeping Indians in line.

Crook tells about it in his *Autobiography*.

"My men were scattered, more or less, collecting material for building purposes," he wrote of the October 17, 1857, incident when word was received that the nearby Indian agent had been killed. "I at once had the 'long roll' beaten, and in less than half an hour I was at the agency with all of my company except two. We made short work of the disaffected Indians, killing several of them."

Crook's men were not about to be left behind when action called: the two who missed the boat swam across the river, fully clothed and armed, to catch up with their lieutenant.

Apparently the Indians had tried to trap the agent. In the confusion of their attack the agent was able to hold off his position until help came. Crook estimated that 10 warriors were killed and "this put an end to the trouble."

Actually Crook had expected trouble from another direction. Shortly after arriving at the new fort site he had been alerted by friendly Indians that the local tribe was going to make an attack on his life.

"These Indians got up a conspiracy to murder me and destroy the boats that ferried the river, and then kill the agent and his employees, sack the place, and then return to their own country," he wrote. "They reasoned that if I was killed the soldiers would be without a head, and they would have nothing to fear from them."

Crook devised a one-man defense. "I laid my rifle on one side of me, and my shotgun on the

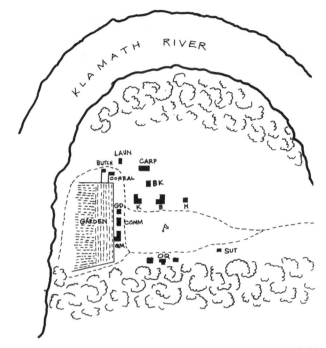

FORT TERWAW was described by Inspector General Mansfield after 1859 visit: "The men were comfortably quartered in a log barrack shingled, and slept in double bunks two tiers high; and had a good mess room and kitchen also built of logs and shingles; and they appeared cheerful and contented." Noting bend-of-river location, Mansfield predicted "the parade will be covered with water" in high water, somewhat of an understatement. (Redrawn from Mansfield Report, 1859.)

other, with my pistol and bowie knife under my head . . . I felt so confident that I would be more than a match for them that I hoped they would make the attack."

The Army's bold response at the agency convinced the Indians that this was not the best place to pick a fight. The warriors ran away.

Crook was able to concentrate on completing the post which he called "Terwaw" after the Indian name for the site. The barracks went up first, a garden was planted, and the remainder of the buildings were almost finished when Company D was called to the Coeur d'Alene War in 1858. Company B took over the post temporarily while Crook's company vigorously campaigned in eastern Washington and Idaho.

Four months later Crook returned to Terwaw to find Company B "had pushed the building of the quarters fairly, but the garden that we had expected so much from was a failure." Crook seemed to be jinxed on the matter of gardens; he always had one planted and, as consistently, was unable to reap a worthwhile harvest.

Once the post was built, the troopers had little to do. "It was the happiest part of my life," Crook remembered, "and never in my life enjoyed myself so much." Crook could stay abreast of what was

"TERWAW IS 30 miles from Crescent City, amidst the grandest old forests my eyes have ever beheld or my fancy conceived," wrote California Volunteer in 1862. Fort site is in center of picture on what Crook described "a beautiful, grassy flat."

happening by talking to Indians who were frequent visitors to the post, and by observing the canoes passing on the Klamath River.

Inspector General Joseph Mansfield visited Terwaw in May, 1859, calling it "very creditable to Lieutenant Crook . . . it is well commanded and he is a highly meritorious officer." He was pleased with everything that he saw—troops at drill, the financial records and the other items with which he found much fault at other posts. His only complaint was that his canoe capsized enroute to the post "and I lost my sword, rifle, and all my baggage except a small carpet bag containing my uniform."

Terwaw was abandoned in June, 1861. The citizens immediately called for its reestablishment, citing that most of their men had gone to the gold fields leaving their families unprotected.

On August 31, Company C, 4th Infantry, returned to find the barracks and garden in good order. It was even able to buy back some of the property disposed of when Crook left.

The future was not happy for Terwaw. Four times during the next rainy season it was underwater and 17 buildings were lost. In March, 1862, Company G, 2d California Infantry, reported. "The post will require an immense amount of labor and material to rebuild." The Indians caught on, and refused to work unless paid well, even charging four cents per man each way to row the soldiers across the river.

With the decision that a new post had to be established 20 miles north near a new Indian reservation, it became obvious that Fort Terwaw had served its purpose. On July 11, 1862, it was ordered to be abandoned for good.

DEADLY KLAMATH River has flooded Fort Terwaw site more often than when Army was there. Floods in 1964 left only fireplaces of town of Klamath Glen and this boulder marker to Fort Terwaw. At time of photography a year later, town was starting to rebuild.

TO GET THERE: From Eureka, California, go north on U.S. 101 about 70 miles to Klamath. Take Terwaw Valley Road east 3.7 miles to Klamath Glen Road. Turn right (south) .2 miles to marker in center of Klamath Glen, site of fort.

FORT TERWAW was sketched by California Volunteer George E. Young when post was trying to recover from floods in 1862. After inspection of district, commander ordered "peaceful" policy with Indians causing one settler to charge officers with being "nothing more than military figureheads, the soldiers picnic parties, the forts tenting grounds for military parades." Renewed depredations reversed policy.

(Col. Fred B. Rogers Collection)

FORT BRAGG, CALIFORNIA

A young lieutenant's respect for his first company commander provided the name for Fort Bragg. The respect of others for the same officer caused that name to be retained throughout the Civil War.

Second Lieutenant Horatio G. Gibson was fresh from West Point when he joined the 3d Artillery in time for the Battle of Chapultepec, Mexico, in 1847. A lasting impression was made on him by his captain, Brevet Lieutenant Colonel Braxton Bragg, three times brevetted in 15 months.

Ten years later when First Lieutenant Gibson established an Army post on the Mendocino Indian Reservation in northern California, he had no hesitation regarding a name. Colonel Bragg had left the Army in favor of the life of a Louisiana planter, confining his government service by 1856 to serving as his state's Commissioner of Public Works. By naming the new camp after this hero of Buena Vista, Gibson felt that at least the Bragg name was back in the service of the Army.

For an artilleryman, the early days of Fort Bragg were especially trying. Men who had been recruited and trained as cannoneers of the 3d Artillery found themselves performing the age-old Army chores of artisans, masons, and hewers of wood.

"It is slow work, owing to the scarcity of proper tools," reported Gibson on June 18, 1857, a week after officially establishing the post. "I do not expect to have all necessary buildings completed before the beginning of the rainy season."

Three months later Gibson could report some progress and the hope of having his command under cover before winter. "I have to report the erection and occupation of three buildings, all of which however are unfinished," he wrote. "The men are now at work on the officers' quarters, which ought to be completed within a month. A stable, guardhouse and storehouse have yet to be built."

The artilleryman came through in this report with a request that the post be provided with its allowance of howitzers.

Fort Bragg was a year old when almost all of the garrison was suddenly rushed to eastern Washington for the Coeur d'Alene War. Gibson was sick when the call came. He ordered 15 of his men to respond to the call. Ten days later he followed them, placing a non-commissioned officer in temporary charge of the post.

Gibson returned to Bragg for a short time after the end of the Coeur d'Alene War, then moved on to be the quartermaster of his regiment. After Civil War duties as a colonel and brevet brigadier general of the 2d Ohio Artillery Volunteers and a hero at Antietam, Gibson returned to the 3d Artillery. He was its regimental commander for the last eight years before his retirement in 1891.

The infantry took over Fort Bragg in early 1859 with a 20-man detachment from Company D, 6th Infantry. The entire company arrived in September. This permitted the garrison to seriously pursue the problems of keeping the Indians peaceful and the settlers at a distance. A small detachment was outposted in Round Valley, 40 miles to the northeast, when it became obvious that the rugged terrain and seasonal floods prevented any rapid movement from Fort Bragg.

Complaints were received at various forts in March, 1861, that the Indians were plotting to exterminate the whites. The Fort Bragg garrison was ordered to take to the field. "Keep actively engaged moving over the country requiring pro-

INSPECTION AT Fort Bragg was highlighted in this 1858 painting by Alexander Edouart. View looks to northeast across parade ground; three enlisted barracks are in rear to left of flagpole, officers' quarters at right. Lieutenant Gibson presented a copy to Braxton Bragg, but it was destroyed when mansion was burned by Federals in 1864.

(Col. Fred B. Rogers Collection)

tection," the 60-man expedition was told. The detachment in Round Valley was moved to a halfway point, lessening the resupply problems and putting it closer to supposed threats.

The company was supplied with several members of a newly recruited 30-man company of Volunteers who signed up for three months. Acquainted with the area, they were employed as guides. "They proved to be of invaluable aid to the regular forces, which, indeed, would have been worthless without them," according to a contemporary and probably exaggerated account.

Soon counter-charges were leveled against some of the settlers who were clamoring for Army protection.

"There are several parties of citizens now engaged in stealing or taking by force Indian children from the district in which I have been ordered to operate against the Indians," reported Lieutenant Edward Dillon, commander of the Fort Bragg field detachment. "As many as 40 or 50 Indian children have been taken . . . This brutal trade is calculated to produce retaliatory depredations on the part of the Indians . . . These men keep the Indians constantly on the alert, attacking and chasing them before us and following in our wake for the purpose of obtaining children."

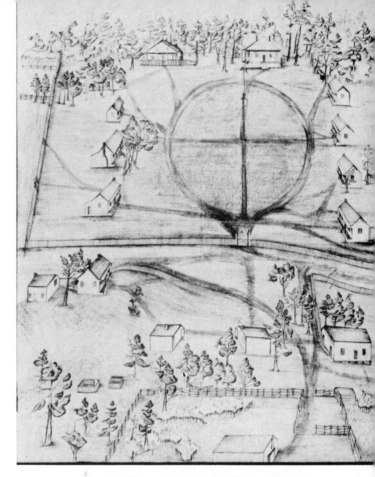

(Bancroft Library and Col. Fred B. Rogers Collection)

BIRD'S EYE VIEW of Fort Bragg by unknown artist probably dates from 1863, matches 1863 newspaper description: "Fort Bragg is merely a smooth, sloping, open piece of ground in a pine forest, with the various buildings encircling the open space, which is about 10 acres extent. . . . Around the space thus enclosed is a circular carriage way, and intersecting each other at right angles across the plaza are raised walks, and in the center a magnificent flagpole." Officers' quarters were at far end; barracks flanking both sides of parade; hospital left foreground (with cemetery enclosures in left corner); guardhouse, commissary, and quartermaster in right foreground. Commissary burned in May, 1864.

FORT BRAGG was comfortable post by time it was finished. In 1862, regimental commander made surprise visit to post, found "the discipline and instruction of the garrison at Fort Bragg (Company D, Second Infantry California Volunteers) in a highly satisfactory state." No mention was made that when the company arrived two months before it had only 40 of its 80 men; the rest had deserted. (Redrawn from data provided by Colonel Fred B. Rogers, USA (retd).)

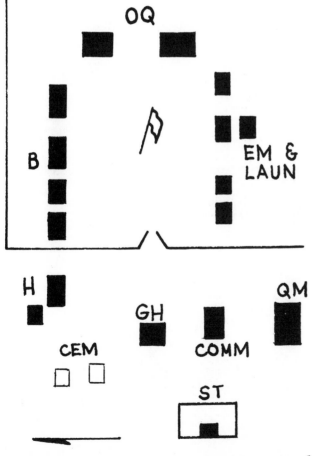

After three months of operations, it appeared that the settler complaints had been satisfied. They were willing to admit that the Army's conduct of the campaign "inspired a hopeful confidence in their good judgement and soldierly qualities," said a contemporary account. When this resulted in the discharge of the 90-day guides, the writer was quick to announce that the Army had "seized the first opportunity to make a serious mistake . . . The regular soldiers could not fight without the aid and encouragement of the Volunteers, and the Indians knew it. They feared the Volunteers only."

The regulars had similar feelings about the Vol-

STEAM SAWMILL employing 60 men nestled here in this pocket next to Noyo River south of post in 1863. When the Army was at post, off-duty recreation was spent at John Burns' hotel in Noyo and, illegally, at Indian camps. Commander of post said in 1862 that Indians were "inoffensive and peaceable" except that "the licentiousness of the females causes the young men of the command to be continually under medical treatment." Year later, order against visiting squaws was enforced by placing military guards around lodges and permitting only surgeon and agent to enter.

unteers, usually suggesting that the Indians feared the undisciplined Volunteers because of the brutal punishments they rendered on any unfortunate captive.

Ironically the longtime Volunteers who took over the post from the regulars in November, 1861, had the same opinion of the short-time volunteers. "The mingling of the Humboldt volunteers with the men of my regiment at the same post would be demoralizing and dangerous to the discipline that they have been 18 months acquiring," stated the commander of the 2d Infantry California Volunteers.

One of the final actions of the regular Army before the arrival of the Volunteers was a visit by the Acting Inspector General of the Pacific, Lieutenant Colonel Don Carlos Buell. Noting that outposts were still being sent to Round Valley and the intermediate point, he commented, "Their services are of no value whatever where they are, and I recommend that they be immediately returned to their company."

Buell passed to the Bragg commander "to make no more attacks on Indians except for depredations actually committed." Noting that Indians at Shelter Cove, 40 miles up the coast, had yet to be punished for a recent murder, he ordered Bragg's garrison "to take measures for the effectual punishment of that band."

Buell confined the mission to a Fort Bragg detachment on the theory that even if it were defeated, "the Indians will slacken their vigilance" and other forces could attack them successfully. The expedition did not fail, however, nor did several others that returned to the Shelter Cove troublespot for the next two years.

The garrison was usually suspicious of where the

guilt really lay when Indians were charged. On one Shelter Cove campaign, Captain J. B. Moore relayed the report that a settler "took a child from a squaw who happened to be a little to the rear of the party, tied it to a tree, and shot it." The same man was accused of shooting a defenseless squaw to death on a previous trip. The Army was powerless to discipline the citizens, however, and insisted that certain white men were committing depredations "in order to get employment as guides, packers, and business for the horses, mules etc."

Buell went on to other actions in the Civil War, coincidentally reaching his peak as a major general of Volunteers in command of Federal troops that defeated the Confederate Army of the Tennessee, General Braxton Bragg, C.S.A., commanding.

Bragg's acceptance of a Confederate commission prompted the commander of the 2d Infantry California Volunteers to recommend a new name for Fort Bragg, "which has long enough borne the name of a traitor." Nothing came of the suggestion, perhaps because Bragg was out of the Army when he joined the Confederacy, or because his Mexican War comrade-in-arms, Brigadier General George Wright, could still remember the heroism at Buena Vista.

Until the post was abandoned in October, 1884, the Fort Bragg name was retained, one of the few named after Confederates that did so.

TO GET THERE: Town of Fort Bragg grew up on Army site after area was opened to settlement in 1867. It is on State 1 about 150 miles north of San Francisco. Parade ground was bounded by modern Laurel Street on north between Franklin and McPherson; point about 100 feet south of Redwood street was southern boundary. Main street bisects parade somewhat west of center; state marker for fort is on stone near hospital site at 321 Main Street.

WIND SWEPT TREES overlook mouth of Noyo River south of Fort Bragg site. Army and Indian Agency used lighters to unload ships here. Army came to area to keep peace at Mendocino Indian reservation but found by 1862 that its reported "several thousand" Indians were only 1,000, later only 280. Many braves left reservation to work as potato pickers at 50 cents a day. To prevent them from wandering "would require a chain of sentinels to be posted completely around" reservation, Army feared.

(University of Wyoming)

THE AGENCY WATCHERS

"All we ask of you is to bring men, not women dressed in soldiers' clothing. You may get this and tear it up and tell your Father that we are all quiet and receive your presents and by this means keep peace and fill your pockets with money, while our Great Father knows nothing of what is going on, but is like a blind old woman who cannot see. We beg you for once tell our Great Father what we say and tell him the truth."

—Uncpapa Chiefs to Indian Agent, 1862.

THE plea of the Indian was taken up by spokesmen throughout the land but went unheeded more often than not. The settler took his land, the store keeper cheated him, the miner ignored or injured him, the soldier tamed him.

As the Westward surge pushed the past before it, the question was: what to do with the inhabitants of the land? A nomad and a hunter, the Indian had no real roots as evidence of permanent residency.

Treating with the Indians as foreign nations was attempted, but seldom worked. What one chief said did not really bind his tribe. And, unfortunately, what the white man said in peace councils did not bind his Congress.

The solution finally adopted, good or bad, was the reservation system. The tribes were moved onto reservations with an agent to watch over them and provide for them, and the Army to protect them. The success of the system was in direct proportion to the honesty and skill of the agent. The Episcopal priest-agent at Fort Simcoe, Washington, was so well liked that he was called "father" in respect that crossed over religious lines; his wards usually showed a profit from their endeavors.

The record of the agents before the Civil War was not always in this tradition however. "Political hacks" was so common a synonym for the agents that attempts were made continually to turn the responsibility over to the Army and its career, honor-bound officers. Indicative of the trouble was the example of the agent of Siletz, Oregon, who left his three-year tour with a profit of $40,000.

Guarding the agencies—to keep the Indians in, the whites out, and the employees safe—were the nearby Army detachments. Some of these are visited in the section that follows.

131

FORT OSAGE, MISSOURI

Built for trading rather than fighting, Fort Osage was the westernmost extension of one of many schemes for handling the Indians. Its ultimate defeat was not at the hands of lurking savages, but through the collective efforts of politicians and trading syndicates.

President George Washington and his Secretary of War, Henry Knox, were the instigators of a plan to use trade as the weapon for dealing with the Indians. Known as the "factory" system, the idea was for the government to establish fortified trading houses—or "factories"—at which the Indians could exchange their furs for the white man's goods.

Idealistically speaking, the plan presented the picture of a well-managed enterprise at which the Indian could receive fair treatment for his labors and not fall prey to the whiskey keg. Practically speaking, President Thomas Jefferson considered that there was more to it than that. He expected that the Indians would develop a taste for the factory's goods and willingly go into debt to the government. What better way to satisfy these debts than for the Indians to sell land to the new settlers?

Twenty-eight combination factory-forts were built, most of them in the East or Midwest. Bellefontaine, near St. Louis, had a factory, but only until it could be moved further west to Fort Osage.

The Lewis and Clark Expedition's leaders played major roles in the early days of Fort Osage. Meriwether Lewis was the Governor of Missouri in 1808 when the fort was founded and it was he who drafted a treaty with the Osages regarding the site and surrounding area.

William Clark played an even more direct role. He selected the actual site 300 miles up the Missouri River from Saint Louis, remembering a spot "I had examined in the year 1804 and was delighted with it and am equally so now." In 1808 Clark sat on a hill overlooking the site and sketched a floor plan; below him 81 men of the 1st Infantry and 80 30-day militia dragoons set to work felling timbers.

Clark's connection with Fort Osage did not end at this point. As the Superintendent of Indian Affairs at Saint Louis, his interest was continual. Later Clark became the governor of Missouri, another role which kept him concerned with the affairs of Fort Osage.

In charge at Fort Osage from its first day was George Champlin Sibley, a conscientious and honest New Englander who had been the assistant factor at Bellefontaine. The successes of Fort Osage were Sibley's doing; the failures were despite his best efforts.

RESTORATION OF Fort Osage started in 1941, factory (background) was finished in 1954, and remaining buildings were completed in 1961. Post was sometimes called Fort Clark, probably after leader of founding group, but official name was adopted at christening in 1808. Credit for restoration is shared by Court and Park Department of Jackson County, Mo., and Native Sons of Kansas City, Mo.

The start of construction required every effort that Sibley could muster. The militia troopers were so tired after their 300-mile tramp from Saint Louis that, as Clark noted in his *Journal*, it was difficult to make them do anything. It was five days before all hands were enthusiastically employed. By this time seven civilians and the reluctant laborers had put up most of two blockhouses and cleared much of the land. Within five more days the two blockhouses were almost finished, three more were well along, a blacksmith shop and workshop were finished.

Hints as to Sibley's success in obtaining soldier cooperation appear in his list of expenses for build-

ing the fort. In addition to $196.75 paid to "soldiers for work done by them," Sibley notes "Whiskey to encourage Fatigue men while digging cellar, etc. $31.75."

Sibley and Clark did not wait to finish the fort before summoning its charges. The same day that he arrived at the fort site, Clark sent Nathan Boone, son of the famous Daniel, to the villages. His message was that the government had invited other tribes to war on the Kansas and Osage Indians, but would provide protection if they camped next to the fort. Within a week more than 3,500 Indians set up two villages near the fort.

Nine days after his arrival, Clark signed a treaty with the Osages that gave them annuities and other rewards in return for half of Missouri and Arkansas. Clark wrote that his four cannon "Boom! Boomed!" at the ceremony and the tribes danced, especially pleased because he had passed out $314 worth of weapons to the chiefs, and paint, tobacco and blankets.

On November 10 the treaty was renegotiated because Congress refused to ratify it. Governor Lewis re-wrote the treaty and sent it upriver for signature, not making a big thing of the fact that he had added the remainder of Missouri to the area ceded by the Indians.

Business was brisk from the start, but not always calm. As early as October, 1808, Sibley could record in his diary: "About the 12th they commenced trading and about the 16th I was induced to shut the store against them on account of their insolent and violent conduct."

Captain Eli B. Clemson's 81 infantrymen provided Sibley with his strength to counter the Indians. "Captain Clemson had the ordnance put in firing order and posted in the most advantageous

ORIGINAL CANNON in Blockhouse No. 1 overlooks Missouri. From here Army could control navigation on river and first see approach of many expeditions that passed Fort Osage. Steamboat "Western Engineer" that led Stephen H. Long's Yellowstone Expedition of 1819 probably was strangest sight. "The bow of this vessel exhibits the form of a huge serpent, black and scaly, rising out of the water from under the boat, his head as high as the deck, darted forward, his mouth open, vomiting smoke, and apparently carrying the boat on his back," newspaper reported. "The brass field pieces, mounted on wheel carriages, stand on the deck." Speed was three miles an hour, draft was reported variously between 18 and 30 inches. The first steamboat to ascend Missouri, "Western Engineer" reached vicinity of Council Bluffs, Iowa, before low water forced expedition to shift to keel boats.

FORT OSAGE'S white-oak stockade protected it from Indians who camped outside—as many as 5,000 during trading seasons. Security it offered was especially reassuring in 1811 when 145 Osages talked Army into ferrying them across river, then embarked on war with Iowa Indians. While warriors were gone, sentries at stockade heard strange noises indicating Iowas were nearby; loss of 24 horses proved this. One night Factor Sibley was awakened by Osages who filled his bedroom, dangling over his bed severed head of Iowa caught within 300 yards of post and promptly "cut into at least 50 pieces."

HISTORIC FLAG floating over reconstructed Fort Osage has 15 stars and 15 stripes, dates from 1795 through 1818, bulk of fort's life. Same Stars and Stripes flew over Fort McHenry to inspire Key's "Star Spangled Banner" in 1814. This flag is replica. Officers' quarters porch is at left, blockhouse No. 2 next to flagpole, barracks at right.

THIS IS three-and-a-half story factory house, despite appearance from front (note rear view in sketch). Sibley had his bachelor quarters here until his marriage in 1815; bedroom, dining room, kitchen were at this end, offices, trade room, and storerooms at opposite. Indians brought their furs and other goods here to exchange for manufactured products. Replica rests on original footings. Interior is furnished to represent trading days, includes second-floor museum on factory system.

manner around the hill occupied by the guard, which commands the bottom in which the camp is," wrote Sibley on September 23, 1808. "Our camp is now surrounded by Indians, who, tho friendly, might notwithstanding be tempted by the prospect of getting possession of the factory goods and other stores, to commit some violent outrage."

As it did at most factories, it was not long before friction developed between the soldiers and the civilian employees. One employee packed up in 1811 and took his family away, causing Sibley to write in his diary: "It is easier for a camel to go through the eye of a needle, than for an independent American to live near an outpost like this, and keep on good terms with those who command the garrison."

The departing civilian might also have been piqued by the fact that wolves had eaten almost half of the 180 pigs he had been raising to sell the Army. It was suspected that "two-legged wolves" from both the barracks and wigwams were more to blame than the four-legged variety.

The split was official in 1809 when Clemson filed charges against Sibley for inciting the Osages to violence. Actually Sibley had been trying to quiet a large group of disorderly Osages, but Clemson believed otherwise.

War clouds moved over Fort Osage in 1812.

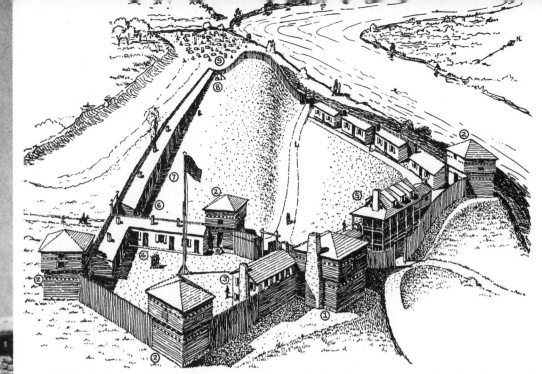

SKETCH BY George Fuller Green depicts Fort Osage at its peak. Blockhouses are numbered 2, except for largest blockhouse, No. 1. No. 3 is officers' quarters; no. 4 barracks; no. 5 factor's house; no. 6 mechanics; no. 7 blacksmith; no 8 well. Interpreters, guides, traders and others lived in huts at no. 9.

(Clarence Burton and Jackson County, Mo., Park Department)

to show a profit—and in 1823 the post was abandoned.

TO GET THERE: Town of Old Sibley on Missouri River is site of restored fort visited by as many as 100,000 annually. From Kansas City, take U.S. 24 east through Independence to Buckner. Turn left (north) and follow signs to site, about 4 miles. Tables, water, restrooms are available on site; caretaker lives in restored barracks year-round.

BARRACKS OFFERED few luxuries for soldiers, although single-man bunks were exception to the double-bunks common to most forts, practice criticized by surgeons. In these barracks lived many men who were to attain fame later: Jim Bridger, "Old Bill" Williams, Manual Lisa and other fur traders including Astoria overland expedition that founded Fort Astoria.

Amid stories that six other frontier forts had been taken by the British or had fallen to the Indians— as had Fort Dearborn in modern Chicago—it was obvious that 63 infantrymen could not hold off a determined attack. In June, 1813, the fort was closed temporarily.

Brevet Major James Dorman brought his company of the 8th Infantry back to Fort Osage in 1816. The Army's stay was short. In 1819 Colonel Henry B. Atkinson stopped on the way west to establish Fort Atkinson and when he left, he took the garrison with him.

Trading continued at the post for three years, but on a limited scale. The head of one wagon train reported that he arrived at the fort at 10 p.m. one evening in 1822 and had to sleep on a porch because he could not rouse anyone in authority. The next day he was given a bed in the "garrison," an empty room because, as the "commander" said, both of his soldiers had deserted a few days before "and carried off all his amenetion."

By this year the fate of Fort Osage and the factory system had been decided. Despite the support of both the Army and Indian Bureau, Congress was convinced by Senator Thomas Hart Benton and the fur trading interests that the competitive factories should be abolished. The profits shown by Fort Osage were ignored—it was one of the few

FORT HALL, IDAHO

A singular fact about Fort Hall is that it was once attacked and surrendered and another singular fact is that the only loss suffered was one barrel of whiskey, superior quality.

Rufus B. Sage's 1846 *Scenes of the Rocky Mountains* tells the story with sufficient caution that it may be apocryphal. Regardless, it is one of the legends of this historic emigration landmark and through it is imparted some of the reactions of the American frontiersman to the presence of the Hudson's Bay Company.

Although Fort Hall was founded in 1834 by an American, Nathaniel Wyeth, within two years it was sold to the Hudson's Bay Company. The appearance of the British flag overhead hardly 20 years after the War of 1812 was not taken kindly by several trappers. They demanded that it be removed—or at least the U.S. flag be flown beside it.

Refused, the mountainmen announced they would remove the flag by force. The gates were closed and brisk firing started—but no one shooting at one another. The trappers shot at the unwelcome flag. "The garrison, feeling ill-disposed to shoot down their own friends in honor of a few yards of parti-colored bunting, elevated their pieces and discharged them into the air," according to Sage's account. He did not add that most of the 60 occupants of the fort were French rather than English.

After the stockade was stormed, the commandant was given an ultimatum: fly the American flag and "treat his captors to the best liquors in his possession," or the fort would be looted. The short and bloodless campaign ended around a barrel of the commandant's best in the center of the fort.

Liquor was present at an earlier occasion at Fort Hall, the day in August, 1834, when Wyeth named his trading post after the oldest man in his party and then "wet it with villanous alcohol." A scien-

(Idaho State Historical Society)

FORT HALL is depicted here after it was abandoned. When Wyeth first built it he had few tools and less time, but result was 80-foot square 15-foot high stockade with two blockhouses. All buildings were of cottonwood. Apparently Hudson's Bay Company put adobe over log construction. Description in 1849 said: "It has a fine court in the centre, with a fountain of water in the middle. There is an entrance on the south side and one on the north. Around the inside are little rooms with one small window to each, which are to keep their furs and fur stores." Agent lived in apartment on second floor "with a portical on the north side and steps running from the court."

tist in the party compared the christening to a riot, "the free and uncontrolled use of liquor" resulting in "gouging, biting, fisticuffing, and 'stamping' in the most 'scientific' perfection," he said.

Wyeth did not stay long at the fort. Announcing, "Its bastions stand a terror to the skulking Indians and a beacon of safety to the fugitive hunter," he moved westward. "It is manned by 12 men and has constantly loaded in the bastions 100 guns and rifles," he added.

Wyeth's absentee managership did not prosper. His men bickered among themselves, and in 1836 he sold out to the Hudson's Bay Company for $30,000. This put the HBC at a key point where the Oregon Trail split to California and Oregon. Anxious to keep the number of Americans at a minimum in Oregon, the company advised emigrants that the Oregon Road was impassable to wagons. The road to California was recommended.

Many emigrants followed the company's advice, but equally as many were unwilling to make last-minute changes in their plans. Disposing of their wagons, the emigrants walked overland to the Pacific Northwest.

The military arrived at Fort Hall on August 5, 1849, in the persons of Colonel William W. Loring and his Regiment of Mounted Riflemen. Loring did not tarry. He was supposed to have been met by a supply train that did not arrive, so he moved on before all of his men could desert from the sudden diet of short rations. He left two companies to establish Cantonment Loring three miles up the Snake River from the Fort.

The cantonment's reports frequently carried the

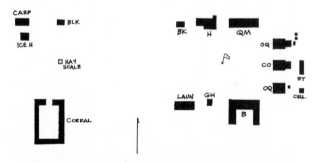

MILITARY FORT HALL, 1870-1883, usually kept Indians on reservation. Notable exception started Bannock War in 1877. Another outbreak was threatened in 1878 but was ended by timely arrival of three 5th Cavalry companies to surround Bannock camp. Most buildings including 90- by 26-foot barracks, were of lumber, except for guardhouse and shops of logs. (Redrawn from plat in National Archives.)

FORT HALL site about 2 miles in distance, was located by Oregon Trail expert Ezra Meeker before it fell victim of Snake River water projects. Army's Fort Hall site was 25 miles northeast of Wyeth's fort. Soldiers left it in 1883 despite protests of settlers, but it was believed that settlements had grown strong enough to protect themselves.

"Fort Hall" heading, adding to the impression that this was the source of military protection. Emigrants were surprised to find that Fort Hall was not a military fort; after the cantonment was abandoned on May 6, 1850, they were disappointed that no escorts were available.

"Uncle Sam's boys were not there, not even one that we saw," complained a traveler in 1851. His train spent the night in front of Fort Hall where the Indians gave visible proof of their presence. "The night we tarried in full view of the fort they came ... about midnight when the guards were being changed, and took three horses," he said.

The Oregon Volunteer Cavalry patrolled the road to Fort Hall in the Civil War. From August, 1865, to May, 1866, Company B, Oregon Volunteer Infantry, garrisoned a temporary Camp Lander "on Snake Creek a little north of Fort Hall," using scrap logs and adobe from the fort for their shelters.

The Army came in full force in response to an Indian Bureau request and officially adopted the Fort Hall name on May 29, 1870. The mission being to watch over the Shoshone and Bannock reservation, the military Fort Hall was located 25 miles northeast of Wyeth's post. The success of the fort is suggested by the fact that from here the Bannocks started their war of 1877.

TO GET THERE: The four sites of Fort Hall (Wyeth's, Loring, Lander, U.S.) are virtually impossible to locate without guides. U.S. Fort Hall is 12 miles east of Blackfoot, Idaho, on Lincoln Creek. Parade ground still is outlined by trees from Army days. Marker for original Fort Hall is reached from town of Fort Hall. Take Sheepskin Road west at north edge of town for 7.1 miles. Turn left, go 3 miles. Turn right on dirt road, continue 1.8 miles to marker, right side. Original site is inundated 2 miles south of marker.

MARKER FOR fort site is 2 miles from location, but at least on dry ground. It memorializes the many emigrants who passed fort, including missionary Marcus Whitman and family who later were victims of infamous massacre. National Park Service placed marker to establish status of Fort Hall as National Historic Site.

FORT BERTHOLD, NORTH DAKOTA

"Since the Indians never attack a fort, even though most of these forts are nothing but a fence of palisades surrounding the buildings, the whites are safe, even without a military garrison."

The author of these words, Colonel and Brevet Major General Philippe Regis Denis de Keredern de Trobriand, may have been a hero at Gettysburg, but apparently in 1867 he did not know his Indians around Fort Berthold.

Only five years before de Trobriand's arrival in Berthold territory, the Indians did exactly what he said they never did. Doctor Washington Matthews, post surgeon for most of Fort Berthold's Army days, is one of the best sources on the incident.

"On Christmas Eve of 1862," he wrote in his official report, "while most of the friendly Indians were absent at their winter quarters, the post was attacked by a large party of Sioux, who reduced the old fort and the greater part of the village to ashes, and nearly succeeded in capturing the inhabited stockade. The citizen garrison, however, defended itself bravely, and aided by the timely arrival by some Indians from winter quarters, succeeded in driving off the Sioux with great loss to the latter."

It did not take de Trobriand long to adjust his thinking. As the commander of the military in the Dakotas, he quickly learned that the Sioux Indians were not particularly cowed by soldiers and stockades.

Fort Berthold was a good teacher on the subject of Indians, especially in terms of Sioux depredations. Its history reached back far beyond the Christmas Eve attack of 1862. Even the site to which the history is traced was different.

The American Fur Company was responsible for the establishment of the first Fort Berthold in 1845 on a bluff overlooking the Missouri River. Nearby were the villages of the Gros Ventre and Mandan Indians, prospective customers for the fur trade.

Fourteen years later, this stockaded post was

(North Dakota Historical Society)

FORT BERTHOLD'S plains were alive with artillery activity when 1864 Sully Expedition camped next to post. Sully's use of a dozen 6-pound smoothbores and 12-pound mountain howitzers was a successful experiment after campaign moved from here.

joined by another fur fort. The opposition apparently decided that there was business enough for two so they built a wooden quadrangle complete with bastions and named it Fort Atkinson. To insure that they had first call on the Indian business, the post was closer to the village.

It appears that the advantage of being next to the village was not outweighed by the disadvantage of being distant from the river landing. By 1862 Fort Atkinson was taken over by the owners of the first fort.

Berthold's staff quickly recognized the advanages of living in a three-year-old fort over one that was nearing its second decade of feeding termites and harboring fleas and bedbugs. Although the shift did not solve the latter problem, in 1862 the fur company moved to the buildings of Fort Atkinson as "New Fort Berthold."

It was the original Fort Berthold that the Sioux attacked on Christmas Eve. Virtually destroyed by the attack, the stockade continued as living quarters for employees and Indians. When Doctor Matthews first arrived in the area in 1865, the Indians identified "one or two houses of hewn logs, occupied by Indians," as the sole remains of the first trading post.

Berthold's importance as a trading post quickly was overshadowed by its role with the Indian Bureau. With hundreds of Indians living nearby

INTERIOR OF fort, trading post when photographed in 1870 by Stanley J. Morrow, shows corner resembling sketch (opposite page). Shortly before Morrow visit, Indians had suffered scurvy attack, an estimated 25 dying before Army could augment their diet with sauerkraut and pickles.

(Museum of the University of North Dakota)

INUNDATED by Garrison Reservoir, Fort Berthold lives only in memories. Site is underwater in distant center. Indian Agency last used fort, frame buildings having replaced Army's log structures. Graves of Son-of-the-Star and White Shield, two friendly chiefs, and more than 100 Indian soldiers, scouts were silent sentinels at former fort site.

(National Archives)

ENGINEER'S CONCEPTIONS of Fort Berthold show rude construction of "merely a palisaded square of buildings constructed of squared logs, all of those opening are on the interior court," General de Trobriand described in 1867. "Two high, massive gates, which close on hinges and are strongly barred on the inside, give access. To defend the outer facades, two projecting blockhouses are placed at corners opposite each other; these are pierced with loop-holes, from which the line of fire covers the outer walls, and they have an upper story which juts out over the ground floor to protect it." De Trobriand pointed out that approach to fort was through cemetery of "aerial tombs of the redskins" where bodies were placed on platforms. Indian village surrounded fort.

who were frequent recipients of Sioux visitations, the fort had a quasi-military function. Annually the agent petitioned for "a small force" of troops to protect both himself and his charges.

The records are dotted with accounts of Sioux raids into the friendly tribes gathered around Berthold. The redman was not the only objective; the steamboats plying the river were fair game, too. Three men were killed when the *Shreveport* was attacked while at the Berthold landing in 1863; the first mate was killed and two crewmen wounded in 1865 when the *St. Johns* was sniped at below the fort.

It is little wonder that the white man took vicarious pleasure in reporting of Indian counter-action on the Sioux. On one occasion the Sioux appeared while commissioners were attempting to convince the friendly Indians that they had nothing to fear from the Sioux. The peace talk broke up as the braves galloped out of the fort in hot pursuit.

"About sunset they returned with five scalps, which they exhibited in front of the store to the gaze of the gentlemanly commissioners," Interpreter and Trader Charles Larpenteur recorded. "Some of the Indian also had Sioux feet and hands tied around their horses' necks."

The ghastly trophies reminded the whites that the significant difference between the friendly and hostile Indians was that the former lived within the fort's protection and the latter did not. The difference had no bearing on the attitudes of the tribes, a fact demonstrated by 1863 incident.

On occasion, spokesmen of the Sioux approached the Berthold Indians about an alliance against the whites. "The two parties met at a ravine about three miles from the post, when, instead of advancing to shake hands, a Ree brave suddenly fired upon the Sioux, and a battle ensued, in which two Gros Ventres and nine Sioux were killed." The reporter was Surgeon Matthews.

The increase in depredations from this affair caused General Alfred Sully to send Company D, 6th Iowa Volunteer Cavalry, to establish a military Fort Berthold in 1864. His plans to send two companies were reconsidered when he learned the accommodations could handle only one. The soldiers moved into the stockade for a short time but an altercation with the traders resulted in the Army moving into log huts next to the fort. The troopers could not fight the eviction because the Army never got around to buying or even commandeering the stockade.

New troopers arrived at the post in 1865 when Company C, 4th U.S. Volunteer Infantry relieved the Iowans. Fully 10 per cent having deserted enroute to the Dakota forts, the 4th Infantry was an unhappy lot, especially when the term "Galvanized Yankees" was used. All enlisted men of the regiment were former Confederates. None of these was overly enchanted with the prospects of fighting Sioux, the Dakota winters, and the bedbugs and fleas that by then had taken up residence in the long, low poorly ventilated barracks that also had to serve as mess rooms.

To their credit, the ex-Confederates of Company C measured up well at Fort Berthold. "The best I have inspected belonging to the U.S. volunteers" was praise given them by the Inspector-General in 1866.

Soon after this inspection, the company left to be mustered out. Regular troops of the 13th Infantry replaced the Volunteers, manning the decrepit defenses. Their tour was short; a year later the troops moved 17 miles to the west to a so-called "New Fort Berthold" that soon was officially named "Fort Stevenson."

TO GET THERE: Although in 1952 the combined efforts of the National Park Service, Corps of Engineers, Smithsonian Institution and North Dakota State Historical Society raced against rising water to successfully locate the sites of both Forts Bethold, they are now under the waters of the Missouri River Garrison Reservoir. To go to overlook of the site, take Interstate 94 west from Bismarck, N. D., for 43 miles past Mandan to the turnoff north to Beulah and State 49. Pass through Beulah at 31 miles and continue straight north on gravel road to its deadend at reservoir. Fort site is straight north in mid-reservoir.

FORT WINGATE, NEW MEXICO

Ration Day in September, 1861, had been going so well at the Army post near Bear Springs that a carnival spirit prevailed during the horseraces between the Navajo and Army mounts. Before the day was out the carnival turned into a massacre.

The last race was between a quarter horse owned by Surgeon F. E. Kavenaugh and a pinto pony belonging to a popular brave, Pistol Bullet. Both animals started well, but after 100 yards it was obvious that Pistol Bullet was in trouble. His pinto twisted and weaved without direction and suddenly stopped dead. The Army horse streaked across the finish line to the cheers of the soldiers who had bet heavily on the outcome.

Howls from the Indians soon drowned out the soldiers. Apparently the reins of the Indian mount had been cut with a knife so they would part as soon as Pistol Bullet yanked on them. The charges of foul were rejected by the judges—all soldiers.

As the exalting soldiers crowded back into the fort, a shot rang out, possibly from a sentinel who saw an Indian try to sneak in. Firing became general.

"The Navajos, squaws and children ran in all directions, and were shot and bayoneted," remembered a sergeant. "I saw a soldier murdering two little children and a woman. I hallooed to the soldier to stop. He looked up but did not obey my order. I ran up as quick as I could, but could not get there soon enough."

An order was given for the mountain howitzers to be rolled out, but the artillery sergeant pretended not to hear. By the time the sergeant was

goaded into action, the Navajos had disappeared, scattering about the valley where they attacked the post herd and ambushed the mail runner. A dozen Navajos were dead.

The Army post was Fort Fauntleroy, the forerunner of Fort Wingate. Located at the site of a treaty signed in 1846 between Colonel Alexander Doniphan and the Navajos, it was founded in 1860 to stop depredations by both Indian and Mexican desperados. Earlier a post at Cebolleta—70 miles to the east—had tried this, but with little success. An 1850 Inspector-General's visit noted that most of the commanders at the town garrison seemed to wind up under arrest.

At first, Fort Fauntleroy was a tent camp outpost of Fort Defiance, Arizona, 35 miles to the northwest. The camp was reinforced when Lieutenant Colonel Edward R. S. Canby conducted a campaign against the Navajo in 1860 and signed a treaty there with 34 chiefs in early 1861. It assumed the role of Fort Defiance when the latter was abandoned and turned over to the Navajos in April, 1861.

New Mexico Volunteers were called up at the start of the Civil War so that most of the regular Army troops could be rushed to blocking positions against an expected Confederate invasion. Companies A, B, and C of the 2d Regiment of New Mexican Volunteers were garrisoning Fort Fauntleroy at the time of the horserace incident.

"With the exception of five or six, they are all of Hispano-Mexican descent, speaking the Spanish language almost exclusively," was how William Need described the new troops at Fauntleroy. A former soldier who enlisted in the New Mexico militia, Need wrote a lengthy letter to the Secre-

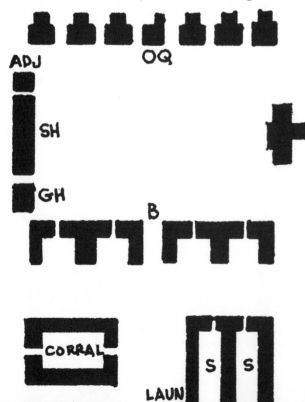

"FORT WINGATE . . . is garrisoned by five companies of the 13th Infantry and two troops of the 4th Cavalry, all comfortably quartered in adobe buildings," noted report of overnight visit by General of the Army William T. Sherman during his pre-retirement tour in 1883. "The clay from which these adobes are made gives the buildings a grayish-blue tinge, very neat and pleasant to the eye." This is how post was laid out by 1875 after plan for circular arrangement was disapproved. Another visitor to post was Lieutenant John G. Bourke, aide to General Crook, who was surveying Navajo reservation. Bourke was especially impressed by Post Surgeon, Washington Matthews (formerly of Fort Berthold who became noted ethnologist), and sutler store of Lambert Hopkins. "My national pride was aroused," Bourke recorded, "by the display of goods at the very best quality, and put up in excellent style. These included raisins, almonds . . . and varieties of wines and liquors, all of California production. . . . The proprietor, Mr. Hopkins, evidently understands his business." Bourke was wrong about this; Hopkins went bankrupt in 1882, had to sell $4,000 house to chief creditor for $1. Bourke was less impressed by Fort Defiance Agency where he described agent as "a psalm-singing hypocrite whom the Navajos despised and whom they tried to kill." He noted that agency school, which agent claimed had 60 children, was "one miserable squalid dark and musty adobe dungeon . . . nine (9) cottonwood bunks, in which, if he had made them double up, 18 little children could be made wretched." (Redrawn from National Archives plat.)

tary of War "at intervals snatched from military duty as a sentinel on the watch tower" at Fort Fauntleroy. He sent a general indictment of almost all political and military authority in the territory, suggesting they were agents of the Confederacy.

Need's words began to ring true as the Civil War came closer. Fort Fauntleroy's namesake—the departmental commander—had already resigned in order to join the Confederacy. The owner of the winning horse at the race, Kavenaugh, was so obviously pro-Southern that he soon left. When next heard from he was the leader of a four-man detail that captured the 50-man Volunteer detachment at Cubero, 60 miles to the east.

On September 25, 1861, Fort Fauntleroy was renamed Fort Lyon, one of several posts to honor the recently killed Nathaniel Lyon. This was anticlimactic, however. Two weeks before, the garrison had been withdrawn to meet the Confederate threat along the Rio Grande. A mail station remained but its occupants throughout the war continued to use the old name, as Need did in his letter written after the redesignation.

Continuing trouble in this northwestern corner of New Mexico prompted the founding of a new post in the valley of Ojo del Gallo, 50 miles southeast of Lyon. Four companies of the 1st New Mexico Volunteers arrived in mid-November, 1862. "It is to be surrounded by a defensive stockade

OLD AND MODERN Fort Wingates bear some resemblences. In 1890's, Post Surgeon M. B. Kimball, wrote: "Fort Wingate lies on a vast sandy plain surrounded on one side by mesas cut by frequent canons, and on the other side by the towering foothills of the Rocky Mountains . . . From the top of the nearest mesa the landscape, dotted with bristling pinon trees and broken by the jagged walls of the rocky canons, looked depressing and repellent. We saw no trace of life . . . The Navajo, once notorious bandits, are now peaceful shepherds . . . frequent visitors at the fort, for they soon learned what a good market it was for blankets." In old view (above) officers' quarters are in foreground, barracks in rear. Only one of the double-story barracks is obvious in modern view (below). An Indian school, post was one of best examples of frontier fort until its adobe officers' quarters and most other buildings were replaced in early 1960's by modern construction. Fort Wingate garrison was withdrawn in 1910. Buildings became Wingate Ordnance Depot in 1918, largest of its type in world. Buildings were turned over to Indian Bureau in 1925 when depot moved closer to railroad. Entire stock of depot was sold to British for World War II in 1940. Depot was redesignated Fort Wingate Ordnance Depot during centennial in 1960.

whose north and west sides are flanked by an enclosure containing the magazine, and the south and east sides of the corral and stables," reported one of the officers.

Named Fort Wingate even before it was erected, to honor an officer killed in the Battle of Glorietta, the post was built quickly under the command of Lietenant Colonel Jose Francisco Chavez, the governor's stepson and Kit Carson's second-in-command. He had 25 civilian laborers and 75 soldiers to put up a "defensive stockade 4,340 feet long, 8 feet high; one million feet of lumber; 9,317 feet of adobe for buildings, 13 feet high and 2 feet thick; and 1,800 feet of adobe walls to surround

BARRACKS IS only major building remaining from Army days. It was rebuilt following fire of June, 1896, that started in band barracks. "The wind rose," surgeon wrote, "and in a short time the whole parade ground was surrounded by blazing quarters. All the barracks, the public buildings, as well as five sets of officers' quarters, were destroyed." The garrison "camped on the parade ground, cooked their supper with planks from the half-burned sidewalk, and ate in a jolly mood."

the officers' quarters, 1 foot thick and 8 feet high."

"The fort looks vastly fine on paper, but as yet . . . we live on, or rather exist, in holes or excavations, made in the earth, over which our cloth tents are pitched," wrote an officer in December, 1862. "Our camp presents more the appearance of a gipsy encampment than anything else I can compare it to."

Wingate's main Civil War occupation was rounding up Navajos for the agricultural experiment at Fort Sumner, N. M. Along with Fort Canby—on the site of Fort Defiance—it was a headquarters for General Kit Carson's Navajo Campaign of 1863. When this ended, the Wingate records showed that 8,491 Navajos passed through the post on their "Long Walk" to Fort Sumner.

Patrolling for stragglers and raiders was continual. One company was ambushed in 1863 at China Springs, four miles north of modern Gallup. According to a Navajo version, an Indian "shot the captain right in the middle of the back of the neck and the bullet came out through his eye." Other patrols were less fatal and more successful for the soldiers, including one in 1865 that became snowbound and subsisted for the last three days on boiled water.

The 1868 treaty that ended the Fort Sumner experiment also called for the relocation of Fort Wingate. In June the soldiers shifted to the Faunterloy-Lyon site. Because the buildings had provided a quarter million feet of lumber to build the first Fort Wingate, the troops spent the summer in little more than a tent camp. The post trader set up shop across a counter of planks spread between two boxes. Temporary buildings were rushed at the same time that the garrison processed 6,913 Navajos returning to their new reservation.

Construction of the second Fort Wingate was delayed while authorities debated its design. The proposal for 18 buildings to be in a circle facing into the flagpole was disapproved by the district headquarters as being too costly and hard to defend. It was 1870 before work could begin in earnest on the usual rectangular plan.

As the only post in Navajo land, Fort Wingate was both important and active until after the turn of the century. The Indians understandably resisted sending their children to distant reservation schools and frequently the Army was called out when this resistance became warlike. In every case the tact of the troops prevented bloodshed until the opposition melted away. "The sight of so many soldiers seemed to overawe them," one report suggested.

Fort Wingate was midway between its two main sources of entertainment, Gallup to the west and Coolidge, to the east. The latter, population 100, was a newcomer to the area with the arrival of the railroad in 1881. Its distance from the fort, 14 miles, was equalled by the number of its saloons "catering to the riffraff that followed on the heels of the new railroad," an old-timer remembers in Frank McNitt's *The Indian Traders*. "Outlaws and drunken Navajos purchased intoxicants openly. Eventually a series of killings terminated in the execution of seven outlaws."

When the Wingate troopers were not involved in tearing up the 14 saloons, they were busy preventing others from doing the same thing. On two occasions, barrels of beer belonging to the railroad were stolen by desperados who took over the town. The justice of the peace telegraphed to the fort for help. He feared that the railroad company would carry out a threat to level the town with several hundred construction men unless the beer were returned.

The town was leveled of its own accord by fire

in 1890. Nine years later Hans Neumann occupied the site with a trading post that specialized in Navajo blankets and rugs. He had a backroom stocked with liquor for Wingate officers, but soon found that this was a mistake. While the officers played cards at his bar, the wives were in the rug room pretending interest in the goods—thereby involving the laborious spreading and folding of many heavy rugs by Neumann and his staff.

A lieutenant named John J. Pershing was a frequent visitor at Neumann's. Pershing also passed part of his Wingate assignment on a trip to the Grand Canyon in which he lost his horses and equipment twice and almost died from thirst in the desert. "If nothing else we have discovered the way not to go to the Grand Canyon" he announced upon returning.

The interest in off-post entertainment increased when an 1889 regulation prohibited alcoholic beverages from being sold at any Army installation. Brevet Brigadier General Eugene A. Carr, who had conducted a vigorous campaign to rid the reservation of Navajo bootleggers, announced that the prohibition was backfiring.

"A number of groggeries have been set up on the edge of the reservation," Carr reported. "They are usually supplied with harlots; and soldiers visiting them are drugged with vile liquor, wheedled out of their money, clothing, and arms, and sent back drunken, demoralized and with venereal diseases, to be tried, put in hospital, etc."

Ultimately the regulation was modified so that canteens could sell alcoholic beverages. Not only were the profits returned to help the soldiers, but the incidence of drunkenness fell off—now that the beverages were readily available. The hog ranches quickly went out of business.

Wingate companies were called south for the Apache campaigns of the 1880's. The return of 13th Infantry from a year-long campaign, 1885-86, was described by a corporal in Don Rickey's *Forty Miles a Day on Beans and Hay:* "The band met us at the foot of the mountains and played us in," said Corporal F. J. Gehringer. "We were a sight to behold, hardly a uniform on a man—many had just coveralls."

The Navajo agency headquarters at old Fort Defiance needed Wingate help periodically. In 1875, Brevet Brigadier General William R. Price took a four-man detail to assist the agent and his assistants in leaving. The agent had resigned after his charges questioned his right to what he claimed was his personal property. "I believe I can then with very little trouble find out what belongs to the Government," said Price, if the agent would identify what was his out of 3,000 pounds of flour, 54 pounds

POST CEMETERY has many markers scattered around, most of them unmarked. "Unknown" is most common name that can be read. At least 60 markers bear names of Mexicans who died at Fort Wingate when 4,000 refugees from Pancho Villa revolution were interned here in 1914. Marker at right bears name of Mexican General Gazetano Romero who died at Wingate on July 22, 1914; body was moved to Mexico in 1920's.

of coffee, 240 tin pails, 75 pair of children's shoes, and other assorted items that appeared suspiciously akin to annuity goods.

Ten years later the troops assisted in the hunt for two Navajo murderers, but were only able to find the grave of one of the victims. Two suspects were brought back to the Wingate guardhouse. One turned out to be the father of a guilty man; he gave himself up to protect his son.

In 1905 a Defiance trader recognized silver bracelets on a customer as those that had been stolen the day before. With a revolver on the counter, the storekeeper demanded his property. The Indian refused, insolently suggesting that there was nothing that could be done. From mid-morning until after dark, the store's doors were kept locked except to admit more Navajos. By dusk the store had 25 Indians inside. As he lit the oil lamp the trader whispered to his wife, "I've got a varmint by the tail and I don't know how to turn him loose."

Answering a knock on the door, the trader recognized two men, a Wingate officer and a Navajo chief. Behind them was a detail of men from the fort. Although they were at Defiance for a different purpose, the troopers returned to Fort Wingate with several prisoners.

Asked later how many soldiers were in the detachment, the trader answered: "If you had asked me then I would have counted 40 for every man, it was such a relief to have them there."

TO GET THERE: From Gallup, N.M., take Interstate 40 (U.S. 66) east to Fort Wingate turnoff, 12 miles. Three miles south on State 400 is site of Second Fort Wingate (Fauntleroy and Lyon), now Indian school. Returning to Interstate, continue east 48 miles to Grants. Turn right (south) on State 53 to San Rafael. Old Fort Wingate site is a mile west and slightly south of village.

CAMP RADZIMINSKI, OKLAHOMA

Radziminski was a 15-month post that knew two major battles and three sites but never got around to becoming permanent.

Brevet Major Earl Van Dorn arrived at the first site of Camp Radziminski on September 23, 1858, at the head of four companies of the 2d Cavalry, one of the 5th Infantry, and a detachment of 135 friendly Indian Scouts led by Sul Ross, some day to be governor of Texas. Van Dorn's mission was to lead a punitive column against the Comanches, and thereby convince them that the quiet life on the reservation was preferable to raiding into Texas.

First he sent out scouts while work started on a picket stockade on the southeast bank of Otter Creek. Six days later the scouts returned with news that there was a Comanche encampment of 120 lodges 40 miles away. The scout did not know that the Indians had just completed a peace conference at Fort Arbuckle and were returning to their home reservation.

Van Dorn hustled his supplies into the half-completed stockade, left the infantry to keep watch, and trotted off with his cavalry and the Indian Scouts. With only 40 miles to make, he planned to hit the Comanches at dawn.

The 40 miles turned out to be 100, but Van Dorn still attacked at dawn a day late. The Comanches knew he was in the area, but were not especially alarmed because of the recent talks at Arbuckle. Two hours after dawn 70 Indians were dead. Lieutenant Cornelius Van Camp and three troopers were dead and 10 more were wounded, including Van Dorn who was struck by two arrows.

One of Van Dorn's arrows pierced his stomach and was expected to be fatal. The surgeon cut off the arrow point and withdrew the shaft, insisted that Van Dorn not move for five days from the battle ground, and then returned him to Camp Radziminski on a stretcher between two horses.

Van Dorn survived to lead Radziminski's second conflict, an attack in May, 1859 about 20 miles from modern Dodge City, Kansas. Fifty Comanches were killed and 36 captured with the Army suffering nine dead, including three Indian scouts, and 17 soldiers wounded. Lieutenant Fitzhugh Lee was one of these, an arrow piercing his lung and sticking out his back. He survived, carrying the arrowhead in his chest through careers as a Confederate general, governor of Virginia, and a Spanish-American War U.S. general.

Van Dorn was not wounded in the second battle. He was destined to become a Confederate major general, lose the Battles of Pea Ridge and Corinth, and be shot to death by a jealous husband in 1863.

After the first fight, the initial Radziminski site was occupied until mid-November when grazing gave out. A new site higher up Otter Creek was used until March, 1859, when the troops moved to a better spot across the creek where two granite peaks protected them from the weather.

Here they put up temporary sod walls, topped by their tents. Makeshift stone chimneys provided some warmth but also caught one tent on fire, burning two soldiers fatally.

Most of the winter was spent in training the recruits sent to fill out the companies. When the snows deepened, the cavalrymen felled cottonwoods so that their horses could eat the bark. Another winter occupation is suggested by artifacts found on the site by Colonel W. S. Nye, as noted in his *Carbine and Lance*: "Several marble poker chips and parts of champagne bottles."

NAMED AFTER First Lieutenant Charles Radziminski, 2d Cavalry Officer who died of tuberculosis in 1858, Camp Radziminski was at this site until December, 1859. Texas Rangers then used it for year. Custer's 1869 "Winter Campaign" camped in sod ruins. It is most famous of three sites, reputedly is location of buried treasure.

TO GET THERE: First site is near Tipton, Oklahoma, on State 5 probably at same location as 1874 "Fort" Beach, supply redoubt for Fort Sill campaigns, also called "Fort Otter." Third site is reached by taking U.S. 183 for 3 miles north from Snyder, Oklahoma, to Mountain Park; turn left (west) for 4.2 miles; right (north) 1.1 mile to where road becomes dirt. Continue 1.1 miles more to dirt road to right (east). General site is .5 mile down this track.

FORT HOSKINS, OREGON

Although not the usual thing at Western forts, a popularity poll was conducted by the commander of Fort Hoskins when it was suggested that the Army's presence was unwanted.

The results indicated that everyone was happy about having a fort nearby. Everyone, that is, except a farmer named Allen. Mr. Allen said that the income from selling eggs and milk did not equal the losses in his pig population.

Or, as a Civil War Oregon trooper at Hoskins put it, everytime that bear meat was served, the local pig count was decreased. "We threw out rich greasy slops at our back door and the pigs from the neighboring farms were attracted thither," explained Corporal William M. Hilleary. "The farmer laughed to see his porkers growing fat so fast on so small amount of wheat."

Then the "guard reported one night a fight with a bear," added Hilleary. "Short and decisive was the battle. The breakfast table was loaded with 'bear steaks'" that resembled ham and bacon.

The reason that Captain Christopher C. Augur conducted his poll was a derogatory report by a special inspector of Indian affairs, J. Ross Browne.

Browne visited the fort in 1858, and announced

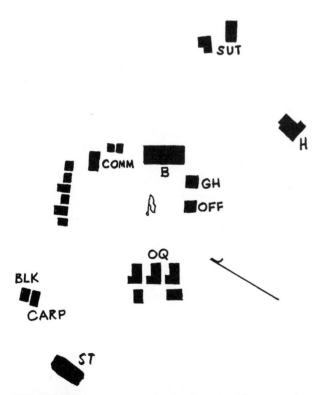

"THE BUILDINGS were arranged around a square known as the parade grounds, barracks on the north, officers quarters on the south, quartermaster and commissary, bakery and laundries on the west and guardhouse and hospital on the east," according to Corporal Hilleary. Barracks was double-storied, with mess rooms on first floor. (Redrawn from plat in **A Webfoot Volunteer,** Oregon State University Press.)

that its location was "ill-advised and unfortunate." He said that he had "made diligent inquiry of the principal settlers . . . without exception they agreed it was a nuisance, and are opposed to its continuance there . . . As to any practical protection, they consider such an idea preposterous. Expensive quarters for the officers and men are being built near the present site, which is on a private claim.

"I beg earnestly, in behalf of common sense, that this unnecessary expense may be discontinued, if it be in any way designed to benefit the Indian reservation. Each soul at the agency might be murdered a week before the tidings could reach Fort Hoskins."

Although Browne's investigations of the Pacific Coast Indian reservations exposed many abuses and improved the lot of the Indian, his greater fame was as a popular satirical writer. Apparently he was not averse to bending the facts slightly to score a sensational point. Augur wrote all of the settlers within a three mile radius of Hoskins and found that Browne had spoken to only one. The pig farmer's complaint was the only adverse comment that vaguely matched Browne's report.

As to the matter of protecting the agency, Augur already had established the blockhouse at the Siletz reservation headquarters. This was the primary protector of the agency. As is described elsewhere, Siletz Blockhouse bore the brunt of Indian troubles. Hoskins provided the detail to man the blockhouse, changing the personnel every two months.

When Fort Hoskins was founded on July 26, 1856, it was supposed to protect the eastern entrance to the Siletz reservation. It was also to guard the point where the reservation road opened into the settlements, except that there was no reservation road.

This road became the special project of Lieutenant Phil Sheridan, a member of Hoskins' first garrison. As Sheridan tells it in his *Memoirs*, he was less than successful in this regard. "The work was both tedious and laborious, but in time perseverance surmounted all obstacles and the road was finished, though its grades were very steep," he recorded. "I wished to demonstrate its value practically, so I started a Government wagon over it . . . I took the wagon to its destination, but as it was not brought back, I think comment on the success of my road is unnecessary."

Sheridan would have taken little comfort from the report of the fort's commander in 1862: "There is no wagon road from here to the Siletz blockhouse."

The military activities of Fort Hoskins centered

around keeping the Indians on the reservation and the settlers at a distance. Some Indians tried to camp near the fort, but this was discouraged after a settler announced that he would shoot the next redman he found "peeking in his windows." Momentary trouble arose when an agency employee killed an Indian, but payment of $200 to the relatives salved the hurt feelings.

Old John, one of the chiefs, was a leader of the Indian opposition. Old John was arrested at least three times, once with 50 rifles aimed at him, and the final arrest resulted in exile to Alcatraz in San Francisco Bay. On the way to this island prison, the chief forgot that he was aboard ship and tried to escape. His war whoops brought both passengers and crew to assist the soldier guards. Old John spent several years at Alcatraz, returning an enlightened Indian.

The Civil War brought volunteer troops to man Hoskins. Captain J. C. Schmidt of the 2d California Volunteer Infantry relieved Captain Fred-

erick T. Dent and immediately announced that secessionist feeling was rife in the valley. He wrote headquarters that the settlers "exulted in the withdrawal of the troops" and "the late commander aided the inhabitants in their nefarious designs on this garrison.."

Schmidt said that Dent gave one Jerry Evans "a box of ammunition containing 1,000 rounds of rifle musket catrridges; that he knew the said Evans to be a rank secessionist." Dent, of course, was U. S. Grant's brother-in-law. The aspersion on his loyalty apparently went no further, possibly because one of Schmidt's sources was the same farmer Allen, the unhappy supplier of pigs to the first garrison.

"Things do not look very pleasant in this vicinity" was how Schmidt summed up his first impressions of Hoskins in 1861. "There is at this post one 12-pounder . . . about 15 old flint-lock muskets (useless), 11 pistols nearly all unserviceable," he said, adding that the only working weapons were those brought by the company "but they are all poorly guarded."

Life with the volunteers at Fort Hoskins has been described in at least two diaries. Both Corporals Royal A. Bensell and William M. Hilleary kept records that are informal accounts of their "adventures" at the post. Hilleary took much interest in the dining problems, noting in many entries that meals frequently consisted solely of "bread and water" or "bread and molasses."

"We buy our own vegetables," Hilleary noted, to satisfy "ravenous appetites . . . There was not a crum (sic) left on the table after meals." His diary mentions a "Great Bread Riot" when "21 men belonging to Co. B Infantry called on Captain Palmer and complained of the scarcity of bread. The Capt. promised a reinforcement. Still stormy. Co. F Infantry have enough to eat when they furnish their own potatoes."

Company F sponsored "Bread Riot No. 2 . . . a few days afterward" when they "found a 'square

PARADE GROUND of Fort Hoskins recalls hours of drilling by Volunteers. "Our captain did not seem to enjoy the drill very well and whenever he went out with us we knew it would be play," remembered Corporal Hilleary. The commander of Hoskins' other company "drilled his company in person and was strict in discipline but never shirked his duty, never turned the company over to subordinate officers when he should have been there himself."

meal' awaiting them . . . It consisted of a piece of bread about two inches square and a cup of water to each man."

When the volunteers arrived they found that the post had stores of rations at least 10 years old. Pork, for instance, bore 1852 quartermaster markings. An attempt to use it caused a scent that was discernible for miles around. The ration storage solved for the volunteers the riddle: why Fort Hoskins?

"The only object that appeared to a raw recruit of sending us to this place was to consume a lot of old stores which the regulars had not been able to make way with," concluded Hilleary.

Bensell's diary is sprinkled with references to the off-duty activities of the garrison. Apparently these were considerably exhuberent on occasion; records show that one lieutenant resigned rather than face courtmartial for his actions at the New Year's Eve celebration welcoming 1863.

The fort had a dramatic club—the "Lyceum Society"—, glee club, bible class, and debating club. Considerable attention was paid to rifle marksmanship. Even the nearby churches provided diversion. Bensell's diary suggests ulterior motives to his religious interest. "Go to church" he noted for a Sunday in 1863. "Find some good looking girls, fat and saucy." And for another Sunday: "Some very pretty girls in attendance, objects of general observance and interest."

A number of marriages occurred between local girls and the soldiers, an indication that by the time Fort Hoskins was abandoned in 1865, it had won general acceptance with the settlers.

TO GET THERE: From Corvallis, Oregon, take U.S. 20 west 11 miles to intersection with State 223. Turn right (north) about 5 miles to turnoff (left, west) to Hoskins 1 mile. This near-ghost town is adjacent to fort site, on private property on slight plateau behind main street.

FORT HOSKINS might have looked like this, although this sketch is believed ot have been made after fort was abandoned. Long building was barracks, three small ones in foreground, officers quarters; hospital was at far right corner. Butt of flagpole was dug up in 1964 revealing document buried in bottle that showed flagpole was dedicated on January 19, 1859, and that "ladies at post" were Captain Augur's wife and six children.

(Mrs. Harriet Moore and Oregon State University Archives)

FORT UMPQUA, OREGON

If the Army expected to fight when it camped at the mouth of the Umpqua River, it was not disappointed. It was probably surprised, though, when the fighting had less to do with Indians than it did with property rights.

Captain Joseph Stewart brought Company H, 3d Artillery, on July 28, 1856, to the abandoned site "of what was once called Umpqua City." The question of property rights seemed remote at the time. The site was completely surrounded by 30-foot high sand bluffs that were kept from the new buildings only by a windbreak of pine and fir trees.

"These are being covered in rapidly," reported Inspector General Joseph K. F. Mansfield in 1859, "and the northwest winds which blow all summer, will in less than 5 years cover the post up entirely unless timely removed."

The post was near the mouth of the Umpqua River where, it was theorized, it could provide protection to both white man and Indian at the southern entrance to the Grand Ronde and Siletz Indian Reservations. Mansfield considered that it failed in this objective, because there was only a "mule trail" inland, regardless of Phil Sheridan's road-building efforts between Siletz and Hoskins.

The abandonment of Fort Orford 90 miles to the south provided the new post with ready-made buildings. The blockhouse, hospital, and two officers' quarters were moved to Fort Umpqua. Other quarters and the barracks were built from logs or lumber obtained locally.

By November, 1856, the post was ready for the winter when an unexpected visitor arrived. Amos E. Rogers informed Stewart "that the land which had been taken for military purposes at Fort Umpqua belonged to me . . and stated to him that I should expect and endeavor to obtain compensation therefor from the Government if it was reserved and occupied by Military purposes by the United States."

Rogers said that he had filed on the land in 1854, resided there for the required period, and happened to be absent on business when the military arrived. It took awhile for the government to admit that Rogers had a point. By that time the Government agreed with Mansfield's opinion: "It

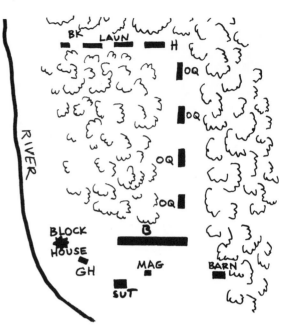

FORT UMPQUA was sketched by Inspector-General J. F. K. Mansfield after his 1859 visit. "The company was comfortably quartered in a one story frame building with piazza, and with a good mess room and kitchen," he reported. "The men slept in double bunks, two tiers high." Long building between magazine and officers' row was barracks. Blockhouse was used as office and storeroom by quartermaster. Sutler was in building between guardhouse and magazine. (Redrawn from Mansfield report, 1859.)

(George Eastman House and Col. Fred B. Rogers)

OFFICERS' ROW in 1859 shows long barracks building in rear, almost hidden by trees. Box in foreground suggests post was not neatest in Army, but markings on side help confirm that this is Fort Umpqua. Both old photographs here of Fort Umpqua were in album compiled by Surgeon Edward Perry Vollum, but style suggests they were taken by Lieutenant Lorenzo Lorain, Fort Crook's photographer. Lorain was stationed at Umpqua as quartermaster and commissary officer.

might be proper to pay him a small rent, for it is of no value otherwise to him, but I would not advise a purchase, as the post must be removed in less than five years.

The "small rent" started as $53 total in fiscal year 1858. By 1861 it had been renegotiated to $500 annually, a sum which also included the privilege of cutting timber on the property.

Although the post was increased to a two-company installation after its first winter, the addition of Company L, 3d Artillery kept it at this level for only six months. Stewart's company left for the inhospitable heat of Fort Yuma, California, in January, 1858. Company B, 3d Artillery was at the site for a month until called to the Coeur d'Alene War. For the remainder of its history, Umpqua seldom boasted more than a single company.

The start of the Civil War resulted in the immediate reduction of the garrison to one lieutenant and 12 men. Rumors that the post would be abandoned caused Judge R. E. Stratton to warn headquarters that the Indians were ready to return to their "old haunts" but "the presence of a very small force at Fort Umpqua would effectively prevent it."

Judge Stratton cited another reason for keeping the fort. Suggesting that the governor was pro-Southern, Stratton said that abandonment of the post would permit the governor to re-occupy it

MOUTH OF Umpqua River was treacherous to ships trying to land passengers at fort. In 1859 George Crook was aboard steamer **Columbia** when she had to land new surgeon here. "We encountered a fearful storm as we neared the mouth of the Umpqua," he wrote in diary: "and in crossing the bar before entering the harbor a heavy wave struck us aft and combed at least 15 feet above the deck, pouring down upon it like so much lead, sweeping everything before it. The railing, steering wheel, snubbing posts, lockers, and in fact everything on the deck was swept off, the two men at the wheel included." One man later was rescued. Ship lay off shore a day, making repairs and waiting for sea to abate, finally gave up and dropped passengers at next port.

with state troops "such as only he could rely upon."

Stratton was assured in August, 1861, that the fort would not be abandoned, a decision that was reconsidered the following June. In the face of orders that the post would be closed, pressure was exerted by J. W. Drew for the troops to remain. Drew had bought the property from Rogers and had a good reason for the Army to stay, contradicting the opinion of his brother, the former Indian Agent, that "the detachment of troops there was of no use."

Brigadier General Benjamin Alvord personally visited the site, giving credence to local legend about its abandonment. Supposedly the paymaster stopped at Fort Umpqua in the summer of 1862 but could find no one around. The story is that he reported to Alvord, the department commander, that everyone was away on a hunting trip and "there were no Indians requiring a post here."

The pressures were sufficient for division headquarters to alert a San Francisco company to be ready to re-garrison the post. At the last minute, the order was suspended until Alvord's opinion could be solicited.

The general did not mince words. His telegraphed reply, quoted here in full, spelled the end of Fort Umqpua: "There is, in judgment, no necessity for troops at Umpqua."

TO GET THERE: Site of military Fort Umpqua is on peninsula directly north of Winchester Bay, Oregon, but it must be approached from U.S. 101 about 4 miles north of Reedsport, Oregon.

HISTORY OF Umpqua area includes this story near fort site of Jed Smith, early fur trader. Post should not be confused with other forts of same name that were trading posts. One was founded in 1832 about 40 miles to east to trade for Indians' beaver and furs. It included four log buildings enclosed by 12-foot high picket stockade, with bastions at two corners. Indians attacked it several times, besieging it for several hours in 1839 until discouraged by casualties inflicted by French trader and his Indian employees.

BILLIARD HALL was pride of Fort Umpqua in wing behind hospital (foreground). This 1859 view, probably by Lorain, looks down laundress row; bakery is at end of row. Umpqua river is in background. Many buildings remained at site after abandonment, prompting visitor in 1864 to describe post "among these bleak sand hills . . . the remains of the garrison can be seen . . . The officers quarters were expensive buildings. Some neat conservatories still stand, monuments of useless extravagance."

(George Eastman House and Col. Fred B. Rogers)

LARGEST FORCE ever assembled against plains Indians camped at Fort Berthold, North Dakota, near end of Alfred Sully's 1864 Sioux Expedition.

OFF TO THE SIOUX

"We do not consider any property safe on this river, or lives either, any longer, as the Sioux, we think, have commenced their war on the traders, as well as the soldiers."

—Deseret News, March 5, 1855.

IT is said by some that the bloody Sioux Wars were started by an over-eager lieutenant and a drunken interpreter. This so-called "Grattan Massacre" was more of an effect than a cause, however.

The cause of the Sioux War was simply that the white man was moving West and a primary route—the Oregon Trail—cut through Sioux country. The white man's treatment of the Indian was unsympathetic, to put it mildly. The Indian reciprocated in kind.

The Grattan incident occurred in 1854 when Brevet Second Lieutenant John L. Grattan went to a Brule Sioux camp near Fort Laramie, Wyoming, to investigate a stolen cow. With him were 29 soldiers, two 12-pound howitzers, and Auguste Lucien, the post's interpreter.

A combination of Grattan's inexperience and Lucien's prejudiced and possible drunken interpretations soon complicated the meeting to such an extent that a musket was fired by a soldier. Before the firing had ended, the entire Army detail was dead or dying, and another Sioux War had started.

At least three major expeditions were launched against the Sioux before the end of the Civil War. The first, Harney's 1855 Sioux Expedition, was a direct result of the Grattan incident. With 600 men Brevet Brigadier General William S. Harney "severly chastised" the Sioux at Ash Hollow, Nebraska, and later reached a treaty with the tribes at Fort Pierre, South Dakota.

A period of unrest continued into the Civil War. Massacres in Minnesota and along the trails finally reached the point that the government, despite its commitments on the Eastern battlefronts, had to take action.

One expedition under Brigadier General Henry Hastings Sibley moved against the Sioux in 1863 and met them in two engagements. Brigadier General Alfred A. Sully, a veteran of the Harney expedition, defeated the Sioux in the Battle of Whitestone Hill the same year.

A year later Sully took the largest expedition of the Indian Plains Wars across the Dakotas. He had 4,000 men, a dozen cannon, and 15 supply steamboats.

Sully's victories were thorough and, for the Army, relatively painless. The Battles of Killdeer Mountains and the Badlands inflicted such casualties on the Indians and so scattered them that Sully predicted, "I think they will never organize for resistance."

Sully was no prophet. A year later both he and General Connor led campaigns against the Sioux. But still the depredations continued along the trails and against the forts. After the Custer Massacre in 1876 the Sioux were subdued only when a Sully-style, full-scale campaign again was launched against them.

FORT GRATTAN, NEBRASKA

"I caused a small field work to be thrown up near the mouth of Ash Hollow, and left, as a garrison to the same, Captain Wharton and his company (I) of the 6th Infantry; leaving also, at the same post, a portion of the prisoners and property captured in the engagement of the 3rd instant on the Blue Water."

With these words Colonel and Brevet Brigadier General William S. Harney announced on September 26, 1855, that he had left a detachment of troops at one of the major landmarks of the Oregon Trail, the entrance to Ash Hollow.

"My object in establishing this post," he continued, "was to afford a point of support for the public and emigrant trains and the monthly mail passing between Forts Kearny and Laramie, and also to have the means of furnishing escort to the same."

September 8, 1855, was the official founding date of Fort Grattan. This was six days after the opening battle of Harney's Sioux Expedition, known variously as the Battle of Ash Hollow, the Battle of Blue Water, or Harney's Massacre. The fort was near the camp from which Harney began his march on September 2.

With 600 men in his force, Harney was ready for battle when his scouts reported an Indian village on Blue Water Creek, six miles from his North Platte River camp. Colonel Philip St. George Cooke, of the Mormon Battalion fame, led his four mounted companies of the 2d Dragoons out of camp at 3 a.m. Quietly Cooke worked his way around the Indian camp rear.

At 4:30 a.m., Harney took the infantrymen from camp on a course paralleling the creek. Twice the Sioux sent emissaries begging peace—or, at least, providing delaying tactics—while they hastily packed up their camp. Harney refused to stop, unless the Sioux gave up their young men who had committed depredations—a condition he knew that the Brule Sioux chief, Little Thunder, would not be able to meet.

"We attacked them with our rifles," described one infantryman, "while their arrows or the bullets from their poor flintlocks could not reach us. They were forced to flee. But they ran straight into the hands of the dragoons, who followed them as they turned back toward us."

Another infantryman added, "When the infantry saw the dragoons coming down in such beautiful style, they gave a yell which resounded far and wide. The Indians threw away everything they had in the world ... I do not suppose the Indians in this country had such a perfect clearing out as

ASH HOLLOW Cemetery includes this 1849 gravestone (inside glass-faced larger marker) for Rachel E. Pattison, 18 years old, who died on June 19, 1849. Original stone, found on grave years later, bears legend: "She was enroute to Oregon Territory over the Old Oregon Trail." Lions Club is credited with preserving stone and grave.

FORT GRATTAN barely can be discerned in slight mounds covered by riverside brush in center. Harney's camp was nearby before Battle of Blue Water. Cooke left his camp standing when his dragoons left for battle; they returned here after fighting ended. Indian wounded were treated at the new fort. Many immigrant diaries make note of Fort Grattan or "old sod fort" at mouth of Ash Hollow.

" A LARGE NUMBER of ash trees grow here, from which it gets its name," wrote Oregon Trail traveler in 1849 of Ash Hollow. "The hills are sandy and traveling difficult . . . The bluffs are naked and sandy and the whole country presents a desolate appearance except near the river. We have been much teased and severly bitten by the buffalo gnats which swarm in thousands around us."

on this occasion. They will have cause to remember General Harney for some time."

Harney's report said that 86 Indians had been killed, five wounded, and about 70 women and children captured. Nearly all of the Sioux provisions and camp equipment had been taken. The Army losses included four killed, seven wounded, and one man missing.

After the battle and the detachment of Captain Henry W. Wharton and Company I to build a fort, Harney took the remainder of his force to Fort Laramie. Wharton's troopers did not lose time. Just in case another band of Sioux appeared, quickly a 100-foot-square earthwork was built with bastions at two of the corners.

The speed had another advantage. Because of it there were some appreciable remains to mark the site when Harney sent word down the trail on October 1 to abandon the short-lived fort. He had parlayed with the Sioux near Fort Laramie, decided that the main threat was over, and recalled his troops.

The remains of Fort Gratton, remembered more because of the unhappy name than the surface remains, were landmarks on the Oregon Trail. Harney remembered the post in later years when he was in command of the early stages of the Mormon Expedition, and ordered that the location would be a rendezvous for the troop columns.

One officer on the Utah expedition described it in 1857. "A little enclosure made of sods, close upon the bank of the river about a hundred paces from me," he wrote, "occupied for a while after the affair of Ash Hollow or Blue Water as it is called, by two companies of Infantry, but long since deserted, bears the name of Fort Grattan—in its loneliness and abandonment a fit symbol of the fate of him from whom it was named."

TO GET THERE: From Scottsbluff, Nebraska, go east on U.S. 26 about 90 miles to where it crosses North Platte River below Lewellen. Go to Ash Hollow Cemetery on right. Fort is a left turn from highway across from cemetery. Go on county road 4 miles across sand draw, angle northeast across hay meadow to south bank of old river channel. Site is large mound covered with brush alongside old river bank.

FORT PIERRE, SOUTH DAKOTA

Buying forts sight unseen was a practice seldom indulged in by the U.S. Army. The experience at Fort Pierre may explain the reason.

Its location on the upper Missouri river provided Fort Pierre with the geographical advantages desired by the Army. This was noted during the planning of the Sioux Campaign in 1855, and the American Fur Company was approached about the possibility of selling the post.

After a suitable period of considering the question, the company agreed to sell its "valuable" trading post for $45,000. This was in April, 1855, three months before any soldier was to visit the place to see what had been purchased.

Fort Pierre's main selling point was its reputation as the leading trading post on the upper Missouri. It had been in the center of the Missouri fur forts since 1832 when it replaced 10-year old Fort Tecumseh, a mile downstream. The latter post was the Columbia Fur Company's leading fort when founded in 1822, but the American Fur Company quickly recognized the unfortunate riverbank site upon taking it over in 1827.

Flooding of the surrounding area usually cut Tecumseh off from the outside at least once a year, so in 1831 a new site on higher ground was selected.

(Smithsonian Institution)

WHEN PAINTED by Bodmar in 1834, Fort Pierre was described as "Each side of the quadrangle is 108 paces in length; the front and back . . . each 114 paces; the inner space 87 paces in diameter. From the roof of the block-house, which is surrounded with a gallery, there is a fine prospect over the prairie; and there is a flag-staff on the roof, on which the colors (sic) are hoisted . . . The situation of the settlement is agreeable; the verdant prairie is very extensive, animated by herds of cattle and horses." This view is closeup of post.

Company officer Pierre Chouteau visited the company's headquarters in 1832, providing a ready-made name for the new location.

Prince Maximilian visited in 1833. He noted a "decayed old house, the only remains of Fort Tecumseh," and the replacement, "a large quadrangle, surrounded by high pickets . . . At the northeast and southwest corners there are blockhouses, with embrasures . . . the fire of which commands the curtain; the upper story is adapted for small arms, and the lower for some cannon . . ."

Twenty-two years later Fort Pierre was still in existence, but barely so. The fur trade had passed its peak, partly because the beaver hat was no longer in vogue and partly because the beaver population was almost trapped out of existence. The Indians had been decimated by smallpox, and the survivors were becoming more and more hostile. These factors, coupled with the fact that wooden forts were not designed to last 22 years, convinced the fur company to accept the $45,000 before the Army changed its mind.

The first troops arrived at Pierre in July, 1855, while General Harney was moving overland toward Ash Hollow. Five companies of the 2d Infantry were added to the post's garrison by August, 1855, although the term "garrison" is a misnomer. Major William R. Montgomery quickly realized that the flea ridden, termite infested, rotting establishment was unsatisfactory for his 450 men.

He also realized that there was little he could do about it. For eight miles in every direction, both

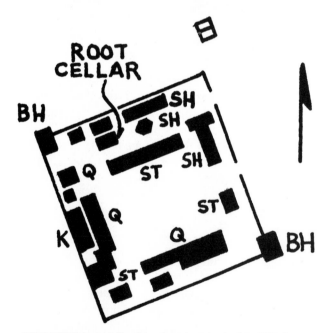

FORT PIERRE looked like this when Army arrived in 1855 for two-year stay, although most troops were quartered elsewhere. Post often is called Fort Choteau to differentiate it from second Fort Pierre built upriver when employees moved upon Army's arrival. Latter post was equally large, measured about 225 feet on east and south sides, 195 on west, 227 on north; it had one bastion, was abandoned in 1863. This ground plan shows post occupied by Army until May 16, 1857. Lower quarters row was 122 feet long, had seven sets of quarters; left-hand quarters row was 91 feet, story-and-a-half, with five sets. (Redrawn from Army plat at South Dakota Historical Society.)

ARMY'S FORT Pierre was at this site, marked since 1930 by this stone, present of Des Moines, Iowa, Doctor Raymond A. Burnside. Army left fort in custody of D. M. Frost trading company, but within two months post was gutted; what Army and "custodians" did not want, others took. By 1860, remains included only shell of one row of houses.

the timber and the grass had been stripped by the years of fort use. Details were sent out to bring lumber and forage to the fort, but with little luck. It was estimated that $20,520 would be needed to put the place into useable order—if the materials could be obtained.

When Harney arrived in November, bringing the population up to more than 900, he found that nothing had been done to prepare for the winter. Pasteboard pre-fabricated huts were brought up-river and the soldiers were given permission to build log huts on both sides of the river below and above the fort. Companies set up camps as distant as 19 miles upstream in an effort to protect themselves from one of Dakota's severest winters.

Although some men died, many cattle froze to death, and the cavalry lost a third of their horses, the scattered camps had one advantage. One trooper wrote that many Sioux were encamped near his winter quarters. "We fraternized with them in the friendliest way, often went into their tents, and gave them a lot of food; and in this way we learned to make ourselves understood by them," he said.

The rapport between both paid off in March, 1856, when Harney parlayed with the tribes. By this time he realized where the true blame lay for the Grattan Massacre, and he was more amenable to discussion. Before the talks ended, both sides agreed to peace.

MISSOURI RIVER at this point saw Fort Pierre's first troops arrive in July, 1955. Troops passed through fort site in later years, Sully Expedition using it as rendezvous—although probably second Fort Pierre was used. In 1843 Fort Pierre was described as "enclosure of strong picket planted close together to the depth of 4½ feet and 22 feet high above the ground. The entire enclosure is 235 feet square, occupying therefore more than an acre of ground."

Harney provided each chief with an official commission designating him the leader of his tribe and told the assemblage: "I hope the Great Spirit will take care of you, and that He will put good in your hearts, and that you all may have plenty, and keep your hands and hearts clean, that you may not be afraid to meet the Great Spirit hereafter."

When the 7,000 Sioux prepared to leave the council ground the next day, they first filed up to Fort Pierre. "Tremendous applause" augmented by Indian drums and horns greeted Harney as he appeared at the gate, signaling a temporary recess before the great Sioux wars to follow.

TO GET THERE: From Pierre, the capital of South Dakota, take U.S. 14 west across Missouri River. Do not turn south into town of Fort Pierre; instead continue west on U.S. 14 for 1 mile beyond U.S. 83 to right-hand turn into road 514. Go north 1.3 miles; fort site marker is .3 miles east (right) of road in field at end of dirt road across private property.

CAMP EDWARDS, SOUTH DAKOTA

Troops were stationed twice at Camp Edwards, each time as an indirect result of an Indian massacre. Although more than five years separated the two garrisons, the opposition and the mission were unchanged: keep the Sioux from molesting the settlers and from returning to their old haunts in Minnesota.

"It is situated on the Upper Lake of the Ti-Tanka-The group and within six miles of Lake Preston, Minnesota," is almost the sole clue to Camp Edwards in War Department records. The only other references are in the muster rolls of the units concerned and a few hints in the *Official Records* of the Civil War.

Translating this location into modern terms puts the camp next to Round Lake on a narrow spit of land between Lakes Tetonkaha and Oakwood in the Oakwood Lakes area of eastern South Dakota. Until it became the site of the short-lived town of Oakwood in 1877, the area went by the Indian name of "Tetonkaha," meaning "Big Summer Lodge."

French Scientist Joseph N. Nicollet and his young assistant, Lieutenant John C. Fremont, employed the Indian name during their 1839 Dakota expedition. They spelled it "Titankahe," commenting that this signified an area of importance to the Indians; villages and ceremonial and burial grounds scattered about attested to that.

The Spirit Lake Massacre took place in Iowa about 150 miles southeast of Titankahe Lakes. Resentment over settler encroachments on ceremonial lands, coupled with hunger after a hard winter, boiled over on March 7, 1857. The 14 warriors of renegade Sioux Inkpadutah slaughtered 40 whites and kidnapped several women in a week-long frenzy.

Pursued by three companies of Volunteers, Inkpadutah headed for the Oakwood area. Twenty miles to the southwest, the murderers were confronted by a party of Santee Sioux. The Santees were determined to take Inkpadutah and convince the whites that only he and his renegades were guilty. Inkpadutah escaped in the confusion, but two of his sons were killed.

In May, a detachment of Company I, 2d Infantry, was rushed to the Spirit Lake area from the Missouri River post of Fort Randall. The troops left without their company commander, Captain Delozier Davidson. He had been on leave and at the time was carried as "absent without leave." This was a common occurrence of the period when parent units failed to learn that higher headquarters had approved requests for additional leave. When Davidson rejoined his company, he found it doing not too well; 10 of his soldiers deserted in June.

A year later, after the Sioux had ceded the southeastern corner of South Dakota, two companies of the 2d Infantry stopped at Oakwood Lakes and founded Camp Edwards. Davidson had his Company I. With First Lieutenant Henry B. Hendershott and Company H, the total was two officers and 107 enlisted men. The officers and their companies campaigned together before, including several battles in the Mexican War in 1846 and 1847. They were together at Fort Yuma, California, 1850-53, and in 1855, were part of the first garrison at Fort Pierre. Their headquarters post by 1859 was Fort Randall.

The significance of the Edwards name is uncertain. The two officers may have selected it to honor Captain Oscar Edwards of the Voltigeur Regiment whose bravery impressed them during the Battle of Chapultapec. They were with two Edwards in Cali-

CAMP EDWARDS site can be seen in clearing across Round Lake (left picture) while Lake Tetonkaha is in background of picture at right. At least six small water bodies make up Oakwood Lakes, state recreational park once site of Oakwood, second town in Brookings County. Samuel Mortimer built cabin near fort in 1871, using remaining timbers for construction or firewood. Thriving community of Oakwood, on eastern shore of Lake Oakwood, was founded in 1877, began to die when railhead passed seven miles south. Post office was closed in 1894. Soldiers returned to lakes one more time before end of town—for encampment of Grand Army of the Republic in 1880's.

EARTHWORKS OF Camp Edwards are outlined by mounds and stockade-type posts around historical marker. During second occupation, commander was told to "keep his men under strict discipline and prepared at all times for an emergency." Men could not leave post but had to devote spare time to drill and "school of instruction" so winter would not be spent in idleness. Headquarters inspected monthly, reports were submitted weekly, and route between posts was patrolled every two days.

fornia, either of whom might have been in mind: Second Lieutenant John Edwards of the 3d Artillery—which frequently served with the 2d Infantry—or H. B. Edwards of the Indian Agency in the San Joaquin Valley. Davidson may have been honoring Assistant Surgeon Lewis A. Edwards, a fellow District of Columbia native.

The troopers arrived at Camp Edwards on June 3, 1859, and left on July 4. Earthen breastworks five feet high about 100-feet square were erected around a single log hut. Although cannon parapets supposedly were built, there is no indication that there was any artillery along.

Troops returned to Oakwood partly as an after-effect of the Fort Ridgely and New Ulm Massacres of Minnesota in 1862. More than 750 whites died and 269 were taken prisoner in these events. Direct results included the sentencing of 306 Indians to death, with the ultimate hanging of 39; the removal of the Sioux to the Missouri River reservations; and the annual Sioux Expeditions of the 1860's.

After General Sully's 1864 expedition—in which one of his opponents was the same Inkpadutah of Spirit Lake infamy—he returned to the Sioux City area and announced his plan "to place the force in the district in the most efficient state of preparation for early spring movements."

Two hundred men, mainly from the much esteemed Brackett's Minesota Cavalry Battalion, were to be outposted at four locations selected by Major General John Pope, the department commander. "These posts, of course, are temporary in their character," Pope explained, "and only the shelter actually necessary for troops will be put up by the troops themselves and at the least possible expense to the United States."

Forty men of Brackett's Company D were taken by First Lieutenant Joseph H. Porter to the Camp Edwards remnants on November 11, 1864. Originally Porter was to locate at Lake Poinsett, seven miles north. Officially he was reported as being at Lake Preston, 15 miles west. The fact that Edwards already existed, surrounded on almost three sides by water, ruled in its favor.

Porter spent the winter at his "Camp near Preston Lake." Frequent patrols were sent out to return Indians to the reservation and to prevent illicit trading. The whiskey sellers were special targets of General Sully. Porter was told that "the presence of such whiskey traders would be discouraged as much as possible" and to inform them "they will receive no protection whatever from the military."

Except for violent storms in February, 1865, the winter passed relatively quietly. On April 8, 1865, the Minnesotans abandoned the camp to join Sully's Northwest Expedition. Within four months, they marched 575 miles to the Devil's Lake area of North Dakota, then to Forts Berthold and Rice.

Inkpadutah again was one of the hostile Indians. As usual, he escaped punishment—as he did 11 years later when he faced Custer at the Little Big Horn.

TO GET THERE: From Brookings, S. D., take U. S. 77 north 8 miles to County 30. Turn left (west). Go through Bruce, 4 miles, for 3 more miles to right turn into Oakwood Lakes. Follow marked road north between three lakes to site of Camp Edwards on left.

SULLY'S BASE CAMP, NORTH DAKOTA

Alfred A. Sully had so many men in his 1864 Sioux Expedition—more than 4,000 plus a dozen cannon—that he could leave some of them behind to set up supply camps. His forwardmost base camp was on the Heart River in North Dakota, a 10-day post manned by 125 soldiers, 250 emigrants, and a Quaker cannon.

The emigrants and their 123 wagons joined Sully on July 4, 1864, happy to be under the care of the massive troop movement. When Sully arrived at the Heart River on July 25, he left both his supply tail and the emigrants. Under Captain William Tripp, Dakota Cavalry, the wagon train was corralled and defenses set up. Sully's main body moved on the next day.

Accustomed to the overwhelming size of the main force, the wagon train was unhappy to have only one company for their protection. The scouts had reported a 6,000-warrior camp to the front, easily enough to massacre everyone at Heart River if the Sully troopers were on a wild goose chase.

The wagons were circled on the north side of the Heart and rifle pits were dug all around. The quartermaster suggested a Quaker gun would help so a large log was hollowed out, reinforced with iron bands, and several test rounds fired through it. The impromptu field piece appeared serviceable, inspiring some degree of security in the settlers.

Twice the camp was thrown into a frenzy. On July 27 the mules stampeded, but were brought back with no indications that lurking Indians had been responsible. The next night the rifle pits were manned, but a rumored attack did not materialize.

The troopers returned in a rainstorm on July 31, jaded and bedraggled, to report the defeat at Killdeer Mountain of the 6,000 Indians. As was to be the case at the later Battle of the Badlands, Sully's cannon were the decisive weapons, inflicting heavy

HEART RIVER (foreground) "contained very poor water for drinking, strongly impregnated with coal and minerals" commented Iowa cavalryman during his short stop at Base Camp. Sully abandoned it on August 3. He moved his forces west to a near-disaster in torturous Badlands even though he defeated Indians there.

casualties on the Indians with few soldiers losses.

A wolf's yell cut through the Base Camp's night silence on July 31, shortly to be followed by a chorus of "piercing, harrowing sounds," remembered one soldier. "A picket gun was fired, and then another and the men seized their arms, and, because they were awakened, damned everything . . . The firing was kept up all night long, and only the warm sunshine of the morning dispelled the delusions of the night."

TO GET THERE: Take I-94 east 27 miles from Dickinson, North Dakota, to Antelope turnoff. Go south on gravel road for 14.3 miles. Sully Base Camp was in field to left (east) just before taking bridge across Heart River.

STORY OF Sully Base camp, the Heart River Coreal, is told on marker in center of site. Other traces obvious in field are many shallow rifle pits and a number of boulders with soldiers' names and July, 1864 dates crudely carved on them.

FORT DAKOTA, SOUTH DAKOTA

When Captain Daniel F. Eicher and the troopers of Company E, 6th Iowa Cavalry, arrived at Sioux Falls, South Dakota, in 1865, they concluded that they were just three years too late.

If they were at Sioux Falls to protect its residents, as their orders specified, the soldiers could see that there was one problem: no residents. The burned out houses were vacant, as they had been since the Sioux ransacked and burned the town in 1862. There were enough settlers in the general area to warrant protection, however.

Most of the settlers made an early excursion to the site of the new fort to see for themselves that the Army really was there. If, in the process, the soldiers could be sold some vegetables, bread, dairy products, or meat, well, that was all right, too. Between grasshoppers, unfriendly Indians, unpredictable politicians, incompleted railroads, and four years of drought, times were not the best, any extra income was welcome.

Sioux City had fallen from its earlier days of 1858 when it was the "squatter capital" of the territory. The town was founded in 1857 by both the Western Town Company and the Dakota Land Company. Shortly after settlers started arriving in the spring of 1858, a town organized by the Dakota company was raided by Indians. This made the settlers aware that they had no government.

The next step was for the people to organize their own government. A representative was sent to Washington to petition Congress for formal status, but with no luck. With the leadership of the town companies, a mass convention was held at Sioux Falls in September, 1858 and the election of an impromptu legislature was ordered.

PLAQUE MARKS site of Fort Dakota on Philips Avenue, Sioux Falls. Post was abandoned in 1869, sold in 1870. Date of 1873 probably tells how long after Army left that building was used. Tiny cemetery, containing bodies of three soldiers, a discharged soldier, and "a laundress named Gallagher," blocked downtown progress until moved by city to its cemetery in 1881.

Realizing that respectability and the semblance of legality would be essential if they were to have any success in being recognized, an actual election was held. Its validity was not lessened by the fact that the same 50 Sioux Falls residents voted many times over in order to guarantee a large turnout. Actually the settlers divided into three or four-man teams and roamed the countryside, stopping every few miles to have a drink of whiskey, proclaim the location of a voting precinct, and then vote several times by putting the names of friends and relatives on the ballots.

The newly elected assembly proclaimed itself the government "of that portion of Minnesota without the state limits, now called Dakota." The assembly held another election and session the following year. By this time the novelty had worn off and other towns, desirous of being the capital themselves, strongly opposed the Sioux Falls "vigilance committee."

Chosen governor by the second assembly was its speaker, Samuel J. Albright. Albright was the founder and editor of Dakota's first newspaper, the occasionally-published *Dakota Democrat*. When the

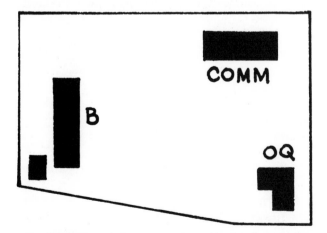

NOT DESIGNED as defensive work, Fort Dakota was log depot from which troops could operate. When finished, post had log barracks and hospital 170 feet long, 20 wide, 8 high; a 21- by 20-foot stone blockhouse; two wooden buildings 91 feet long by 21 wide, used for storage and guardhouse; a second barracks 80 feet long by 20 wide, and a 200-foot-long stable. (Redrawn from South Dakota Historical Society plat.)

TWO MONUMENTS overlook Sioux Falls from bluff above city. Shaft was dedicated in 1949 by County Historical Society as "Memorial to the Pioneers of Minnehaha County 1856-1889." Smaller marker at right is to Judge J. B. Amidon and son, killed by Indians in 1862. Before Army arrived at Sioux Falls, Yankton Indian Agent was authorized to enlist 50 Yankton Indian Scouts. Indian Scouts patrolled near Sioux Falls in 1864, captured several ring leaders of Nebraska and Minnesota massacres, "and shot them on the spot."

squatter government faded and Albright left town, the paper continued publishing but as *The Northwestern Independent*. Democrats were out of vogue, especially in view of the Republican federal government that was responsible for patronage in such federal territories as Dakota. Besides, Albright took the old nameplate with him.

In August, 1862, Sioux Falls was on the fringe of the Minnesota Sioux outbreak. In the face of tales of the Minnesota ravages, the settlers abandoned the town in favor of the stockade at Yankton. A detail of Militia Cavalrymen that had been in Sioux Falls accompanied the settlers.

The Sioux attacked the town, killing the only two whites they saw: Judge A. B. Amidon and his son. The buildings were fired and the printing press of *The Northwestern Independent ex-Dakota Democrat* was thrown into the Big Sioux River. The Indians kept the metal type as decorations for their peace pipes.

"A general alarm pervades our settlements," Governor William Jayne—a real governor was in authority by 1862—wrote to military headquarters. "Family after family are leaving our territory and whole settlements are about to be broken up. We must have immediate aid and assistance from you or else our Territory will be depopulated."

Jayne asked for 300 muskets for the state militia he was mustering, three 6-pound cannon with ammunition for three blockhouses being built, and "three companies of cavalry . . . to be stationed where they will afford the most protection to our people."

The Army's strategy called instead for aggressive expeditions to run down the Indians in their haunts.

The settlers would have preferred a series of small forts that provided immediate defenses against attack along with a payroll and quartermaster purchases to boost the economy. Politicians and businessmen charged that the notoriety of the large-scale campaigns was discouraging emigrants from settling in the Dakotas.

By 1865, with the Sioux Expeditions behind them, the Army was ready to establish small posts for local protection. General Alfred Sully said again that the Sioux were convinced that large-scale battles were futile. Guerilla-type actions might occur, he suggested, "whereby citizens who live on the borders or are traveling unconscious of danger will be the sufferers more than the troops."

Lieutenant Colonel and Brevet Brigadier General John Pattee, in command of Iowa Volunteers at Sioux City, Iowa, was directed to survey the southeastern part of Dakota for two military posts. The results were Fort James, 60 miles west of Sioux Falls, and a post at Sioux Falls.

Although only three buildings surrounded by a rail fence, the new fort was the key to the resurrection of Sioux Falls. Some settlers returned to the townsite and gathered close to the Army to satisfy the demands of both protection and good business.

Fort Brookings was the name selected by General Pattee for the site, probably in honor of politician W. W. Brookings, manager of the company that founded Sioux Falls. The choice was disapproved by headquarters in favor of the Dakota name. Immediate confusion resulted with Post Dakota that had been at Dakota City, Nebraska, five miles south of Sioux City, Iowa, for a year.

The providing of security from an occasional real foe—along with a continuing sense of security against an imagined foe—occupied the garrison of Iowa volunteers.

The Volunteers were relieved in June, 1866, by Captain and Brevet Lieutenant Colonel Kilburn Knox and his Company D, 22d U. S. Infantry. Knox published new post orders upon arrival, requiring each man to have two sets of uniforms but permitting "straw or felt hats" to be worn when on duty in the hot sun.

A month later the Army proposed to abandon both Forts James and Dakota. More than 16,000 Indians had agreed to treaty proposals of a Peace Commission during the winter, making it likely that the posts had little reason to continue. Reaction to the idea was so pronounced that the Army compromised. Only Fort James was closed in 1867.

More so than Indians, liquor was a main troublemaker at the garrison. Knox permitted the sutler to

STILL BEING constructed when this photograph was taken in 1866, Fort Dakota was inexpensively built for short-time use. Ultimately 12 buildings were at post but only three show here: barracks, left; commissary, center; half-finished officers' quarters, right. Rail fence was to keep livestock and carriages off of parade ground. Officers' house was "of hewed logs set upright," had dirt roof, ceilings nine feet high, two rooms 16 by 15 feet and two 16 by 10 feet. Fort had its own version of World War II "See Here Private Hargrove." Private Hargraves arrived at post under arrest, was released from guardhouse once for two days, spent next 14 weeks behind bars, then settled matter by deserting.

sell only two drinks a day to each enlisted man, one in the morning and one in the afternoon. Men on the sick list, or excused from duty, were reported to the sutler so that nothing could be sold them. The post surgeon would provide from his official stocks for sick men "who are really in need of stimulants," Knox decreed.

All liquor sales to enlisted men were stopped on October 26, 1866. "A great disturbance and disorder has been caused by the sale of liquor at this post," Knox explained.

A year later, Captain and Brevet Lieutenant Colonel William A. Olmstead, the new commander, went even further. "The practice of teamsters, ambulance drivers, and other enlisted men bringing liquor *of any description* to this post will be no longer tolerated," he announced (the italics were his).

Olmstead was commanding officer for 14 months until he was suddenly relieved on March 15, 1869. Captain and Brevet Lieutenant Colonel John M. Duffy arrived with orders to assume command and place Olmstead under arrest. Two months later Olmstead was still at the post, living in two rooms behind the barracks, until permitted to resign rather than be courtmartialled over his operation of the post.

Duffy was Fort Dakota's last commander. He encountered new problems in May, 1869, a month before the post was abandoned. Settlers had heard that the post was to be given up and several, "mostly Norwegians," moved on the reservation. Three were arrested by Duffy who supplied their names to the Land Office "to insure they are not permitted to hold their claims."

The Territorial Legislature suggested in 1868 that the troops at Fort Dakota be moved to another location. The Army responded without delay. Everything movable was shipped to Fort Randall, on the Missouri River. This displeased the district commander and his quartermaster, neither of whom considered what was salvaged as worth the $3,000 shipping charge.

TO GET THERE: Sioux Falls is on Interstates 90 and 29 in southeastern South Dakota. Fort Dakota marker is at Hollywood Theater, 218 North Philips Avenue in downtown Sioux Falls. Across street was fort site; barracks location was on Philips with south end about 125 feet north of 8th Street.

FORT JAMES, SOUTH DAKOTA

Closer than most posts to the romanticized version of western stockades, Fort James was built solidly of stone under the supervision of a professional stone mason. From the blockhouse at one corner to the heavy wooden gate and forbidding outside walls pierced by rifle slits, the work met most of the prerequisites for a permanent installation of the Army.

It lacked only one major requirement: a reason for being. Although this was not always critical at Western forts, it was in the case of Fort James. The post was only 13 months old when it was abandoned; most of the construction was hardly nine months old.

Brevet Brigadier John B. Pattee selected James' site on the same trip in which he surveyed a location for Fort Dakota. James' location gave him more trouble than Dakota's. First he could not find a spot sufficiently wooded for timber and fuel purposes, probably because the Indians burned the prairie every spring. Then when he arrived at the James River, the stream was running high and he had to go 23 miles upstream to find a crossing.

"Crossed the river by carrying our equipment on our heads," he reported, "the water about four feet deep, the banks very muddy."

Still hunting for a wooded location, Pattee walked downstream 17 miles to a wide flood plain in the bend of the river. There was a spring around which the fort could be built and large outcroppings of quartzite, so-called "Sioux Falls Granite," with which to build. A nearby bluff afforded observation in all directions.

Pattee put Lieutenant George W. McCall, a stone mason in civilian life, in charge of building the

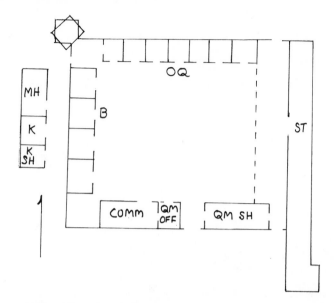

CAMP NEAR Firesteel Creek, as this plat is listed in National Archives, was built by Companies I and C, 7th Iowa Volunteer Cavalry. "Blockhouse is to be made of stone, 8 feet high, and then one story of hewn logs reversed as shown by the plan," General Pattee ordered. "The corner of the stable marked bastion is arranged so that if loop holes are made for small arms, the east and south may be separated from the bastion or blockhouse. The general says he will send a howitzer this fall." Blockhouse was 20 feet square. Stable yard was graded to one foot lower than parade ground. (Redrawn from plat in National Archives.)

fort. The detailed instructions received by the lieutenant ended with this laconic sentence: "If you build laundress's quarters put them outside of the fort."

The fort was officially established in September, 1866, but only construction troops and transient escorts for the stage road were there. It was not until January, 1867, that the garrison arrived—the 95 men of Company M, 7th Iowa Cavalry.

Ten men under a sergeant were outposted 63 miles southeast at Yankton, the supply depot for the post. This was also the closest source of recreation, a fact that made the entire post wonder when the Yankton sergeant deserted in March.

With little to do but escort stages and battle the Dakota weather in message deliveries, the Iowans

SOUTHWEST CORNER of Fort James is shown in this 1866 sketch. Commissary and quartermaster building is on left, barracks on right. Each barracks room was designed for 20 men. Behind barracks, outside of stockade, was 82- by 20-foot building used as mess, kitchen, and storeroom. Fort burned in 1868, a year after Army left, "and the impression is that persons must have wantonly fired the place," contemporary newspaper article reported.

(National Archives)

INDIANS ONCE fired on fort from atop this bluff west of site. Although legend says firing was more in jest than to inflict harm, soldiers shot back. Bluff was beyond effective rifle range, so troopers rolled out howitzer. Single round killed one Indian, wounded another. Quartzite slab (foreground) helps locate vicinity of Fort James.

INDIAN AND soldier observing Fort James from atop nearby bluff suggests peace that prevailed during 1866-67 era of fort. Post went by several names before adoption of river's name: Camp near Firesteel Creek was used by headquarters; builders called it Fort Des Roche or Fort La Rouche after rocky area.

(South Dakota Historical Society)

were hard put to keep interested and out of trouble. The war was over and, as far as most of the Volunteers were concerned, so was the reason for staying in uniform.

The 70 regulars of Company F, 13th U. S. Infantry, relieved the Volunteers in May, 1867. A month later the new men were told that they, too, would be leaving; the post was to be abandoned in October.

JAMES RIVER no longer flows through barren plains that greeted first soldiers. Army's arrival stopped Indians from annually burning fields. Oldest trees in area date back to that 1866 period. Town of Rockport grew up around fort ruins in 1872. It became county seat, had newspaper, school, churches. Bachelors complained of female shortage—ratio was 10 to 1 in 1879—and suggested importing them. Town disappeared after it became Hutterite Colony in 1890.

TO GET THERE: From Sioux Falls go west on I-90 about 55 miles to Alexandria turnoff. Go west on county road from north edge of town. At 5 miles, turn south for 5.3 miles, then turn east for 2 miles. At bluff, drop down to first right. Pass through Hutterite Colony. Just past colony is site of fort on left side, between road and river.

FORT DILTS, NORTH DAKOTA

Providing a postscript to the history of the 1864 Sioux Expedition is the story of Fort Dilts. It is a tale of heroism and foolhardy speculation. Coming as it did immediately after General Sully claimed that the Sioux would never attack again, it probably helped to put the results of the expedition into proper perspective.

The story began in June, 1864, when Captain and Assistant Quartermaster James Liberty Fisk announced that he was going to lead a wagon train of emigrants to Idaho. A former private in the 3d Minnesota Volunteer Infantry, Fisk was commissioned in 1862 and successfully led trains to Oregon in 1862 and 1863. In the process he usually incurred the enmity of the Army "as he was both too reckless and too ignorant to be trusted," according to Major General John Pope, commanding the Department of the Northwest.

Regardless, when Fisk said he was going to lead another train, Pope directed that the Army commanders along the way "accompany and escort his train. . . . If you can spare a piece of artillery (without horses or men), please let Captain Fisk have it." Pope knew that Fisk's expeditions had Congressional approval, even though it was claimed that most of his emigrants were deserters and draft dodgers.

Fifty cavalrymen guarded the train as far as Fort Rice on the Missouri. Here Fisk attempted to exercise his Army rank to keep the escort with him. Signing himself with the awesome title of "Commanding North Overland Expedition for Protection of Emigrants," Fisk issued new orders to the escort commander.

"I call upon you to continue to perform for me, with the detachment you have, such scouting and guard duty as may be required from here to the mouth of the Big Horn," Fisk wrote. "You will provide yourself with 30 days' rations for 45 men, and be in readiness to start with me on Monday next, the 22d instant. What seems to me to be an absolute emergency impels me to make this demand, and I trust you will cheerfully comply."

The escort replied that their horses were "entirely

unfitted for a march of that distance" and, besides, they had specific orders from their commanding officer, "the ranking officer," not to continue.

The commander at Fort Rice mustered a 50-man detachment to stay with Fisk. Mainly men whom Sully had kept behind because of poor health, the detail was on poor mounts that Sully had rejected.

Boasting that with 50 men he could go any-where, Fisk headed straight west. About 165 miles from the Missouri, his rear guard was attacked and slaughtered by a band of Indians—survivors of the Bandlands Battle. Former Corporal Jefferson Dilts, a guide, died with three arrows in his body and six dead Indians sprawled around him.

The next day Fisk covered 10 miles before camping. The following morning he moved three more miles until the emigrants' pressure finally forced him into setting up a defense. Several oxen were harnessed to plows and a six-foot high, two-foot thick sod wall was erected outside the circle of wagons. The fortified corral was named after the heroic Dilts.

Fisk could see that his situation was serious.

FORT DILTS saga is told on this monument in center of shallow earthworks. When Fisk returned to Fort Rice, Army wanted to courtmartial him for "gross military offenses." Fisk's arrogant attitude did not endear him to Army, but his expedition was part of Congressionally approved and financed "Emigrant Overland Escort Service" administered by Secretary of War. Service's activities were curtailed and Fisk resigned nine months later. Unsuccessful in organizing privately supported expedition in 1865, he led his largest in 1866 with 160 wagons carrying 325 persons. At least 1,400 followed Fisk's routes between 1863 and 1866.

Sniping Indians hovered around. The bare Dakota plains could not support the animals, so Fisk broke into his meager bread and flour supplies to keep the stock from dying. The emigrants wanted him to turn back, but this would have spelled financial ruin to his enterprise. He was not about to do that.

Under cover of a storm the first night, the escort commander and 14 men were able to slip out for Fort Rice. Fisk told them to report "he was corralled and fortified, and was surrounded by Indians, and that he must be reinforced to enable him to go forward." The detail got to Rice after three days and nights of hard riding. Sully arrived the next day. Overcoming his anger at the news of Fisk's "folly of so small a party going into an enemy's country," Sully "thought it my duty to do all in my power to save them . . . on account of the women and children and my soldiers, if no one else, who were innocent."

Colonel Daniel J. Dill, the Fort Rice commander who had provided Fisk's escort, commanded the 900-man relief expedition. Fort Dilts was reached

MINNESOTA CAVALRYMEN and infantrymen who died defending emigrants are memorialized by these five markers, although bodies are elsewhere. Markers for Jefferson Dilts and two Iowa cavalrymen are near flagpole. Emigrants arrived here on September 5, 1864, three miles after moving from campsite where several of them left poisoned hardtack. Reportedly 25 Indian scavengers died from eating it.

LONELY FORT Dilts site probably is little changed from 1864 appearance. During siege, a letter was found on stake in front of fort. It was written by Mrs. Fanny Kelly, prisoner of Sioux for several months, who was told by Indians what to write—and then wrote what she wanted. Fisk offered to give Sioux two loaded wagons and teams in exchange for her, but deal fell through when Indians insisted on delivery before giving her up. Mrs. Kelly was returned to Army three months later because Sully refused to talk peace with tribes until she was freed.

after 10 days. Dill reported that the Indians had given up the siege and "Fisk told me that he had been trying to get the emigrants to break the corral and move forward, but he could not get them to do it."

"The emigrants told me that they never intended to move one mile forward without a strong escort," Dill added. He informed the train that he "had come to relieve them and escort such as wished to go back to Fort Rice to that point."

Fisk pleaded for two companies to take him through the Badlands "which he claimed would put him beyond danger." Dill, already having felt the bite of an unhappy Sully, "refused to grant any such request, knowing the folly and madness of such a move as that." Fisk announced he was going on without an escort even though only 20 emigrants said they would stay with him.

"After sleeping on the matter and finding that a number of the 20 had changed their minds and were going back with my command," Dill reported

that Fisk "concluded to return with them."

The 10-day trip was not without incident. Four days from Fort Rice, a small party of Indians charged through the picket line and made off with 15 horses. These, plus 15 oxen that were left along the way as they wore out, were Dill's main losses.

Dill had one more casualty. A muster revealed that a soldier of the 8th Minnesota Volunteers was missing. Apparently he had obtained whiskey from the emigrants at Fort Dilts "and became intoxicated the morning we left the corral and supposed to have laid down and left behind," explained Dill to strike a final sour note to the unhappy enterprise.

TO GET THERE: From Rhame, on U.S. 12 in the southwestern corner of North Dakota, go west 5 miles to a hard right turn onto gravel road. After 2.5 miles turn left onto single track dirt road. Site is on left side, 2 miles further.

CONTINENT AWAY, attack of Fort Sumter was felt in West.

(Harper's Weekly)

THE STORM GATHERS

"Outwardly everything is quiet in this country, but I know that there are many men on this coast who are traitors at heart, and who are at this moment writhing under the defeats of the rebels. They are harmless because so greatly in the minority now; but such men require close surveillance."
—Brigadier General George Wright, April 30, 1862.

THE shot at Fort Sumter started it all and was heard across the country. Often thought to be unconcerned with the Civil War, the West had a vital stake in its outcome and many effects during its progress.

Volunteers mustered in every Western territory were disappointed to learn that their services were more valuable in the West than on Eastern battlefields. Regular Army units were relieved by the Volunteers—with the few exceptions such as the San Juan Islands and part of San Francisco Bay—and sent Eastward. A famed "California Column" of Volunteers marched across the desert to insure that the Confederacy withdrew from Arizona and New Mexico.

A Federal government preoccupied with the Bull Run defeat and a Confederate menace to the capitol was slow in providing Indian annuities. This provided another reason for some tribes to fight the white again. Quick to realize the weakened defenses, some tribes took advantage; others, however, stayed true to their treaties and even aided the Volunteers in their work.

In Northern California, the commander decreed that hanging would be the penalty for Indians involved in depredations of the whites. Expeditions were mounted against marauding tribes in Eastern Oregon and Washington, in Wyoming and Nebraska, in Northern and Central California, in New Mexico and Arizona.

Many posts were abandoned and new ones established, often temporary and crude affairs erected "by the labor of soldiers at no expense to the government." The new camps, and none was more than a camp even though more elaborate titles were used, watched for both Indians and secessionists.

Many took the names of Civil War heroes or leaders. The result was several named after Brigadier General George Wright, the department commander on the coast; former Senator Edward D. Baker, killed early in the war; and Nathanel Lyon, the first general killed. Posts also were named for officers killed at the Battle of Valverde, Captain Alexander McRae, a cavalryman who fell while commanding the artillery; and Captain Benjamin Wingate, an infantryman.

The next few pages visit some representative Civil War Posts. Their temporary, transient nature reflects a pioneer West entering both a period of Civil War and the first days of a new era.

DETACHMENT MARE ISLAND, CALIFORNIA

"In view of the exposed and defenseless condition of the powder magazine at the Navy yard, Mare Island, California . . . I would most earnestly request that General Sumner may be instructed to locate a company of soldiers there, in the absence of Marines," wrote Secretary of the Navy Gideon Welles to Secretary of the Army Simon Cameron on September 21, 1861.

The outcome of the request was the four-month detailing of soldiers to perform the security missions of Marines at the Pacific Coast's most important Navy yard. Indications are that the naval assignment was not overwhelmingly successful.

The Army was the first to suggest that the Navy needed help at Mare Island. On May 9, Brigadier General Edwin Sumner offered the loan of a battery of light artillery to put the yard "beyond danger, or to move the temptations presented by its apparent defenseless condition." The next day the offer was modified when General Sumner came to the "conclusion that a company of foot artillery will form a better force for the yard than the light battery." He wrote the commandant that he would, "if the guard is wished by you, send the foot."

At first the Navy doubted the need for soldiers but the exchange of letters was passed to Washington. With many other reports on hand of Confederate designs in the West, the Navy's Secretary decided that help would be appropriate, just in

(Colonel Fred B. Rogers Collection)

USS INDEPENDENCE (foreground) was berthed at Mare Island from 1855 to 1906 as barracks for Navy Yard sailors and Marines. Soldiers also lived aboard from November 5, 1861, to March 14, 1862, finding hammocks, cramped quarters, and other novelties more uncomfortable than unusual.

case. His request of September 21 was the result.

The new yard commander, Navy Captain William H. Gardner was happy to receive soldier aid. Events of the summer had suggested there was some basis for concern. When he arrived in June, Gardner received a Pony Express message ordering him to relieve the captain of the USS St. Mary's not "allowing him to remain an hour on board than is absolutely necessary to enable you to place a loyal officer in his stead."

Several reports in August suggested that secessionists were plotting to blow up the yard's magazines, so Gardner erected a high picket fence around them. The Coast Survey steamer *Active* was anchored near the magazines, her guns at the ready.

A Sergeant Poe reported to the Navy Yard on November 5 with two corporals and 14 privates of the 3d Artillery. As far as the soldiers were concerned, the duty was a considerable improvement over the island of Alcatraz where the rest of their company was stationed. Ten more men arrived a few days later.

Swinging hammocks aboard the USS *Independence* was a novelty that soon wore thin. The sailless sailing ship that had been at the yard for six years as a barracks ship, provided quarters that were even more cramped than those at Alcatraz. Then, too, the troopers found the duties were neither less time-consuming nor more interesting. Round-the-clock guard posts were established around the magazines, duties not calculated to

ADMIRAL FARRAGUT supposedly lived in this house during early days after he started building Navy yard in 1854. Civil War hero of Mobile Bay, commander at time, found that available funds were inadequate for work after first month. Both Farragut and Naval Agent Richard Ashe borrowed on their personal credit to keep work going and workmen labored without pay in hopes that cash would arrive. California's senators brought yard's plight to Washington attention, resulting in arrival of first funds in two months along with reprimand for Farragut for using Congressional channels for relief. Reprimand apparently did not hurt his career; he became Navy's first full admiral in 1866.

arouse enthusiasm by their complexity or novelty.

The artillerymen realized that they had been better off on Alcatraz where, at least, they were able to work with cannon and occasionally respond to alarms. They were quick to agree when an Army inspector reported in January, 1862, that they were of little service at the yard.

Although the Navy may not have agreed at any suggestion that its discipline was questionable, the Army suggested to Gardner that the soldiers be returned to their company "where they could be brought under strict discipline."

Gardner agreed, "The guard as they are, without an officer, are, as you say, of little, if any real service in the protection of the public property." He said he could do nothing about relieving them, however, because the Secretary of the Navy had arranged for them to serve in the absence of Marines.

This situation resolved itself smoothly on March 7 when the *USS Lancaster* arrived for repairs. As soon as the Army learned that the ship had a large company of Marines aboard, the suggestion was made that they could relieve the Army detachment in the Marine mission of protecting the Navy yard. Gardner had the same idea. The day that the Army letter was received, he ordered Sergeant Poe to gather his troopers, march aboard the steamer *C. M. Webber,* and head for Alcatraz and home, "with many thanks for the services of the detachment."

REMINDERS OF PAST are in Mare Island gun park. Figurehead (left) of **USS Independence** aboard which Army detachment was stationed, dates from ship's launching in 1812. Figurehead and several guns in park are only traces left of former barracks ship. Dahlgren 10-inch smooth bore (right) is part of collection that includes guns from **USS Kearsarge,** that sank Confederate blockade runner off France in 1864, and two from Farragut's flagship at Mobile Bay. Naval guns are offered to Army to protect San Francisco during Civil War, but absence of ground carriages was major problem.

TO GET THERE: Mare Island is in San Francisco Bay adjacent to Vallejo, California, which is about 25 miles north of San Francisco on Interstate 80. Enter Navy Yard by Tennessee Avenue. Permission must be obtained prior to visit due to security restrictions.

BUILT IN 1857, this is one of several magazines around which soldiers marched in 1861-62. Marine detachment of five officers and 100 men left Washington in February, 1862, to relieve soldiers. Captured by Confederates, Marines were exchanged for $261,000, finally arrived in January, 1863. Workmen also provided protection by organizing 28-man "Mare Island Reserves," to fire yard's howitzers; two-company, 175-man "Mare Island Guards," as infantrymen; and eight-man sharpshooter squad. Earthworks and battery of two 24-pounders also were emplaced.

CEMETERY includes graves dating from 1850's, including that of daughter of Francis Scott Key. Six Russians were buried here in 1863. They died of injuries received when several hundred Russian sailors and Marines aboard ships being repaired at island, marched, singing, into San Francisco to fight fire that threatened city. Russians also had a victory while at Mare Island: a lieutenant married daughter of yard's commandant.

CAMP WRIGHT, CALIFORNIA

California's only Civil War battle was fought by Camp Wright troopers, but the honor is somewhat minimized because no shots were exchanged and the rebels were civilians. The affair bore a considerable resemblance to other secessionist disturbances in the state except that Confederate agents were involved and Dixie was their destination.

Hardly a week after Camp Wright was founded on October 18, 1861, Major Edwin A. Rigg, commanding, was alerted that 40 rebel sympathizers were heading his way. Their leader was former State Legislator Dan Showalter, admitted secessionist who recently had killed a fellow assemblyman in a duel over politics. His disappearance after the duel was explained by common gossip that he held a Confederate commission and was on his way to Dixie.

On October 27 Rigg dispatched an 11-man patrol "to intercept someone passing out through here," but no one was found. Faced with the possibility of attack, Rigg decided to test the alertness of his new garrison. He was not disappointed.

"At 1 o'clock this morning I had an alarm," he wrote Colonel James H. Carleton at Los Angeles; "the long roll was beat, and with every soul in camp, ignorant of such an intention, the companies were under arms in good order in eight minutes... I was very much pleased with their conduct, and am satisfied that they are ready at a moment's warning for service."

After dusk on October 28 Rigg was told that a party of 16 to 20 men was nearby. A 50-man detail was sent "to hem them in" while a 20-man contingent "crossed above them to close in on them and capture them." The opponents turned out to be several stray horses.

When Rigg was informed that two Confederate groups already had made their way out of California, he knew that it was vital to capture Showalter for both political and morale purposes. The previous parties had included Albert Sidney Johnston, former commander of the Pacific Department, and Judge David S. Terry. The surviving half of the 1859 Broderick-Terry duel, Terry had gathered recruits for Dixie as he made his way into Arizona.

"If any party... attempt to pass you," Rigg was directed, "stop it, search the persons and baggage if you suspect them of being enemies of our country, and cause them to take the oath of allegiance to our Government. If you find upon them evidence of their being disloyal, hold them in confinement... We have had enough of the bullying and treason of such men... Keep your own coun-

OAK GROVE Stage Station was where Camp Wright moved in early December, 1861, because wind near Warner's Ranch "blows in a perfect gale (not a moderate breeze) more than half the time, driving the dust in clouds, and blinding the eyes of everyone, and infiltrating into every coffee pot, camp kettle, water bucket, etc.," surgeon reported. Food could not be cooked because wind put out fires. Gales blew down all tents and tipped over tables and inkstands so that company reports could not be written. Stage Station was used as hospital and officers' quarters at Oak Grove camp.

sel; act with great circumspection, but with great firmness."

A month of observing Carleton's directive to "keep a sleepless vigilance," was rewarded on the morning of November 27. A civilian brought in a letter that he had been asked to deliver but, as the recipient was missing, he had read instead. Reference to a group of 18 at Temucla, 20 miles away, left little doubt that the waiting was almost over.

Several detachments were sent out. A cavalry patrol under Lieutenant C. R. Wellman learned that the Confederates were hiding at the ranch of John Minter.

Taken by surprise early on November 29, Showalter and company knew it was too late to fight. They tried to bluff, as Carleton predicted they would. Showalter, in particular, refused to be taken to Camp Wright, preferring instead to "take the consequences." He agreed to go without a fight after Wellman promised that the party would be freed if no evidence of disloyalty could be found.

Rigg questioned each of the 18 prisoners and received from each a statement of pro-Union sentiments and a sworn oath of allegiance. Despite this, Rigg told Carleton, "there is no doubt but every one of them is a rank secessionist, and are on their way to lend aid and comfort to the enemy."

CROSSROADS OF Southern California branched off here in three ways: to Los Angeles, San Luis Rey, and San Diego. Site of Camp Wright after it was moved an eighth of mile to high ground nearer Warner's Ranch in November 1861, was passed by Army as early as Kearney and Cooke expeditions of 1846-7. Both forces rested here after crossing desert. "A poor location," Kearney officer wrote, "with a hot spring and a cold one." Camp Wright commander was less tactful 15 years later: "Climate is unfavorable, very windy, with hot days and cold nights, and in winter said to be very inclement and unhealthy."

"They now regret that they did not resist," Rigg added. "If they had they would have given us a hard fight ... They have pack-mules and are well fitted out, and a desperate set of men."

The papers found on the party convinced Rigg that they planned to do more than just head south into Mexico. All were arrested while Rigg awaited instructions from Carleton.

It was not until December 13 that orders were issued for the prisoners to be marched to Fort Yuma. By this time, Rigg also had been transferred to Yuma. The new Camp Wright commander was complaining that his 118-man garrison was "rather a small force for our situation, having 20 secession prisoners to guard." His concern was increased by a reliable report from San Bernardino that a party of 75, "armed with shotguns and revolvers ... intend to attack your camp at night ... in order to release Showalter and party."

The rescue plot was abandoned. The Showalter party was taken to Fort Yuma by soldiers whose instructions from Carleton included: "You must be on your guard against attempts to rescue these prisoners, and against their rising on and overpowering them men set to guard them. There must be no escape and no rescue."

The prisoners spent six months at Yuma fairly quietly, except for two men who had to be chained after trying to escape. When their release was directed, the party was given back their property and the loan of transportation. In this fashion, and on his promise not to steal the borrowed horses and equipment, Showalter once again passed Camp Wright. His destination was the same as before, Dixie, but this time Showalter made it in time to serve as a Confederate regimental commander.

TO GET THERE: From San Diego take U.S. 80 east to State 79, about 40 miles. Turn left (north). Stay on State 79 for about 40 miles to intersection with San Felipe road. From this point, sites of first two Camps Wright are to left in valley. Continue north on State 79 about 16 miles to Oak Grove site, marked on left side.

CAMP WRIGHT marker claims post was abandoned in 1866, but records indicate no permanent garrison was assigned after Carleton's California Column took troops from it in May, 1862. Tents were pitched under trees at edge of nearby meadow which had 60-foot pine flagpole in its center. This was where Company A, 1st California Infantry mutinied in February, 1861, when all of its privates but one "refused to obey the order this morning to 'drill with their knapsacks on,'" commanding officer reported. Carleton wrote C.O., "Give them one hour to reflect on the consequences of their conduct" then discharge hold-outs without pay. All but 13 obeyed. Guardhouse terms were awarded to holdouts.

171

CAMP CHEHALIS, WASHINGTON

The early days of the Civil War revealed to the Army that the fastest way to be appreciated was to move away. Not that this was any news, for every departure of troops from established forts always had generated storms of protest.

Resistance was not expected at Chehalis, however, a post singularly free of Indian problems during its first year. Founded on February 11, 1860, at Gray's Harbor, the post was "for the protection of the growing settlements in that wild and isolated portion of this Territory," according to Anson G. Henry, surveyor-general of the territory. With both children and grandchildren living at Gray's Harbor, Henry had asked in 1859 that the Army establish the fort.

At first there had been no actual Indian incident to prove the need for troops. Glenn Peterson minded his own business when he was the solitary settler at what he called "Peterson's Point," but the arrival of settlers made some changes. The place was renamed Westport and pressure for Army protection was started.

After the Army arrived, little was heard of Indian troubles until rumors that the post was to be abandoned. Petitions arrived at headquarters to describe "the general hostility of the Indians" and tell of two houses being broken into, property being stolen, and settlers being run off by Indians.

Colonel George Wright, department commander, "had thought of discontinuing the post of Chehalis

(National Archives)

FORT CHEHALIS, as this sketch is labeled, never was officially designated other than as Camp Chehalis, but both terms appear in records. Matching plat, buildings are, left to right, lieutenant's quarters, storehouse, guardhouse, barracks, and commanding officers' quarters. Hospital was planned if post became permanent.

in the spring," his adjutant told the commanding officer, "but in view of the fears of the settlers he judged it expedient that a post be maintained there for some time yet." Wright was quoted as favoring changing the name to Fort Chehalis, but not increasing its size from Captain Maurice Maloney's Company A, 4th Infantry.

Maloney was the founder of the post, locating it on "the only place where buildings could have been put to advantage," he reported. He added that more than logic entered into his choice. It was also free, the gift of Thomas Jefferson Carter, and headquarters was provided with a statement from Carter in which he conveyed the property to the United States "without any emoluments for the same."

Maloney reported that Carter would be happy to provide a deed, too, but had a problem: the area was considered Indian land and Carter could not properly give a deed until his claim was recognized.

As soon as he had Carter's written permission, regardless of its degree of legality, Maloney set to work on a post. Two officers' quarters, one barracks and a storehouse were built at government expense. The soldiers added a small guardhouse of logs to take care of the occasional disciplinary cases. The year 1861 opened with the guardhouse occupied by two men of the 40-man company.

Despite Wright's assurance that the post would be maintained, orders came in June, 1861, to abandon the post. Everything movable was taken away on the reasonable assumption that the post's history had ended. Its career had been short, too short even for a decision to be rendered on changing the name to Fort Chehalis.

A month later, seven affidavits submitted to the

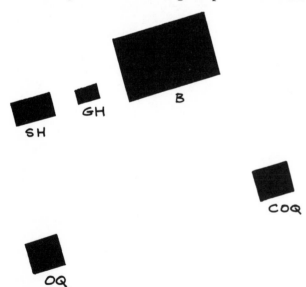

PINE TREES surrounded Camp Chehalis on three sides, with open area in front. Barracks had two large rooms (24 by 42 feet) heated by fireplaces, long porch across front with 12-foot square rooms at opposite ends, and four rooms in rear. Upper half story provided storage. Building was 84 feet long, 50 feet deep. Commander's quarters measured 32 by 43 feet, had six rooms; lieutenant's residence was 15 by 24 feet with four rooms. Storehouse, 40 by 20 feet, included small office. (Redrawn from plat in National Archives.)

CAMP CHEHALIS was in this vicinity and perhaps its buildings looked something like this modern-day Coast Guard station near entrance to Gray's Harbor. Abandoned in late summer, 1861, camp reappeared in Army correspondence in 1868 when it was learned that a caretaker was receiving $50 monthly "simply to look after the buildings." Headquarters had no record of post ever existing and recognized legal problem might occur if buildings were sold without proof of Army ownership. Given choice between selling them or continuing to pay for their care, Army chose former course without much delay.

governor of Washington announced, "The savages have assumed an attitude of hostility, and in some cases have caused the settlers to abandon their farms. Great fears are entertained of further violence."

This was surprising information to the Army. On August 6 a 12-man detachment was sent to the abandoned site with instructions to investigate the complaints. The soldiers were directed to provide themselves with "the necessary camp equipage, including two tents, two axes, and hatchets . . . a small package of simple medicines, with directions for use in case of necessity," headquarters specified. Two weeks of provisions were to be taken and the men "should be prepared to bake their own bread."

Second Lieutenant Campbell D. Emory, fresh out of West Point, commanded the detail. His name was not new to the West Coast: his father, William H. Emory was the original designer of Fort Moore in Los Angeles. Both were to end the Civil War advanced in rank, the father a major general of Volunteers, the son a brevet lieutenant colonel and aide to General George Meade at Gettysburg.

From the territorial surveyor-general came complaints that 12 men were "just enough to provoke the Indians to hostilities, but not enough to afford protection to the settlements." Hinting that the

Army was parly responsible for settlers going to Gray's Harbor, Henry noted, "The establishment of the post promised them . . . an inducement to pitch their tents in that far off wild."

"The life of an innocent babe is not to be put in competition with the cost of supporting a company of soldiers," Henry argued. But his fears were ineffective that "savage barbarity . . . will stain the skirts of those that may have deprived them of protection."

Emory reported that he arrived on August 15. In the absence of the Indian Agent, who had promised to meet him, Emory used his own judgment as to the Indian menace. "The Indians in the immediate vicinity of Camp Chehalis do not number more than 30—men, women, and children," he reported. Another 50 in the general area he termed "peaceful in character."

Headquarters decided that the fears were more imagined than real. With news that the site was 35 miles away from a planned agency headquarters, the district commander's decision was made: "I do not believe that there is any absolute necessity for troops to be there for the present."

TO GET THERE: From Aberdeen, Washington, go west on State 105 about 19 miles to deadend a mile south of Cohasset. Turn right (north) for about 3 miles to Westport and Gray's Harbor lighthouse, approximate site of Camp Chehalis.

CAMP BAKER, OREGON

A continent away and nine months before the opening gun against Fort Sumter, pre-Civil War tension reached a peak at Jacksonville, Oregon, on June 9, 1860. Already seriously split by heated, whiskey-fed debates in its round-the-clock saloons, the dusty mining town was not the kind of place to watch silently while one segment forced its opinions on the other.

UNMARKED FOR many years after post was abandoned, Camp Baker site received this marker from Boy Scouts in summer, 1961. During Civil War post was source of security for area, occasionally also serving as prison for Southern sympathizers. Phoenix man was arrested in 1862 for "hurrahing for Jeff Davis and denouncing the government," according to newspaper, and was put in camp's guardhouse when he refused to take oath of allegiance . . . A few days "laying in the guardhouse" changed his mind and oath was taken. "After the wholesome physic had fairly settled his stomach, he was released." Although originally cavalry post, camp received artillery in January 8, 1862, and first 13 rounds were fired. Two men were injured in March when 13-gun salute was fired, spreading "a deep gloom all through the camp," soldier's diary noted.

Floating lazily in the summer heat over Main Street was the symbol that could ignite the town: the Stars and Bars. Southerners displaced from Virginia, Tennessee and Missouri were outspoken advocates of secession in "J'Ville." The new flag was their answer to the broken heads and jaws suffered by both sides in barroom exchanges.

Main Street was silent. The next step could start a shooting war—and no one wanted to cross the line.

Out from a knot of onlookers stepped the wife of Doctor Ganung. Looking neither left nor right, the little lady made her way to the flagpole.

After pulling down the flag, Mrs. Ganung turned and walked into the crowd. Not a sound could be heard. For some reason no one could take issue with the determined lady. The crisis passed.

But secessionist activities were to be centered in this southwestern Oregon camp throughout the Civil War, their pace mirroring the progress on the battlefields of the East.

"In this end of the state we are about evenly divided as to the national issue," commented Lieutenant Colonel Reuben F. Maury in March, 1862. A witness to Mrs. Ganung's flag incident, Maury could speak as an expert. He and his general store partner, Ben Davis, split up their Jacksonville business a few months before, Davis going south to back his uncle, Jefferson Davis, and Maury serving as one of the founding officers of the 1st Cavalry, Oregon Volunteers.

Maury started raising four companies of Volunteers in September, 1861, with the authority of the state's adjutant general. Captain T. S. Harris' company was full in six days and went into camp near Phoenix, nine miles southeast. Far enough away so they would not stir up trouble, the Volunteers still were close enough to step in if the secessionists got out of hand in Jacksonville.

"Capt. Harris' company of cavalry, numbering 80 men rank and file, left for their new quarters," reported Jacksonville's *Oregon Sentinel* on December 7, 1861. "The point selected is on Coleman Creek, within a short distance of Phoenix, and is said to be a beautiful spot, surrounded by shade trees, and well supplied with wood and water."

Other companies soon arrived at this post named after Lincoln's former law rival and good friend, Oregon Senator Edward D. Baker, recently killed as the Colonel of the 71st Pennsylvania in the Battle of Balls Bluff. An arrival on January 1, 1862, was Hobart Taylor, a member of Captain Sewell True's company and a diary keeper.

FOUNDED AFTER gold strikes in 1851, Jacksonville replaced miners' tents with many permanent buildings in time to fort-up in them during Rogue River War of 1855. Bruner Building (at rear, right picture), second oldest brick building in Oregon, protected women and children hiding behind its iron shutters with orders to "go down with the building before you open the door." Orth Building (right in right picture), built in 1872, was early funeral parlor, included meat market on ground floor, popular dance hall above. Tablerock Saloon (left picture), named after site of treaty ending Rogue River War, dates from 1859, had pool tables brought around Horn. Odd Fellows Hall, started in 1860 as general store, was synagogue before fraternity bought it.

"Arrived here in good trim," Taylor recorded, "found the officers very pleasant but the soldiers slightly inebriated. When the tattoo sounded, I repaired to the walls of a cabin to sleep—slept some and froze the balance of the night."

Conditions at Camp Baker were primitive. Taylor noted that in his log cabin barracks, measuring only 14- by 16-feet, lived 16 men in "eight bunks all up in good order, and as I am writing they are all in and at this time singing Nellie Gray—while I am perched on the upper bunk to keep out of the way."

Rations at the post apparently compared to the housing. "Our dinner consisted of a kind of soup, very good to the taste, and for drink we had some of the best of water served up in fine style," noted Taylor. Supper had a greater variety: "First, bread and meat and water spoiled by adding coffee to it; second, meat, coffee, and bread; third, coffee, bread, and meat."

The regimental quartermaster did his best to improve the situation until stopped abruptly by General George Wright in April, 1862. The department commander noted expenditures for "building quarters, hiring a clerk, etc., all of which is disapproved, and no such accounts or claims will be paid, and what is the most astonishing is that he has hired men to take charge of company horses. What is a cavalry soldier good for if he cannot take care of his horse?"

Wright also criticized the recruiting methods of the Oregonians. He said that too many new men had to be discharged when they arrived at Fort Vancouver "for various causes." He reminded the regiment that all recruits "should, in every case, be entirely stripped of their clothing and critically

MAIN STREET of Jacksonville was scene of secessionist activities until Army's influence was felt. One of town's newspapers, **Southern Oregon Gazette**, was banned from mails because it was "incendiary in character, abusive of the Government of the United States, and treason, open or lurking, in its articles." Masonic Hall (right), still active, was built on site of Eldorado saloon, favorite watering place for miners. Perhaps courage imparted here was with Jacksonville citizens when they joined Lieutenant Phil Sheridan to assist in Rogue River War. "They swaggered about our camp, bragged a good deal, cursed the Indians loudly, and soundly abused the Government for not giving them better protection," general wrote in **Memoirs**. "...The enthusiasm with which they started had all oozed out, and that night they marched back to Jacksonville." Volunteers had encampment at Camp Baker site in 1855.

examined by the surgeon . . . The man's declaration as to his soundness will not be taken." The objective was to assure "that a man is perfectly sound, free from disease, able-bodied, sober, and of good character and habits, before passing him."

Camp Baker was intended only to be a temporary recruiting center. Maury recommended that two companies be left at Baker to guard against Indian depredations, but in May was told to take his companies to Fort Vancouver. Mud slowed the move. A stampede by the horses also delayed matters, especially when they headed in Maury's general direction. "He could not stand the charge and took to a tree," commented Taylor.

Maury arrived at Vancouver to find that his recommendation had been partly approved; he should have left one company at Fort Baker. Urged by the Indian Superintendent, Company C of the 1st Oregon Cavalry was returned to the post under Major Charles S. Drew " for the protection of the inhabitants of that section of country from Indians."

Under the worst of circumstances—for they went unpaid for more than 16 months—the troopers manned the "few old buildings" until May, 1863, when a new post was built. This was Fort Klamath, 20 miles to the northeast.

A small detachment remained at Baker to watch for Indians and secessionists, and to forward supplies to Klamath. A newly organized infantry company stayed three months in 1865 until the roads opened up.

The site was abandoned completely in summer, 1865, and everything given up as being completely valueless.

TO GET THERE: Jacksonville is 4 miles west of Medford, Oregon, on State 238. Phoenix is 3 miles south of Medford at exit 5 from U.S. 99 freeway. Take Coleman Creek Road to Camp Baker Road. Turn right; marker and site are .9 mile west of intersection on left (south) side.

FORT BAKER, CALIFORNIA

Fort Baker was almost overwhelmed by the success of its first assignment, both overwhelmed and overcrowded. Ordered to gather the Indians for movement to reservations, the garrison was outnumbered with 217 prisoners by August, 1862.

The prisoners were the results of a series of successful patrols in Northern California's mountainous forests between the Mad River and "Van Dusens Fork of the Eel River." A temporary post built by the soldiers with whatever was available, Fort Baker was one of three camps founded in March, 1862. Definitely it was not designed to house an assembly of prisoners. The problem was recognized before things got out of hand and the prisoners were moved to the coast.

Baker's problems were waiting for it, as the first commander, Captain Thomas E. Ketcham of the 3d California Volunteer Infantry's Company A, found upon arrival. On April 3, 1862, he described one of them to the district commander.

"I deem it my duty to report to you that a party of whites (citizens) have been out hunting Indians in the vicinity of Eel River, and they say that 17 bucks were killed by the party and the women and children were turned loose," Ketcham wrote. Other citizens, he added, made a living "of killing the bucks wherever they can find them and selling the women and children into slavery."

"One person is said to have made $15,000 last season in the business," the captain charged, at an average price of $37.50 apiece.

During Baker's 20-month history the activities were so intense that little more was said of the slave trade. The post was considered the most important pivot of operations against the Indians in its district and captured 750 of the 835 Indians sent to the reservation during its history.

The post's first successful patrol started on April 23, 1862, with Ketcham taking 25 troopers to a ranch which Indians reportedly had fortified "by felling trees around it." The "fort" was reached in three days, but the Indians had left. A day later the hostiles were found encamped in a ravine. In the fight that followed, three bucks and one squaw were killed and 24 women and children captured. Three Indians escaped.

Ketcham apologized for the death of the squaw, who had been mistaken for a man. He also appealed for the lives of two captured boys, "respectively 16 and 18 years of age, who were found secreted after the firing ceased, and were without weapons," he explained. "... I would respectively request that their lives be spared as it would likely have a tendency to induce others to surrender."

The intensity of operations did not reduce Indian depredations immediately. In July, 1862, four settlers were attacked while moving a herd to town. The soldiers arrived to find one body had been stripped of its clothes, the throat slashed, and the heart cut out.

Humboldt County natives of Company A, 1st Mountaineer Battalion, took over Fort Baker in June, 1863, shortly after one of the garrison's most successful patrols killed 46 Indians.

Twenty tribesmen exacted a measure of revenge from the departing soldiers by ambushing their baggage train, killing one of the guards, and taking the trunks of two lieutenants. The losses included "full dress uniform ... three swords ... four sashes, a valuable gold watch," but not the quartermaster and commissary papers in one of the trunks. These were found discarded near the ambush spot.

TO GET THERE: From Eureka, California, go south on U.S. 101 about 20 miles to State 36. Turn left (east) about 25 miles to Bridgeville; about 14 miles past Bridgeville is Van Duzen Creek, general site of Fort Baker which has been obliterated by frequent flooding.

FOG SHROUDS Fort Baker's site "on a small flat from one and a half to two miles long, and about a half mile wide," according to first description. "The site of the camp is somewhat marshy, but well sheltered being on the west bank of the Van Duzen between high ranges of mountains running nearly north and south. It exhibits signs of having at some period been overflowed." Flooding was common; destructive 1964 damage still was evident when site was visited year later. Fort was abandoned in October, 1863.

FORT ANDERSON, CALIFORNIA

If the men of Fort Anderson expected the citizens to be grateful for the new post's first patrol, they were disappointed. A public meeting drew up two resolutions that charged the troopers with killing peaceable Indians which "will only bring upon us all the horrors of an Indian war," and ridiculed "the madness and folly . . . of attempting the subjugation of 3,000 well-armed Indians by a force of 25 soldiers."

The citizens charged a Fort Anderson patrol with "killing one old man and wounding another belonging to a ranch occupied by three male Indians who have always been of an inoffensive character."

Investigation suggested that the settlers were less than accurate in their facts. "The Indian spoken of as an old man was between 35 and 40 years of age," it was announced, and his death occurred when the three braves "attempted to escape after being fully warned of the consequences."

The Fort Anderson patrol had been tipped off that a band of 200 hostile Indians were at the mouth of Redwood Creek and "very properly went in pursuit of them," according to the report. The three Indians were noticed going in the same direction, so the soldiers arrested them to prevent the band from being alerted. The "old man" was

REDWOOD RANCH, so-called both from its location and building material, is near Fort Anderson site. On road between Fort Gaston, in Hoopa Valley, and coast, it was important way station burned by Indians in February, 1863. Humboldt **Times** reported, "Mr. Minor informs us that all his buildings together with such other improvements as could be burned, were destroyed last week by Indians. They finished their work on the north side of Mad River. From the head of Redwood Creek to its mouth not a building is left. Mr. Minor's house was the halfway house between Fort Gaston and Arcata." This was during period when Army had abandoned Fort Anderson.

killed and a second brave wounded in an escape attempt.

The absence of citizen appreciation did not deter the Fort Anderson garrison from its duties during the seven months of operation in 1862. When the Humboldt county natives of Company B, 1st Mountaineers, reestablished the post as "Camp Anderson" for eight months in 1864, they, too, were unmoved by their fellow citizens' feelings of gratitude or criticism.

On a wide, flat field next to Redwood Creek, Fort Anderson was charged with keeping the peace from that creek, on the south, to the Klamath River on the north. With the abandonment of short-lived Fort Lyon, established midway between Anderson and Fort Baker by the same order in February, 1862, Anderson's area of responsibility was moved south to meet that of Fort Baker.

The vast territory caused Captain Charles D. Douglas to complain, "I have my company in so many places that I have no force to scout with at present." He said that he "had but ten men able to do duty; the rest are sick."

Little sympathy was forthcoming, although district headquarters promised to return an 11-man detachment. "The colonel commanding regrets that he has no men to send you at present," the district adjutant wrote. ". . . You will furnish escorts from your post . . . for all trains with Government supplies, all military expresses, all U. S. mail riders, and so far as practicable for private trains . . So far as possible you will take care to keep always one-half of your effective men at the post."

Douglas took the 50 per cent rule to mean that the other half were to be busy patrolling. This they did with energy, despite the savage terrain that doubled the distance each patrol traveled—considering the up and down mileage.

Fifteen men on a scout in May, 1862, went for seven days without seeing a single Indian and then were attacked by 50 while eating dinner. Pursuit was futile when the forests swallowed up the hostiles.

A week later the patrol chased an Indian to a river which he crossed on a dike. He broke the dike so the troopers could not follow, but a fire fight was waged across the water, seven Indians being killed.

A number of ranches in the vicinity of Fort Anderson were provided with troop detachments until a series of massacres in August, 1862, showed the system to be unsuccessful. Whitney's Ranch, four miles from the post, was attacked on July 28. Whit-

IDEAL LOCATION for Fort Anderson has no traces of Army use, perhaps because of nature of construction. "The troops at this point are now busily engaged in building a temporary log storehouse and quarters," reported soldier correspondent in Humboldt **Times** in August, 1862, "with the view of staying here (which God forbid) all winter." Writer got his wish; his company left in fall, 1862, but spent winter at Fort Wright, experiencing violent snow storms. Many men froze limbs, "in many cases their shoes being torn from their feet," "and patrols ended with scraps of cloth wrapped around feet," according to official report.

ney, a soldier, and a hired man were killed while two other troopers and an Indian boy "bravely held the house (on which 50 bullet holes were afterward counted), continuing to return the Indians' fire till their departure," the official report said.

The next day two express riders were ambushed, but escaped to Fort Anderson with one man and a horse wounded. Two more ranches were attacked and burned the day after. The resident of one ranch was wounded and his wife and child killed.

The district commander, Colonel Francis J. Lippitt, decided to take matters into his own hands and led a company of the 2d California Infantry on a seven-day scout over 80 miles "fully equal to 140 miles over ordinary roads." No Indians were spotted, but there was one casualty when a member of the rear guard failed to answer a challenge and was shot by his sergeant.

After fall, 1862, Fort Anderson was not regularly garrisoned until February, 1864, when the Moun-

taineers arrived. Their wide-ranging patrols met little action, the few Indians remaining off the reservation being too wily by that time. A 10-man scout trailed signs of an Indian cattle drive in August, 1864, in the direction of the post, but noted that it left the trail two miles away in order to miss the Army.

A May, 1864, patrol thought it had captured six Indians, but were disappointed to be handed a pass that permitted the braves to return to their camp and talk other Indians into surrendering.

TO GET THERE: From Eureka, California, go north on U.S. 101 through Arcata to State 299. Turn right (east), go through Blue Lake, 7 miles. About 12 miles further east, gravel road branches off to left (north). Follow this for 4 miles to Redwood Creek, site of Fort Anderson.

FORT WRIGHT, CALIFORNIA

The Civil War battles at Fort Wright were more vocal than physical and usually were fought between the Army and the Indian Bureau. With few exceptions, tribesmen were on the sidelines.

The welfare of the redman was at stake at this post in Round Valley, Mendocino county, when soldiers were dispatched there in 1862. The situation seemed not unlike that of 1858 when troops first camped in the valley, their mission to keep the Indians pacified—and safe from the self-appointed state volunteers who blazed a massacre trail through Northern California.

A detachment of the 6th U. S. Infantry watched over the valley's Nome Cult Agency until 1860, at the same time supervising the cattle herds grazing there from the coast forts. No sooner did the soldiers leave in September, 1861, than rumors of Indian misdeeds filtered into headquarters.

In October, 1862, it was reported that squatters were forcing the Indians from their reservation lands. A quarter of the 2,000 Indians in Round Valley supposedly fled after 22 alleged Indian rustlers were massacred by whites. The Agency Supervisor reported he was fired on twice while in bed.

Captain Charles D. Douglas and his Company F, 2d California Infantry, were ordered to the

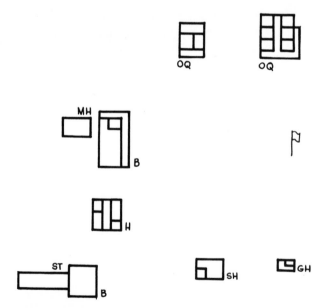

"ERECT BUILDINGS in such a matter as to afford shelter for the entire command in case of attack," founder of Fort Wright was ordered, "as, for instance, by connecting them together by a stockade work, which should be loopholed as well as the buildings." Keeping peace and providing detachments elsewhere left less than dozen men to work on post after doing other duties, but ultimately post took on this appearance. Most buildings were of logs, covered by clapboards, except for adobe barracks and one brick officers' quarters. (Redrawn from plat in Col. Fred Rogers collection.)

valley. This former garrison of abandoned Fort Anderson arrived in December 1862.

Douglas' first official act was to close the valley's only saloon. He was told that it was the "headquarters of the disloyal men of the valley, and to prevent trouble between my men and them just now I thought it was best to close the house," he reported. "The order was obeyed without a word."

Armed with a declaration of martial law, Douglas investigated the earlier reports. The results were not quite what he expected. Apparently the massacred Indians had been camping near the house of one of the Agency Supervisor's sons and everyone but the victims knew what was planned. One son loaned his pistol for use in the massacre, another son moved his family to his father's house "to prevent his wife from being frightened during the affray."

The settlers claimed that they killed the "wild and hostile band" in self defense to protect the peaceful occupants of the valley.

The matter of the supervisor being shot at by the settlers also had an explanation. The two shootings were not anonymous threats against the supervisor, Douglas found, but the work of two men who were unhappy: "because the supervisor took their squaws away from them."

Douglas' first report charged that the agency employees "were grossly neglecting their duties."

"I will here state that the mismanagement of Indian affairs in this valley has brought the Government into discredit, so much so that the settlers of the valley will not sell a pound of provisions without cash in hand," Douglas said. He added that one citizen pledged his personal bond so that the Indians could be given 2,500 bushels of corn to stave off starvation.

Charges followed charges in the next few months while Douglas did his best to protect the Indians and build quarters for his 70-man company. He said that the agent had no idea how many Indians were in his custody, but that this was not necessary because he did nothing for them anyway. The keys to the government storehouse were left with a squaw when the agent left on personal business, Douglas noted.

Every attempt by the Indians to better their lot was frustrated by the agent, Douglas explained. When they tried to build fences to protect crops from the settlers' wandering—and illegal—cattle, the Indians were assigned useless jobs elsewhere. "Utter neglect of duty" is how Douglas summed

"ROUND VALLEY is better adapted by location, soil, and extent for a large Indian reservation than any place I have seen in California," Captain Douglas reported. He added that it "contains, as surveyed, 25,000 acres of as fine land as can be found in the state." Marker at Inspiration Point, near entrance to valley, tells that it was discovered in 1854. Fort Wright—redesignated Camp Wright toward end of Civil War—was located in distant center of this picture.

up the Indian Agency's performance at Round Valley.

Convinced that the fault lay with the agency rather than the Indians and the settlers, in February, 1863, Douglas revoked martial law, except for the matter of selling liquor. For awhile he tried to concentrate on building his post, naming it Fort Wright after the department commander without regard for possible confusion with the Oak Grove Camp Wright.

A murder four miles north of Round Valley in April, 1863, took Douglas on one of the few patrols fielded by the garrison. He led 15 men out of the valley after dark, "to conceal my movements from the every watchful enemy," and marched a day through a driving snowstorm. Two stragglers from the pursued band of Indians were captured the

first night and the main camp was located the next morning.

"I endeavored to make them all prisoners, but could not, as they would not surrender, but fight," Douglas reported. "I therefore gave the order to fire and the entire party were killed, except two old squaws who gave themselves up. Six bucks were here killed, not one of the whole party getting away."

Douglas' methods were effective, but drastic, during the tour. He wasted no time when he learned that a barn burning in July, 1863, was the first step in a plot by the Ukie tribe "to kill all the white men they could, burn their property, and then go into the mountains."

One patrol killed four or five Indians who were routing settlers from their homes. Two Indians,

181

(Colonel Fred B. Rogers and Illinois Historical Society.)

FORT WRIGHT looked like this in 1870, dwarfed by both surrounding mountains and towering oak trees. Guardhouse was at far left, then commissary. Hospital was at left of flagpole, barracks at right. Officers quarters were under trees on right side of sketch. Post was one mile from Indian Agency. Troops were prohibited from visiting it and "no Indians or squaws are permitted to come within the limits of Fort Wright under any circumstances."

including the principal chief, were killed while trying to murder a settler. With the aid of testimony of both settlers and Indians, Douglas was able to identify the five leaders of the plot. In the presence of all Indians in the valley, the five were hung at the new Army post on July 21, 1863.

Douglas was convinced that his firm actions "will have a very good effect on the whole tribe," he explained. "It has already restored quiet among them."

The war with the agency continued, however. In September, 1863, Douglas evicted the Agency Supervisor and appointed another in his place. Soon he was told by headquarters to keep out of Indian Bureau business and to concentrate on preventing escapes from the valley. He responded that the agent never reported any escapes, and he was unable to learn of any because of rules against the troopers visiting the agency.

MODERN SITE of Fort Wright "is near the center of the valley on a high ground, never overflowed, handy to wood and water and to building materials," first commander reported," . . . and in a military and every other point of view by far the most desirable place in the whole valley for a military camp or post." Wright was alerted in 1864 to reported secessionist plot to capture "small force at Fort Wright with their arms, ammunition, and stores," but no attack came.

In April, 1864, the antimosity between agency and Army hit a peak. District headquarters was told to replace the garrison at Fort Wright with another company. The shift was postponed upon the request of the district commander, and then cancelled when the Indian Superintendent for California visited Round Valley. The Agency was reorganized. On the superintendent's recommendation, the fort's garrison was enlarged with a company of Native California Cavalry.

Finally in a position to keep the peace without undue problems with the Supervising Agent, Douglas and his men stayed at Fort Wright until May, 1866, when they were mustered out of service.

TO GET THERE: From Fort Bragg, California, go southeast on State 20 to U.S. 101 at Willits. Head north on U.S. 101 about 24 miles to Laytonville. Turn right (east) 12 miles to Del Rios; continue 16 more miles to Round Valley. Post was in northwest corner of valley.

WEATHER-BEATEN Covelo building dates from 1888, thirteen years after fort was abandoned and year after short reoccupation in 1887. Despite intention to reserve valley for Indians, settlers continued to move in. Congressional committee learned in 1884 that settlers occupied 95,000 of valley's 102,000 acres, reported that since 1873 government spent $241,000 on agency but buildings were in disrepair, herds reduced, and tribes generally demoralized. Settlers grazing illegal cattle on Indian lands, then selling beef to agency to feed actual owners of land, included some employed by agency during Civil War Army disputes.

FORT McRAE, NEW MEXICO

If the founders of Fort McRae had any doubt about its mission—that of protecting travelers on New Mexico's sand-blown "Journey of Death"—the doubt was dispelled enroute to the post's site.

On March 24, 1863, Major Arthur Morrison and Captain Albert H. Pfeiffer's Company H, 1st New Mexican Volunteers, were within 50 miles of the new site when they came upon a wounded citizen. He said he was part of a wagon train that had been massacred by 45 Apaches. Wounded three times, he had been taken for dead.

Morrison took 19 men in pursuit. At dawn on March 25 the detachment came across the 10 wagons, stripped of everything stealable. Within a seven mile radius, they found and buried seven bodies. Further pursuit over a cold trail was tried, but given up when the detail met a party of citizens. They, too, had been alerted by a wounded survivor and defeated by a useless trail.

After a two-day, 150-mile trip, Morrison rejoined the main column and continued to the Fort McRae location. With this graphic example of the threat fresh in their minds, little encouragement was needed to spur the troopers to work quickly in building the new post.

Fort McRae was one of several garrisons established during the Civil War for the dual purpose of protecting the travelers and keeping a close eye on who was traveling. With Army detachments overseeing the routes, secessionists either made lengthy detours in their travels or kept to the regular routes and hoped that they would not be recognized.

The soldiers soon found that the terrain features in the area were not designed to encourage or uplift the spirits of a weary traveler—or fort builder. The Post's mission was to protect travelers on the Jornada del Muerto—the Journey of Death. The

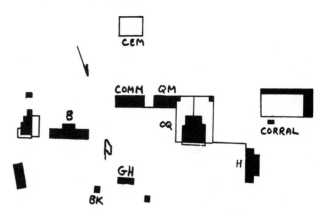

FORT McRAE, as drawn when it was abandoned in 1876, can be compared with contemporary sketch (below). All buildings except bakery were of adobe, dated from 1866 or later. Bakery was of pole jackals. Ruins on site suggest that adobe was on rock base. Barracks capacity was 80 men, though post was intended for one company each of infantry and cavalry. (Redrawn from National Archives plat.)

specific location of the post was midway in the main canyon through which Apaches drove their stolen stock to water at the Oso del Muerto—the Spring of the Dead. This was the source of Fort McRae's water. As the only spring on the 90-mile route, the Oso del Muerto was a frequent point of ambush until the Army arrived.

April 3, 1863, was the official christening date of Fort McRae. Ten weeks later Captain Pfeiffer and his family were the victims when the Indians demonstrated that they were yet to be influenced by

SOLDIER SKETCH of Fort McRae matches official ground plan, including barracks, 120 by 127 feet, left of flagpole, and guardhouse, in front of flagpole. This measured 44 by 18 feet, included guard room, prison room, and 10-foot square cell; in 1870 it averaged two prisoners of post's strength of about 80 men. Prisoners slept on bare boards. Cemetery, behind commissary, was surrounded by adobe wall, measured 60 feet square, included six California Volunteers who died at post. This view is to south-southeast from position 300 yards northwest of flagpole. (For opposite view, see page 7.)

(National Archives)

the new fort. Varying accounts of the unhappy incident are contradictory in their versions, so dependence is placed here on the *Official Records of the War of the Rebellion* and *Army Sacrifices*, a near-contemporary book by Civil War former Provost Marshal General James B. Fry, U. S. Army.

A 41-year-old Dutchman and veteran militiaman, Pfeiffer was also the victim of rheumatic pains. On June 20, 1863, he went to a warm springs eight miles from Fort McRae, hoping for relief in the medicinal waters. With him were his wife, two servant girls, a civilian, and a bodyguard of six New Mexican Volunteers.

The two men posted as sentinels were the first to die when the Apaches attacked. With the women as shields, the 15 or 20 Indians tried to kill the other men.

"Naked as he was," Fry recounts, "the captain, wounded as he ran, flew to his tent and seized his rifle." His wife dropped to the ground on Fry's order, and he shot the Indian behind her.

Pfeiffer tried to get help from the fort, but "the naked, bleeding, and half-crazed victim continued his flight, lacerated by thorns and stones, until he fell fainting in the brush," according to Fry.

Some of the soldiers broke away for help. Morrison mounted a 20-man pursuit with no success in finding the Indians. Mrs. Pfeiffer and the servant girls were found on the trail, badly wounded. Pfeiffer and the civilian also were found, both wounded. Mrs. Pfeiffer and one of the girls died, bringing the toll to four dead and three wounded.

Pfeiffer remained with his company, usually at its head in any scouts. A small touch of revenge for his loss entered into each victory Pfeiffer and his company scored later over the Indian.

Shortly after the massacre, Pfeiffer and the New Mexicans were reassigned from Fort McRae. The new garrison of Captain Henry A. Greene's Company G, 1st California Infantry, pressed the Indian so relentlessly that Greene was carried in the official reports as "the indefatigable Greene."

August, 1863, was busy for Greene. On the ninth he led 20 men on a 12-day, 400-mile patrol that attacked and routed the Indians and captured between 1,600 and 1,800 sheep. No sooner did he return from this affair than Greene took a lieutenant and 22 men 45 miles across the Jornada to make a midnight attack on an Indian camp.

Skirmishing through the underbrush followed until the Rio Grande was reached. Spotting an Indian jump into the water, Private George S. Dickey opened fire. The Indian turned and, as he was dying from his own wounds, fired the only Indian shot of the attack. Dickey fell, mortally wounded.

Morrison and 18 men started after Indian raiders in November. He took 13 men back to McRae after three days. Sergeant Rhodes, a corporal and three privates continued the pursuit for a total of 225 miles. When the patrol reached its objective, one Indian was killed, three wounded, and 150 sheep recaptured.

Recovering stock was a regular event for the McRae garrison. In September the "indefatigable Greene"—it was in this report that the adjective was

"A LARGE CORRAL in which 28 permanent mules, besides transient animals, are kept, is placed 40 yards to the southwest of the medical officer's quarters and hospital, and to the windward of both," surgeon reported in 1869. Stone walls of corral do not match sketches or plot, probably have undergone numerous changes under various owners since Army gave up reservation in 1884. Post herd was driven off in September, 1865, but most of stock was recovered by 20-man patrol under Lieutenant John Slater. Indians resisted with firearms and severely wounded three soldiers, including Slater. Detail was gone eight days, marched 275 miles.

used—took eight men and 18 citizens in recovering 10 cattle. In December, a three-day, 75-mile patrol recaptured 200 sheep, mules, and a horse were left behind by Indians who escaped in the dark. In the same month, Greene led a scout that killed five Indians and captured six, plus 19 head of cattle.

The history of Fort McRae continued through Company D, 1st California Infantry, and its successor, the 1st Battalion of California Veteran Infantry, until July, 1866, when the regular Army took over the post. Adobe buildings were rebuilt or added for the next 10 years of Army use until the post was abandoned in 1876.

TO GET THERE: Private property of Victorio Land and Cattle Company, permission to visit site should be obtained from both the current lessor and the Victorio main office in Bakersfield, California. Site may be reached by boat across Elephant Butte Lake—to McRae Canyon, and walking up it three miles to east— or by vehicle from Truth or Consequences, N. M. Take State 51 for 5.4 miles past Elephant Butte Dam to road intersection. Take right fork (toward Engle) 7.4 miles to dirt track on left. With permission in hand, turn left onto this road for about 4 miles overland past 7TX Ranch. When track disappears completely, continue on foot westward 1 mile down dry arroyo to site. This is dry weather route negotiable only by rough-duty vehicle.

ACKNOWLEDGMENTS

Much of the writing of *Pioneer Forts of the West* had to be done while the author was assigned aboard ship in the Mediterranean. This placed even greater dependence upon the many agencies and individuals that gave of their time to help the author.

He is particularly appreciative of the patience and encouragement of Rear Admirals Robert E. M. Ward and George Pressey USN; Commodore James F. Miller USN; Colonels William R. Burgoyne, Jr., and Bruce F. Meyers USMC; Lieutenant Colonel John L. Helms USA; Majors Richard Esau, Joseph Hoar, Sanborn Warner, George F. Bailey, and Roger Knapper USMC; Chaplains Robert Lang and Bernard Fillmyer USN; Captains Marshall Carter and John Randolph USMC; Lieutenants Tom Mills and William Quigley USMC; Sergeant First Class William Hanna USA, and Yeoman First Class William Hoge USN.

This volume has been dedicated humbly to two retired Army officers who once served at some of the posts covered in the series, and who have been unstinting in their interest and encouragement. The frequency with which their collections are credited with the loan of materials, and their works are cited in the bibliography, makes obvious the debt owed to Colonels George Ruhlen, San Diego, and Fred B. Rogers, San Francisco.

The National Park Service continued to extend maximum cooperation, especially through the help of Robert Utley, Roy E. Appleman, Charles W. Porter III, Jack McDermott, William Brown, Don Rickey, Jr., Charles Snell, John A. Hussey, Michael Becker, Erwin Thompson, Ben Levy, Frank Smith, Edwin Bearss, Jon Montgomery, Robert A. Murray, Dale Giese, Earl G. Harris, Richard L. Holder, Charles L. Peterson, Jess Toth, Harold L. Peterson, and Andrew M. Loveless.

Despite its reorganization, the National Archives still is the primary source of material for the series. Mrs. Sara Jackson has been of particular help, as have Elmer O. Parker, Victor Gondos, Jr., and Garry D. Ryan, Old Military Records Branch, and Milton K. Chamberlain, formerly of that branch; John Porter Bloom, Territorial Papers; May E. Fawcett and Josephine Motelywski, Visual Aids; A. P. Muntz and Pat McLaughlin, Cartographic; Jane F. Smith, Social and Economic Branch; Burford Rowland, Legislative Records.

The task of interpreting the many contradictions and confusions of the "Friendly War" extended from British Columbia to Great Britain. Research in London was patiently done by Gillian Knudsen, assisted by R. F. Monger (Public Records Office) and Helen Phillips (National Maritime Museum). The Royal Marine story was looked into by Captains Nigel Estlick, A. J. Donald, and A. R. Murray, Royal Marines. In North America, help and guidance came from Willard E. Ireland and Inez Mitchell, British Columbia Archives; Robert D. Monroe, University of Washington Libraries; John Hussey, National Park Service in San Francisco; Paul Reitan, at English Camp; and Colonel V. J. Gregory USAF, Port Townsend, Wash.

Fellow members of the Westerners, the Western History Association, the Council on Abandoned Military Posts, and the Company of Military Historians provided much information and many hints.

Military Historians helping were Col. John Magruder and Henry I. Shaw, Marine Corps, and Charles Romanus, Office of the Chief of Military History. Many tips came from Robert Frazer and Father F. P. Prucha, who braved the New Mexico deserts with the author to see forts they have written about in their own fort books.

Material was loaned freely by Lee Myers, Carlsbad, and Marvin King, Arenas Valley, N.M.; Thomas R. Havins, Brownwood, Leavitt Corning, Jr., San Antonio, Jack L. Baughman, Corpus Christi, Walter Knorr, Hondo, J. P. Ephraim, D'Hanis, and Major General George Ruhlen USA, Fort Hood, Texas; Tom Patterson, Mrs. Susie Fountain, Blue Lake, L. Burr Belden, San Bernardino, Calif.; Harriet Moore, Oregon State University Archives, Corvallis; David Blumberg, Miami; Albert Salisbury, Seattle; Francis P. Farquhar, San Francisco; Lloyd Clark, Phoenix, Ariz.; and Fred M. Mazzulla, Denver Colo.

Here, by agency or state, are many others who helped.

Bureau of Indian Affairs: Merrill Tozier. *Gilcrease Collection:* Paul Rossi. *Geodetic Survey:* W. B. Sears and T. R. Custidero. *William and Mary Library:* James Servies. *Marine Corps Education Center Library:* George Mahoney and Mrs. Evelyn Daniels; *Northwestern University:* Florence Stewart; *Denver Public Library:* Alys Freeze. *Bancroft Library:* John Barr Tompkins. *Colorado State Historical Society:* Mrs. Enid Thompson, Mrs. Alice Wallace, Mrs. Kathleen Pierson, Mrs. Laura Eckstrom.

Arizona Pioneers Historical Society: Sidney B. Brincherhoff, Mrs. Yndia S. Moore, Mrs. W. W. Alderson. *Historical Society of S. California:* Mrs. Margaret J. Cassidy. *Yale University Western Collection:* Archibald Hanna. *Museum of New Mexico:* Bruce T. Ellis, Mrs. J. K. Shishkin. *New Mexico Bureau of Mines:* Doctors Robert Bieberman and Robert Weber. *New Mexico Magazine:* George Fitzpatrick; *Westways Magazine:* Patrice Manahan.

Oklahoma State Library: Mary O. Carnahan; *California Beaches & Parks:* Carroll D. Hall (Sutter's Fort), Cliff M. Bisbee (Sonoma), Louis Wakefield (Ft. Tejon), Robert W. Reese (Monterey) and Wayne Colwell (Petaluma, formerly Ft. Ross). *South Dakota Historical Society:* Col. Will Robinson. *North Dakota Historical Society:* Ray Mattison. *California State Library:* Allan R. Ottley. *Idaho Historical Society:* Merle Wells.

State Historical Society of Missouri: Mrs. Elizabeth Comfort, Mrs. Oliver Howard. *Missouri Historical Society:* Mrs. Fred C. Harrington, Mrs. Ruth K. Field. *Nebraska Historical Society:* Donald Danker. *Nevada Historical Society:* Mrs. Clara Beatty. *Oklahoma Historical Society:* Mrs. C. E. Cook. *Oregon Historical Society:* Priscilla Knuth. *Utah Historical Society:* John James. *Washington State Library:* Hazel E. Mills. *Washington State Historical Society:* Anna M. Ibbotson.

The staffs of the Confederate Museum, Library of Congress, Army War College, Newberry Library, Chicago Historical Society and Smithsonian Institution.

Arizona: Ethel Wright and Fred Kuhn, Quartzsite; Kermit M. Edmonds. Mohave Pioneers Historical Society, Kingman. *California:* Msgr. James T. Booth, San Diego Mission; Gerry F. MacMillan, Jerry Schmidt, Mrs. Pearl Lyng (Title & Trust), San Diego; Russell E. Belius, Los Angeles Co. Museum; Ted Garlington, Redding; Mary Pardine, Ft. Bragg; Alto Broggen, Scott Valley; Ethel M. Solliday, Esther Chambers, Monterey; Elbridge Ackley, Laura Pawlus, Bridgeville; John French, Sacramento; R. R. Emparan, William Wetsel, Sonoma; Major R. A. Huntzinger, Captain James Cooper, Lieutenant Earl Rutledge USMC, Mare Island.

Colorado: Edward Bollinger, Ft. Vasquez. *Idaho:* Herbert LeClair, Ft. Hall Tribal Council, Sen. J. Cecil Sandberg, Blackfoot. *Missouri:* Clarence Burton, Ft. Osage. *Nebraska:* Hollis Lamprecht, John Svoboda, Max Coffey, Omaha; Fred W. Penick, Lewellen; Edith Neale, Ft. Calhoun. *New Mexico:* William Mayes, Darlene Lewis, Silver City; Ruth Shaffner, Ft. Wingate; W. Baskin, Gallup; Mr. and Mrs. Carl Hays, Columbus; S. H. Binder, Hurley; Horace Bounds, San Lorenzo; P. W. Christiansen, Mrs. Helen G. Stander, Socorro; Mr. and Mrs. J. Paul Taylor, Mesilla. *Oregon:* Mary L. Hanley, Jacksonville; A. Hindinbisher, Port Orford; Barbara Unger, George DeCloedt, Gardiner; Gene W. Tombe, Siuslaw National Forest.

South Dakota: W. O. Johnson, Ft. Pierre; Carl Norberg, Sioux Falls; David Waldner, Rosedale Colony. *Texas:* James P. Kelley, Laredo; J. Carroll Putman, Cp. Cooper; Ellis Letcher, Benny Rodriquez, Samuel J. Zerr, D'Hanis; Ben E. Pingenot, Harvey Seymour, Eagle Pass; Francis Barger, Mrs. Lucille A. Boykin, Dallas; J. E. Ferguson, Doris Miller, Coleman. *Utah:* Mrs. Myrtle Erickson, Fairfield.

Washington: Joseph Bailey, Paul Thiele, William Eaton, Port Townsend; Shirley Payne, Bellingham; Mrs. Carl Johnson, W. N. Pinkston, Sr., Coupeville; Don Mason, Chehalis; Spurgeon Calhoun, Whidbey Island; James McCash, Lewis County Historical Society; E. M. Weatherell, Tacoma. *Wyoming:* Norman Palm, Elk Mountain.

And, of course, the typing and proof help of Dale and Paula Burmeister, Elaine McDermott, and the author's wife, Teresa.

BIBLIOGRAPHY

To conserve space, certain abbreviations have been used in this bibliography of sources for this volume of the *Forts of the Old West* series.

Only the author's last name and first" initial are given. Titles are shortened by dropping most articles. Places of publication are dropped when they are obvious.

The following abbreviations are used:

Cities: Albuquerque, *Alb;* Caldwell, Idaho, *Cwl;* Chicago, *Chi;* Denver, *Dvr;* District of Columbia, *DC;* Glendale, Calif., *Gdl;* Harrisburg, Pa., *Hbg;* Indianapolis, *Ind;* Los Angeles, *LA;* New Haven, *NH;* New York City, *NY;* Norman, Okla., *Nm;* Philadelphia, *Phil;* Portland, Ore., *Port;* Saint Louis, *StL;* Salt Lake City, *SLC;* San Diego, *SD;* San Francisco, *SF;* Santa Fe, *SFe;* Seattle, *Sle.*

Government Sources: RG, Record Group in National Archives; *NA,* National Archives, Washington, D.C.; *PRO,* Public Record Office, Chancery Lane, London W C 2, England; *QMG,* Quartermaster General; *NPS,* National Park Service.

Other sources: NMM, New Mexico Magazine; *NMHR* New Mexico Historical Review; *TW,* True West Magazine; *FT,* Frontier Times magazine (old or new series); *SW,* Southwesterner newspaper; *GW,* Golden West magazine; *West,* The West magazine; *WW* or *TT,* Westways or Touring Topics, AAA, Los Angeles; *HSSC,* Historical Society of Southern California; *WTex,* West Texas Historical Society *TSHQ* Texas State Historical Society; *SDHS,* South Dakota Historical Society; *Wtr,* Westerners; *Wi-Y,* The Wi-Iyohi bulletin of SDHS; *Mont,* Montana magazine.

OFFICIAL GOVERNMENT SOURCES

Adjutant-General. *List of Military Posts, etc. . . . to Present Time.* DC. 1902.
————. *Outline Index of Military Forts & Stations.* RG 94, NA. 27 vol.
Brown, W. *Santa Fe Trail.* NPS SFe. 1963 (draft).
————. *Cattlemen's Empire* (Suppl. Rpt.). NPS SFe. 1963.
Foreign Office. *General Correspondence, America, United States of.* Series II, Vols. 1466-1474. PRO London.
Foreign Office. *Letters.* Vols. 15-17. PRO London.
House of Representatives. *Permanent Fortifications, Sea Coast Defenses.* 37 Cong. 2d Sess. No. 86. DC 1862.
Inspector-General. *Outline Description of Posts & Stations of Troops . . . in US.* MGen R. Marcy, I-G. DC. 1872.
Lattimore, R. *Fort Pulaski.* NPS DC. 1954.
Mansfield, Col. J. *Inspection Reports.* 1858-59 in NA.
Mare Island Naval Shipyard. *Historical Summary.* 1965.
McCall, Col. G. *Reports of Inspections of Posts, Dept. of New Mexico. 1850.* RG 108, NA.
————. *Reports of Inspections of Posts, Dept. of Pacific. 1852.* RG 108, NA.
Military History, Office of Chief of. *Fort* card & correspondence files. DC.
Miller, Hunter. *Treaties & Other International Acts of the USA.* DC. 1948.
Swords, Maj T. *Report of Inspections of N.M. QM Dept.* House Exec. Doc. No. 2, 32d sess. DC. 1851.
Missouri, Military Div. of. *Outline Descriptions of the Posts.* MGen P. H. Sheridan, cmdg. Chi. 1876.
National Archives. *Preliminary Inventory of Records of Army Posts 1813-1942.* RG 98. DC. 1949.
National Park Service. *Ft. Clatsop.* DC. 1963.
————. *Historic Site Inventory of Military Forts in Western Regions.* SF, Omaha, SFe. 1958-64.
————. *San Juan Island National Historical Park, a Proposal.* SF 1964.
————. *Soldier and Brave.* NY. 1963.
Navy Department. *War of the Rebellion: Official Records of Union & Confederate Navies.* DC. 1894-1927. 2 series, 31 vols.
Pacific, Mil. Div. *Outline Description of Pacific Military Posts.* MGen I. McDowell, cmdg. SF. 1879.
Pacific Station. *Reports of the Commander-in-Chief, In-Letters. 1859-72.* PRO London.
Snell, C. *American and English Camps.* NPS SF. 1961.
Quartermaster-General. *Outline Description of Forts & Stations 1871.* QMG M. C. Meigs. DC. 1872.
————. *Revised Outline Descriptions of Posts & Stations of Troops in Military Division of Pacific.* LtCol R. O. Tyler (ed.). DC. 1872.
————. *A Pictorial History of Housing in Army.* DC. 1927.
————. *Report of Inspections* by BvtBGen Rusling. NA. 1866-67. 2 vols.
————. *Affairs in Utah & the Territories,* from BvtBGen Rusling's Report. House Misc. Doc. 153, 40th Cong., 2d sess. DC. 1868.
————. *Expenditures for Barracks & Quarters.* House Exec. Doc. 93, 35th Cong. 2d sess. DC. 1859.
Surgeon General. *Reports on Barracks & Hospitals with Descriptions of Military Posts.* J. S. Billings (ed). Cir. No. 4. DC. 1870.
————. *Report on the Hygiene of the U.S. Army with Descriptions of Military Posts.* J. S. Billings (ed). Circ. No. 8 DC. 1875.
War, Dept. of. *Official Records* in NA for various posts and commands, including *Letters Sent, Letters Received, Medical History, Muster Rolls,* etc. In addition to spot checking those of the 2d and 4th U.S. Infantry and Brackett's Minnesota Battalion, many post files were scanned and the following searched in detail: Cp. San Elizario, Tex.; Ft. Conrad, N.M.; Cp. Rancho del Jurupa, Calif.;

Ft. Decatur, Wash.; Ft. Grattan, Nebr.; Cp. Edwards, Ft. Dakota, and Ft. James, S.D.; Cp. Chehalis, Wash.
War, Secretary of. *Annual Report.* DC. 1849-92.
————. *War of the Rebellion: Official Records of Union & Confederate Armies.* DC. 1880-1897. 4 series. 128 vols. Atlas.
Whittier, BvtBGen. C.A. Selected *Inspection Reports, 1866.* NA RG 159.

OTHER SOURCES

Adams, E. *To & Fro, Up & Down.* Cincinnati. 1888.
Alexander, T. & Arrington, L. *Utah Military Frontier 1872-1912.* Utah Hist. Qtrly. 1964.
Anderson, C. *Trails of Early Utah.* Cwl. 1940.
Angel, N. *History of Nevada.* SF. 1881.
Ankeny, L. *Salmon Falls Massacre.* FT 1961.
Armes, Capt. G. *Ups & Downs of Army Officer.* DC. 1900.
Army Times. *History of US Signal Corps.* NY. 1961.
Ashbaugh, D. *Nevada's Turbulent Yesterday.* LA. 1963.
Athearn, R. *West of Appomattox.* Mont. 1962.
————. *William Tecumseh Sherman & Settlement of West.* Nm. 1956.
Auer, L. *Ghosts of Old Ft. Leaton.* West. 1965.
Bailey, L. *Long Walk.* LA. 1964.
————. (ed). *Navajo Reconnaissance.* LA. 1964.
Bancroft, H. *History of Arizona & New Mexico.* SF. 1889.
————. *History of Utah.* SF. 1889.
————. *History of California.* SF. 1886-88. 9 vols.
————. *History of Pacific States: Washington, Idaho, Montana.* SF. 1890.
————. *History of Nevada, Colorado, Wyoming.* SF. n.d.
————. *History of Northwest Coast of America.* SF. 1884.
————. *History of British Columbia.* SF. 1887.
Bandel, E. *Frontier Life in Army 1854-61.* Gdl. 1932.
Barret, A. *Western Frontier Forts of Texas.* WTex. 1931.
Barsness, J. & Dickinson, W. *Sully Expedition of 1864.* Mont. 1966.
Bartlett, J. *Personal Narrative.* NY. 1854. 2 vols.
Beattie, H. *Heritage of Valley.* San Pasqual, Cal. 1939.
Beers, H. *Western Military Frontier.* Phil. 1935.
Belden, H. *San Bernardino of Yesterday.* n.d.
Bell, Maj. H. *Reminiscences of a Ranger.* Santa Barbara. 1927.
————. *On Old West Coast.* NY. 1930.
Bender, A. *March of Empire.* Lawrence, Kans. 1952.
Bennett, J. (Brooks, C. & Reeve, F. eds). *Forts & Forays.* Alb. 1948.
Betts, W. *Terrors of Frontier.* West. 1965.
————. *Short Campaign of Lt. Slaughter.* West. 1966.
————. *White River Massacre.* West. 1965.
Biddle, E. *Reminiscenses of Soldier's Wife.* Phil. 1907.
Bieber, R. (ed). *Marching with Army of West.* Gdl. 1936.
Biggers, D. *Five Forts on Texas Frontier.* FT 1940-41.
Billington, R. *Westward Expansion, History of American Frontier.* NY. 1960.
Bledsoe, A. *Indian Wars of Northwest.* SF. 1885.
Boatner, LtCol. M. *Civil War Dictionary.* NY. 1959.
———— Col. *Encyclopedia of American Revolution.* NYC. 1966.
Bourke, J. *On Border with Crook,* Omaha, 1891.
Brady, C. *Indian Fights & Fighters.* NY. 1904.
Brandes, R. *Frontier Military Posts of Arizona.* Globe. 1960.
Bray, L. *Francisco Fort Muesum.* Dvr Wtr 1959.
Brininstool, E. *Fighting Indian Warriors.* Hbg. 1953.
British Colonist. *Misc. Issues.* 1863-72. Victoria, B.C.
Brooks, J. *Mormons in Carson County.* U.T. Reno. 1965.
Brown, D. *Galvanized Yankees.* Urbana. 1963.
Brown, M. & Felton, W. *Frontier Years.* NY. 1955.
————. *Before Barbed Wire.* Ibid. 1956.
Burke, P. *Fremont's Great Blunder.* West. 1964.
Burton, Sir. R. *City of Saints.* NY. 1860.
California Division of Beaches & Parks. *California Historical Landmarks.* Sacramento. n.d.
————. *Fort Ross State Historic Park.* 1965.
————. *Sonoma Mission, Vallejo Home, Sonoma Barracks.* 1965.
————. *Sutter's Fort.* 1959.
Calleros, Cleofas. *El Paso's Missions & Indians.* 1951.
Calvin, R. *Lt. Emory Reports.* Alb. 1951.
Card, V. *Living Ghost Town.* FT. 1959.
Carter, R. *Old Sergeant's Story.* NY. 1926.
Casey, R. *Texas Border.* Ind. 1950.
Chittenden, BGen H. *American Fur Trade of Far West.* Stanford. 1954.
Coffey, M. *Fort Atkinson was SAC of Its Day.* Omaha. 1962.
Colby, C. *Historic American Forts.* NY. 1963.
Collins, E. *Pioneer Experiences of Horatio H. Larned.* N.D. Coll. Vol. VII.
Colorado State Historical Society. *Forts & Camps in Colorado.* Dvr. n.d.
————. *Fort* card file in society library.
Colton, R. *Civil War in Western Territories.* Bm. 1959.
Conkling, R. & M. *Butterfield Overland Mail.* Gdl. 1947. 3 vols.
Connelly, W. *Doniphan's Expedition.* KC. 1907.
Conover, C. T. *Northern Indians Menace to Early Settlers.* Seattle. n.d.
Cooke, D. *Fighting Indians of America.* NYC. 1966.
Cooke, P. St. G. *Conquest of New Mexico & California.* NYC. 1878.

Corning, L. *Private Forts of Presidio County, Texas*. San Antonio. 1967.
Coues, E. *Lewis & Clark Expedition*. Omaha. 1952.
———. *On Trail of Spanish Pioneer*. NY. 1942. 2 vols.
——— (ed). *Charles Larpenteur; 40 Years Fur Trader*. Minneapolis, 1962.
Cowell, R. *History of Ft. Townsend*. Wash. Hist. Qtrly. 1925.
Crawford, C. *Scenes of Early Days*. Petaluma. 1898.
Cremony, J. *Life Among Apaches*. SF. 1868.
Crimmins, Col. M. *First Line of Army Posts Established in West Texas*. WTex. 1943.
———. *Experiences of Army Surgeon at Ft. Chadbourne*. WTex. 1939.
———. *Ft. Elliott, Tex*. WTex. 1947.
———. *California Column in Civil War*. FT. 1938.
———. *Ft. Worth Was Early Army Post*. FT. 1939.
——— (ed). *W. G. Freeman's Report on Eighth Military Dept*. TSHQ. 1948-50.
——— (ed). *Col. J. K. F. Mansfield's Report of Inspection of Dept. of Texas in 1856*. TSHQ. 1938-39.
———. *Old Fort Duncan: Frontier Post*. FT. 1937-38.
———. *Military History of Camp Colorado*. WTex. 1952.
Cropp, R. *Fort James*. Wi-Y. 1962.
———. *Old Fort Pierre*. Wi-Y. 1965.
Cullimore, C. *Old Adobes of Forgotten Ft. Tejon*. Bakersfield. 1941.
Cullum, BvtMGen G. *Biographical Register*. NY. 1879. 3 vols.
Custer, G. *My Life on Plains*. NY. 1962 ed.
Custer, E. *Boots & Saddles*. NY. 1885.
———. *Following Guidon*. NY. 1890.
———. *Tenting on Plains*. NY. 1893.
Danker, D. (ed). *Man of Plains: Recollections of Luther North*. Lincoln. 1961.
Davis, B. *Truth About Geronimo*. NH. 1929.
Davis, E. & T. *Spirit of Big Bend*. San Antonio. 1948.
Davis, W. *El Gringo*. NY. 1857.
De Trobriand, MGen P. *Army Life in Dakota*. Chi. 1941.
Devoto, B. *Year of Decision 1846*. Cambridge. 1943.
———. *Across Wide Missouri*. Ibid. 1947.
———. *Course of Empire*. Ibid. 1952.
Devoy, J. *History of City of St. Louis & Vicinity*. 1898.
Dodge, Gen R. *Plains of Great West*. NY. 1877.
———. *Our Wild Indians*. Hartford. 1882.
Downey, F. *Indian-Fighting Army*. NY. 1941.
———. *Indian Wars of US Army 1776-1865*. NY. 1963.
Drannan, Capt. W. *Chief of Scouts*. Chi. 1910.
Dunn, J. *Massacre of Mountains*. NY. 1886.
Eastman, BGen S. *Seth Eastman Sketchbook 1848-49*. Austin. 1962.
Edwards, E. *Early Mormon Settlements in S. Nevada*. Reno. 1965.
Elkins, Capt. J. & McCarthy, F. *Indian Fighting on Texas Frontier*. Amarillo. 1929.
Emory, Maj W. *Report on U.S. and Mexican Boundary*. DC. 1859. 3 vols.
Evans, E. *History of Pacific Northwest: Oregon & Washington*. Port. 1889.
Evans, M. *Brigham Young & Saints Went Marching*. TW. 1961.
Fabian, H. *Camp Floyd*. Fairfield, Utah. 1959.
Farish, T. *History of Arizona*. SF. 1915. 2 vols.
Farquhar, F. *History of Sierra Nevadas*. Berkeley. 1965.
——— (ed). *Up & Down California in 1860-64*. Ibid. 1966.
Federal Writers Project. *Arizona: Grand Canyon State*. NY. 1940.
———. *California: Golden State*. NY. 1939.
———. *Colorado: Highest State*. NY. 1941.
———. *Iowa: Hawkeye State*. NY. 1949.
———. *Idaho*. Cwl. 1937.
———. *Kansas: Sunflower State*. NY. 1939.
———. *Los Angeles*. NY. 1951.
———. *Minnesota*. NY. 1938.
———. *Montana*. NY. 1939.
———. *Nebraska: Cornhusker State*. NY 1939.
———. *Nevada: Silver State*. Port. 1940.
———. *New Mexico: Colorful State*. NY. 1940.
———. *North Dakota: Northern Prairie State*. Fargo. 1938.
———. *Oklahoma: Sooner State*. Nm. 1941.
———. *Oregon: End of Trail*. Port. 1940.
———. *South Dakota*. Pierre. 1938.
———. *Texas: Lone Star State*. NY. 1940.
———. *Utah*. NY. 1941.
———. *Washington: Evergreen State*. Port. 1941.
———. *Wyoming: History, Highways, People*. NY. 1941.
Fields, F. *Texas Sketchbook*. Houston. 1962.
File, L. *Ghost Town Map of New Mexico*. Socorro. 1964.
Fish, A. *Last Phase of Oregon Boundary Question*. Oregon Hist. Qtrly. 1921.
Fisher, O. *Sketches of Texas*. Springfield, Ill. 1841.
Fitzgerald, A. *Siege at Battle Rock*. West. 1965.
Florin, L. *Western Ghost Towns*. Sle. 1961.
———. *Ghost Town Album*. Ibid. 1962.
———. *Ghost Town Trails*. Ibid. 1963.
———. *Western Ghost Town Shadows*. Ibid. 1964.
———. *Ghost Town Treasures*. Ibid. 1965.
———. *Boot Hill*. Ibid. 1966.
Fohn, N. *Old Fort Lincoln*. Austin. 1960.
Foreman, C. *Cross Timbers*. Nm. 1947.
Foreman, G. *Advancing Frontier*. Ibid. 1947.

———. *Marcy & Gold Seekers*. Ibid. 1939.
——— (ed). *Pathfinder in Southwest*. Ibid. 1941.
Forsyth, Gen. G. *Story of Soldier*. NY. 1900.
———. *Thrilling Days of Army Life*. Ibid. 1900.
Francis, D. *Haunts of Russian Ghost*. TT. 1933.
Frazer, R. (ed). *Mansfield on Condition of Western Forts*. Nm. 1963.
———. *Forts of West*. Ibid. 1965.
Freeman, D. *R. E. Lee: Biography*. NY. 1934. 2 vols.
Fremont, J. *Report on Exploring Expedition to Rocky Mountains & to Oregon & California*. DC. 1845.
Frost, L. *Custer Album*. Sle. 1964.
———. *U. S. Grant Album*. Ibid. 1966.
Fry, Col. J. *Army Sacrifices or Briefs from Official Pigeon Holes*. NY. 1879.
Fulton, M. (ed). *Josiah Gregg Excursions in New Mexico & California*. Nm. 1944.
Furniss, N. *Mormon Conflict. 1850-59*. NH. 1960.
Glassley, R. *Pacific Northwest Indian Wars*. Port. 1953.
Gleason, D. *Islands & Ports of California*. NY. 1958.
Glisan, R. *Journal of Army Life*. SF. 1874.
Goetzmann, W. *Army Explorations in American West 1803-63*. NH. 1959.
Gove, J. *Utah Expedition 1857-58*. Concord, N.H. 1928.
Granger, B. (ed). *Will C. Barnes' Arizona Place Names*. Tucson. 1960.
Grant, B. *American Forts Yesterday & Today*. NY. 1965.
Grant, U. S. *Personal Memoirs*. NY. 1885. 2 vols.
Gregg, K. *History of Ft. Osage*. Mo. Hist. Review. 1940.
Gregory, Col. J. *Divided Waters*. Military Review. 1964.
Grinnell, G. *By Cheyenne Campfires*. NH. 1926.
Grivas, T. *Military Governments in California 1846-50*. Gdl. 1963.
Guinn, J. *Coast Counties (California)*. Chi. 1904.
Hafen, L. *Overland Mail 1849-69*. Cleveland. 1926.
——— (ed). *Far West & Rockies series 1820-75*. Gdl. 1954-62. 15 vols.
——— (ed). *Mountain Men & Fur Trade series*. Gdl. 1965-67.
———. *Fort Vasquez*. Dvr. 1964.
——— & Young, F. *Fort Laramie & Pageant of West*. Gdl. 1938.
——— & A. *Utah Expedition 1857-58*. Gdl. 1958.
Hammersly, T. (comp). *Complete Regular Army Register of U.S. for 100 Years 1779-1879*. DC. 1880.
Hammond, J. *Quaint & Historic Forts of North America*. Phil. 1915.
Hancock, Mrs. W. *Reminiscences of Winfield Scott Hancock*. NY. 1887.
Hanna, P. *Dictionary of California Land Names*. LA. 1951.
Harris, E. *Discovered: Oregon Trail*. Gering, Nebr. 1962.
Harrison, C. *Truth About Ft. Vasquez*. Greeley, Colo. 1965.
Hart, H. *Old Forts of Northwest*. Sle. 1963.
———. *Old Forts of Southwest*. Ibid. 1964.
———. *Old Forts of Far West*. Ibid. 1965.
———. *Military Posts and Camps in Official Records of War of Rebellion, Operations on Pacific Coast; a Working Index*. n.p. 1964.
Havins, T. *Camp Colorado*. Brownwood, Tex. 1964.
Hazard, J. *Companion of Adventure*. Port. 1952.
Heffernan, W. *Edward M. Kern: Artist-Explorer*. Bakersfield. 1953.
Hein, Lt.Col. O. *Memories of Long Ago by an Old Army Officer*. NY. 1925.
Heitman, F. (comp). *Historical Register & Dictionary of U.S. Army*. DC. 1905. 2 vols.
Henry, R. *Story of Mexican War*. Ind. 1950.
Herr, MGen J. & Wallace, E. *Story of U.S. Cavalry*. Boston. 1953.
Heyman, M. *Prudent Soldier*. Gdl. 1959.
Hitchcock, Gen. E. *50 Years in Camp & Field*. NY. 1909.
Hood, LGen J. *Advance & Retreat*. New Orleans. 1880.
Hoop, LtCol O. *Fort Hoskins 1856-65*. Oregon Hist. Qtrly. 1929.
Hoover, M. & Rensch, H. & E. *Historic Spots in California*. Stanford. 1958 (3d ed rev. by W. Abeloe, 1966).
Horgan, P. *Great River*. NY. 1954. 2 vol.
Howard, O. O. *My Life & Experiences Among Our Hostile Indians*. Hartford. 1907.
Howard, R. *Texas Guidebook*. Grand Prairie.
Hunt, A. *Army of Pacific 1860-66*. Gdl. 1951.
———. *James H. Carleton Frontier Dragoon*. Ibid. 1958.
———. *Far West Volunteer*. Mont. 1962.
———. *California Volunteers*. HSSC. 1952.
———. *California Volunteers on Border Patrol*. HSSC. 1948.
Hunt, E. *History of Ft. Leavenworth 1827-1927*. 1929.
Hurt, W. & Lass, W. *Frontier Photographer*. Lincoln. 1956.
Hyatt, F. & S. *Salt War of Texas*. TF. 1956.
Ickis, A. *Bloody Trails Along Rio Grande*. Dvr. 1958.
Ikin, A. *Texas*. London. 1841.
Inskster, T. *International Storm Over San Juans*. Mont. 1967.
Inman, Col H. *Santa Fe Trail*. Topeka. 1897.
Irving, W. *Tour of Prairies*. Phil. 1835.
Jackson County, Mo., Park Dept. *Fort Osage*. KC. n.d.
Jackson, W. *Wagon Roads West*. NH. 1965.
Jocelyn, S. *Mostly Alkali*. Cwl. 1953.
Johnson, BGen R. *Memories of Maj. Gen. George H. Thomas*. Phil. 1881.
Johnson, S. *Sixth's Elysian Fields: Ft. Atkinson on Council Bluffs*. Omaha. 1959.
Johnston, W. *Life of General Albert Sidney Johnston*. NY. 1878.
Jones, E. *Citadel in Wilderness*. NY. 1966.
Jones, G. *Fighting Devil of Ft. Berthold*. West. 1965.

Jones, N. *Journal* (extracts). Utah Hist. Qtrly. 1931.
Judge, B. *Battle at Bear River.* TW. 1961.
Karolevitz, R. *Newspaper in Old West.* Sle. 1966.
Kelsher, W. *Turmoil in New Mexico.* SFe. 1952.
Kelly, L. *Where Was Ft. Canby?* Alb. 1967.
Keyes, MGen E. *50 Years Observation of Men & Events.* NY. 1884.
Kimball, M. *Soldier Doctor of Our Army.* Boston. 1917.
King, J. *War Eagle: Life of General Eugene A. Carr.* Lincoln. 1963.
Kivett, M. *Excavations at Ft. Atkinson, Nebr.: Preliminary Report.* Omaha. 1959.
Keller, J. *Cow Country Stalwart.* West. 1966.
Lackey, V. *Forts of Oklahoma.* Tulsa. 1963.
Lamar, H. *Dakota Territory 1861-89.* NH. 1956.
————— (ed). *Cruise of Portsmouth.* Ibid. 1958.
Lane, L. *I married a Soldier.* Phil. 1893.
Layton, Layton & Associates (ed). *Jefferson Barracks & 6th Infantry.* StL. 1961.
Lee, F. & Hicks, J. *Fort Osage & George Champlin Sibley.* Dvr Wtr. 1963.
Lewis, O. *Sutter's Fort: Gateway to Gold Fields.* Englewood Cliffs. 1966.
Lochamorra, D. (pseud). *Presidio, Texas.* SW. 1965.
Lockwood, F. *Early Military Posts in Arizona.* Arizona Hist. Rev. 1930.
Lott, LCdr A. *Long Line of Ships.* Annapolis. 1954.
Lowe, P. *Five Years a Dragoon.* KC. 1906.
Lowman, H. *California's Mission San Luis Rey.* Covina. n.d.
Mack, E. *Nevada.* Gdl. 1936.
Madison, V. & Stillwell, H. *How Come It's Called That?* Alb. 1958.
Magnuson, Sen. W. *One-Shot War with England.* American Heritage. 1960.
Mahan, B. *Old Fort Crawford & Frontier.* Iowa City. 1926.
Mallon, G. *Murder in Cajon Pass.* West. 1965.
Marcy, BvtBGen R. *Prairie Traveler.* Phil. 1856.
—————. *Thirty Years of Life on Border.* NY. 1874.
Martin, G. *Old San Elizario.* El Paso. n.d.
Mattes, M. *Indians, Infants, Infantry.* Dvr. 1960.
—————. *Scotts Bluff.* NPS DC. 1958.
—————. *Historic Site Archeology on Upper Missouri.* Smithsonian Bureau of American Ethnology. DC. 1959.
Mattison, R. *Army Post on Northern Plains to 1865.* Lincoln. 1954.
—————. *Indian Frontier on Upper Missouri to 1865.* Ibid. 1958.
—————. *Military Frontier on Upper Misouri.* Ibid. 1956.
—————. *Report on Santa Fe Trail.* NPS Omaha. 1958.
—————. *Old Fort Stevenson.* Bismarck. 1951.
—————. *Fort Rice: North Dakota's First Missouri River Military Post.* Bismarck. 1953.
—————. *Report on Historical Aspects of Oahe Reservoir, Missouri River, S. & N. Dakota.* SDHS 1954.
—————. *Reports on Historic Sites in Garrison Reservoir Area, Missouri River.* Bismarck. 1955.
—————. *Upper Missouri Fur Trade: Its Methods of Operation.* Lincoln. 1961.
Mazzanovich, A. *Trailing Geronimo.* Hollywood, Calif. 1931.
McBeth, F. *Lower Klamath County.* Berkeley. 1950.
McCabe, J. *San Juan Water Boundary Question.* Toronto. 1964.
McConnell, H. *Five Years a Cavalryman.* Jacksboro, Tex. 1889.
McKay, C. *History of San Juan Island.* Wash. Hist. Qtrly. 1907-08.
McNitt, F. *Indian Traders.* Nm. 1962.
McRay, G. *Handcarts Across the Prairie.* West. 1965.
Meline, J. *2,000 Miles on Horseback.* Alb. 1956.
Metcalf, C. *History of U.S. Marine Corps.* NY. 1939.
Miles, Gen N. *Personal Recollections.* Chi. 1896.
—————. *Serving the Republic.* NY. 1911.
Miller, F. *Photographic History of Civil War.* NY. 1911. 10 vols.
Mills, A. *My Story.* DC. 1918.
Mills, J. (comp). *Historical Landmarks of San Diego County.* Calif. 1960.
Mission San Luis Rey. n.d.
Moat, L. (ed). *Frank Leslie's Illustrated Famous Leaders & Battle Scenes of Civil War.* NY. 1896.
Monaghan, J. (ed). *Book of American West.* NY. 1963.
Monterey Peninsula Chamber of Commerce. *Path of History in Monterey.* 1961.
Morgan, C. *San Juan Story.* Friday Harbor, Wash. n.d.
Morgan, D. (ed). *Rand McNally's Pioneer Atlas of the American West.* Chi. 1956.
Morgan, L. *Indian Journals 1859-62.* Ann Arbor. 1959.
Morrison, W. *Military Posts & Camps in Oklahoma.* Oklahoma City. 1936.
Mulford, A. *Fighting Indians in 7th U.S. Cavalry.* Corning, N.Y. 1879.
Murbarger, N. *Ghosts of Glory Trail.* Palm Desert, Calif. 1956.
—————. *Ghosts of the Adobe Walls.* LA. 1965.
Murray, R. *Camp at Mouth of Red Canyon.* CAMP Periodical #1. Phoenix. 1967.
Myers, Pvt. F. *Soldier in Dakota Among Indians.* Huron. 1888.
Myers. J. *Deaths of Bravos.* Boston. 1962.
Myers, Lee. *Fort Torreons a Puzzle.* SW. 1962.
—————. *Mangas Colorado Caused Ft. Webster.* Ibid. 1962.
—————. *Fort Webster Life Quite Spartan—Was Too Far Away.* Ibid. 1963.
—————. *El Fortin.* FT. 1966.
—————. *"God and the Apaches."* FT. 1967.

—————. *New Mexico Military Installations.* N.M. Soc. of Prof. Engineers. 1966.
—————. *Fort Webster on Mimbres River.* NMHR. 1966.
Nadeau, R. *Ft. Laramie & the Sioux Indians.* NY. 1867.
Nalty, B. *Leathernecks & Redskins: Fight at Seattle, 1856.* DC. n.d.
Nelson, J. *50 Years on Trail.* Nm. 1963.
Nelson, H. & Onstad, P. (ed). *Webfoot Volunteer.* Corvallis. 1965.
Nesbitt, J. *Old Homes & Families.* Daily Colonist, Victoria, B.C. 1951.
Nichols, R. *General Henry Atkinson: Western Military Career.* Nm. 1965.
Nye, Col. W. *Carbine & Lance.* Nm. 1937.
Olson, W. *Archeological Investigation of Sutter's Fort.* Sacramento. 1961.
Ormsby, W. *Overland to San Francisco 1858.* Van Buren, Ark. 1958.
Orton, BGen R. *California Men in War of Rebellion.* Sacramento. 1890.
Ostrander, Maj A. *Army Boy of Sixties.* Yonkers-on-Hudson. 1924.
Parkman, F. *Oregon Trail.* NY. 1892.
Parks & Rcereation Board. *Jefferson Barracks Historical Park.* StL. n.d.
Patterson, T. *Landmarks of Riverside.* Calif. 1964.
Patton, A. *California Mormons by Sail & Trail.* SLC. 1961.
Paulin, C. *Atlas of Historical Geography of U.S.* DC. 1932.
Payen, L. *Excavations at Sutter's Fort 1960.* Sacramento. 1961.
Perkins, L. *Tillicum Tales.* n.p. n.d.
—————. *Master Whidbey's Island.* Sea & Pacific Motor Boat. 1965.
—————. *Fort Was Built in 1856.* Centralia, Wash. 1966.
Peterson, H. *Forts in America.* NY. 1964.
Pfaller, Rev. L. *Sully Expedition of 1864.* Bismarck. 1964.
Pollard, L. *Lewis & Clark at Ft. Clatsop.* Seaside, Ore. 1962.
Potter, D. (ed). *Trail to California.* NH. 1945.
Porter, E. *Founding of San Elizario.* El Paso. 1964.
—————. *San Elizario, a Century of History.* Ibid. 1964.
—————. *San Elizario—Bower of Eden.* Ibid. 1967.
Porter, V. (ed). *Journal of Stephen Watts Kearny.* Mo. Hist. Soc. Coll. 1908.
Port Orford Chamber of Commerce. *Battle at Table Rock.* n.d.
Port Townsend Chamber of Commerce. *Historic & Picturesque Port Townsend.* n.d.
Price, G. *Across the Continent with 5th Cavalry.* NY. 1883.
Pride, Capt. W. *History of Ft. Riley.* 1926.
Prucha, Rev. F. P., S.J. *Broadax & Bayonet.* Madison, Wisc. 1953.
—————. *Guide to Military Posts of U.S.* Ibid. 1964.
—————. (ed). *Army Life on Western Frontier.* Nm. 1958.
Quiner, E. *Military History of Wisconsin.* Madison. 1866.
Rahill, Rev. P. *Catholic Indian Missions & Grant's Peace Policy 1870-1884.* DC. 1953.
Raht, C. *Romance of Davis Mountains & Big Bend Country.* Odessa, Tex. 1919.
Recruiting News. *Histories of Army Posts.* Governor's Island, N.Y. 1924.
Reeve, D. (ed). *Puritan & Apache: a Diary.* Alb. 1948-49.
Rhoades, C. *Second U.S. Cavalry, 1855-1861.* El Paso. n.d.
Richardson, R. *Frontier of Northwest Texas.* Gdl. 1963.
—————. *Comanche Barrier to South Plains Settlement.* Ibid. 1933.
Rickey, D. *40 Miles a Day on Beans & Hay.* Nm. 1963.
Risch, E. *Quartermaster Support of Army.* DC. 1962.
Rister, C. *Robert E. Lee in Texas.* Nm. 1946.
—————. *Ft. Griffin on Texas Frontier.* Ibid. 1956.
—————. *Southwestern Frontier 1865-81.* Cleveland. 1928.
—————. *Border Command; General Phil Sheridan in West.* Nm. 1944.
Roberts, B. *Mormon Battalion; Its History & Acvhievements.* SLC. 1918.
Robertson, F. *Ft. Hall.* NY. 1963.
Robinson, Col. W. *Digest of Indian Commissioner Reports.* SDHS. 1954.
—————. *Rockport.* Wi-Y. 1951.
—————. *South Dakota Forts.* Ibid. 1953.
—————. *Forts in South Dakota.* Ibid. 1953.
Robinson, W. *Story of San Bernardino County.* 1962.
Rodenbaugh, T. *Army of U.S.* DC. 1896.
Roe, F. *Army Letters from Officers Wife, 1871-1888.* NY. 1909.
Rogers, Col. F. *Early Military Posts of Del Norte County.* Calif. Hist. Soc. Qtrly. 1947.
—————. *Early Military Posts of Mendocino County.* Ibid. 1948.
—————. *Fort Bidwell, Modoc County, California.* SF. 1959.
—————. *Fort Point, California.* Ibid. 1959.
—————. *Soldiers of Overland.* Ibid. 1938.
—————. *William Brown Ide, Bear Flagger.* Ibid.
—————. *Report on Birdseye View of Fort Bragg.* Sebastopol, Calif. 1956.
—————. *History of Ft. Bragg Post.* Ft. Bragg, Calif. 1957.
Rosebush, W. *Frontier Steel.* Appleton, Wisc. 1958.
Ruhlen, Col G. *Fort Thorn—An Historical Vignette.* El Paso. 1960.
—————. *Carleton's Empty Fort.* Nevada Hist. Qtrly. 1959.
—————. *Early Nevada Forts.* Ibid. 1964.
—————. *Compilation of California Forts & Camps.* Unpub. SD.
—————. *San Diego Barracks.* SD Hist. Soc. Qtrly. 1955.
—————. *San Diego in Civil War.* Ibid. 1961.
Rusling, J. *Across America.* NY. 1874.
Ruth, K. *Great Day in West.* Nm. 1963.
Salisbury, A. & J. *Here Rolled Covered Wagons.* Sle. 1948.
—————. *Two Captains West.* Sle. 1950.
Savage, L. *Fort Wingate.* NMM. 1960.

Scanlan, T. (ed). *Army Times Guide to Army Posts.* Hbg. 1966.
Schmitt, M. (ed). *General George Crook, His Autobiography.* Nm. 1960.
———— & Brown, D. *Fighting Indians of West.* NY. 1948.
Schofield, J. *46 Years in Army.* NY. 1897.
Scobee, B. *Old Fort Davis.* San Antonio. 1947.
————. *Fort Davis, Texas.*
Seattle Historical Society. *Seattle Century.* 1952.
Sengle, F. *Whidbey Island Blockhouses.* n.p. n.d.
Sell, F. *Siege at Battle Rock.* TW. 1959.
Settle, R. *March of Mounted Riflemen.* Gdl. 1940.
———— & M. *Thunder on Arickaree.* FT. 1959.
Seymour, H. *Eagle Pass, Maverick County, Texas.* 1961.
Sheller, R. *James H. Wilbur—Indian Agent.* GW. 1967.
Sheridan, Gen. P. *Personal Memoirs.* NY. 1888. 2 vols.
Sherman, Gen. W. *Memoirs.* NY. 1875. 2 vols.
Simpson, Col H. (ed). *Frontier Forts of Texas.* Waco. 1966.
Smith, C. *What a Life! U.S. Army 1863.* FT. 1959.
Smith, G. *Ft. Pierre II.* Smithsonian Bureau of American Ethnology. DC. 1959.
Smith, P. *Sagebrush Soldiers.* Nev. Hist. Qtrly. 1962.
Spotts, D. & Brininstool, E. *Campaigning with Custer & 19th Kansas Volunteer Cavalry on Washita Campaign, 1868-69.* LA. 1928.
Stanley, F. (Rev. Stanley F. L. Crocchiola). *Duke City,* Pampa, Tex. 1963.
————. *Fort Bascom, Comanche-Kiowa Barrier.* Ibid. 1961.
————. *Fort Union.* Ibid. 1961.
————. *Fort Craig.* Ibid. 1962.
————. *Fort Fillmore Story.* Pantex, Tex. 1961.
————. *Fort Conrad.* Ibid. 1962.
————. *Fort Stanton.* Ibid. Pampa, Tex. 1964.
Stanley, Gen. D. *Personal Memoirs.* Cambridge. 1917.
Steele, J. *Frontier Army Sketches.* NY. 1883.
Stern, P. *Robert E. Lee, Man and Soldier.* NY. 1963.
Sullivan, C. *Army Posts & Towns.* Burlington, Vt. 1935.
Summerhayes, M. *Vanished Arizona.* Salem, Mass. 1911.
Sutton, J. *One Day in Southern Oregon History.* Jacksonville, Ore. 1960.
————. *Pictorial History of Southern Oregon & Northern California.* Grant's Pass, Ore. 1959.
Taft, R. *Artists & Illustrators of Old West.* NY. 1953.
Tallck, W. *California Overland Express: Longest Stage Ride in World, 1865.* Van Buren, Ark. 1959.
Taylor, R. *Colorado: South of Border.* Dvr. 1963.
Tebbel, J. & Jennison, K. *American Indian Wars.* NY. 1960.
Temko, A. *Russians in California.* American Heritage. 1960.

Tevis, J. *Arizona in 50's.* Alb. 1954.
Texas State Parks Board. *Fort Griffin State Park.* Austin. n.d.
————. *Data Covering Texas Forts.* Ibid. n.d.
Thomlinson, M. *Forgotten Fort.* NMM. 1945.
Tolmie, W. *Physician & Fur Trader.* Vancouver. 1963.
Toulouse. J. & J. *Pioneer Posts of Texas.* San Antonio. 1936.
Utley, R. *Historical Report on Ft. Bowie, Ariz.* NPS SFe. 1962.
————. *Ft. Davis.* Ibid. 1960.
———— (ed). *Military & Indian Frontier.* Ibid. 1962 (draft).
————. *Custer & Great Controversy.* LA. 1962.
————. *Last Days of Sioux Nation.* NH. 1963.
————. *Fort Union.* NPS DC. 1962.
Virden, Bill. *Affair at Minter's Ranch.* SD Hist. Soc. Qtrly. 1961.
Wallace, E. *Great Reconnaissance.* Boston. 1955.
Ward, M. *Kip.* Las Vegas. 1966.
Warner, E. *Generals in Gray.* New Orleans. 1959.
————. *Generals in Blue.* Baton Rouge. 1964.
Washington Co. Nebraska Historical Society. *Story of Ft. Atkinson.* Ft. Calhoun. n.d.
Watson, M. *Silver Theater.* Gdl. 1964.
Webb, H. *Story of Jefferson Barracks.* NMHR. 1946.
Webb, W. *Buffalo Hunt.* TW. 1961.
———— (ed). *Handbook of Texas.* Austin. 1952. 2 vols.
Wellman, P. *Indian Wars of West.* Garden City, L.I. 1954.
Welsh, W. *Brief Historical Sketch of Port Townsend.* 1963.
Werstein, I. *Kearny the Magnificent.* NY. 1962.
West Point Alumni Foundation. *Register of Graduates & Former Cadets. 1802-1964.*
Westerners Potomac Corral. *Great Western Indian Fights.* Garden City. 1960.
Wheeler, Co. H. *Buffalo Days.* Ind. 1925.
White, H. *Ho! for the Gold Fields.* St. Paul. 1966.
Whiting, J. *Forts of State of Washington.* Sle. 1951.
———— & R. *Forts of State of California.* Sle. 1960.
Whitman, S. *The Troopers.* NY. 1962.
Wilcox, V. *Comprehensive Guide to Westerner Brand Books 1944-61.* Dvr. 1962.
Wiley, B. & Milhollen, H. *They Who Fought Here.* NY. 1959.
Wilson, E. *San Juan Island.* Beaver. 1927.
Wilson, T. (Advertising Agency). *Pioneer Nevada.* Reno. 1951.
Wiltsey, N. *Hawks of Desert.* TW. 1955-56.
Wood, R. *Stephen Harriman Long, 1784-1864.* Gdl. 1966.
Young, BGen G. (ed). *Army Almanac.* Hbg. 1959.
Young, J. *General Sully's Strange Indian Campaign.* West. 1965.
Young, O. *First Military Escort on Santa Fe Trail, 1829.* Gdl. 1962.

INDEX OF FORTS, CAMPS AND STATIONS

This index includes all places with fort-type designations such as camp, depot, post, cantonment, picket post, station, redoubt, detachment, presidio, barracks, blockhouse, and arsenal. Posts covered in detail in other volumes of the *Forts of the Old West* series are included by volume and page number of primary coverage (other page numbers are from this volume). Volumes in the series are *Old Forts of the Northwest* (I); *Old Forts of the Southwest* (II); *Old Forts of the Far West* (III); *Pioneer Forts of the West* (IV); and *Frontier Forts of the West* (the projected volume V of the series, for which page numbers cannot be given).

GENERAL INDEX

191